Cooking Light

Light *and* Easy Menus

Mixed Fruit with Vanilla-Apricot Syrup, page 190

Cooking Light.

Light *and* Easy Menus

edited by Anne C. Cain

Oxmoor
House.

Library of Congress Catalog Number: 2001-131109
ISBN: 0-8487-2383-X
Printed in the United States of America
First Printing 2001

Be sure to check with your health-care provider before making any changes in your diet.

Editor-in-Chief: Nancy Fitzpatrick Wyatt
Senior Foods Editor: Katherine M. Eakin
Senior Editor, Copy and Homes: Olivia Kindig Wells
Art Director: James Boone

Cooking Light® Light and Easy Menus
Editor: Anne Chappell Cain, M.S., M.P.H., R.D.
Assistant Editor: Heather Averett
Copy Editor: Catherine Ritter Scholl
Copy Assistant: Jane Lorberau
Editorial Assistant: Diane Rose
Editorial Intern: Marye Binkley Rowell
Associate Art Director: Cynthia R. Cooper
Senior Designer: Melissa Jones Clark
Director, Test Kitchens: Elizabeth Tyler Luckett
Assistant Director, Test Kitchens: Julie Christopher
Recipe Editor: Gayle Hays Sadler
Test Kitchens Staff: Jennifer Cofield; Gretchen P. Feldtman, R.D.;
    David Gallent; Ana Kelly; Jan A. Smith
Photographer: Brit Huckabay
Senior Photo Stylist: Kay Clarke
Photo Stylist: Virginia R. Cravens
Publishing Systems Administrator: Rick Tucker
Production and Distribution Director: Phillip Lee
Books Production Managers: Theresa L. Beste; Larry Hunter
Production Assistant: Faye Porter Bonner

Contributors
Indexer: Mary Ann Laurens
Recipe Developers: Margaret Agnew; Caroline Grant, R.D.;
    Jan Krahn Hanby; Nancy Hughes; Jean Kressey; Debbie Nakos;
    Kathleen Royal Phillips; Elizabeth Taliaferro

we're here for you!

We at Oxmoor House are dedicated to serving you with reliable information that expands your imagination and enriches your life.

We welcome your comments and suggestions. Please write to us at:

Oxmoor House, Inc.
Editor, Cooking Light® *Light and Easy Menus*
2100 Lakeshore Drive
Birmingham, AL 35209

To order additional copies of this publication or any others, call 1-205-445-6560.

For more books to enrich your life, visit **oxmoorhouse.com**

Cover: Grilled Beef Fajita Salad, page 86

contents

welcome

In a world of cell phones and FAX machines, instant messaging and palm pilots, do you often yearn for the simple luxury of an uninterrupted dinner with your family or friends? Indulge yourself in that luxury—in only 30 minutes! *Light and Easy Menus* shows you how.

Reconnect with your family by sitting down together at the dinner table and enjoying a homecooked meal. You can make the meal in 30 minutes or less. How long you spend at the table is up to you.

5 great secrets

guaranteed to help you get a healthy, homecooked meal on the table in 30 minutes or less

1. Be prepared   2. Multitask   3. Take shortcuts
4. Streamline   5. Get fresh

1 Be prepared: *assemble ingredients and equipment first.*

Avoid dashing around the kitchen pulling out ingredients, bowls, and pans as you need them. Read the recipes in the menu and gather everything you need before you start cooking. If you take a little time to organize your kitchen, you'll be able to start cooking quickly.

7 habits of highly organized cooks

- Clean out your refrigerator, and put the items you use the most in the front and in the door racks.

- Stock your pantry with staples. See "The Well-Stocked Pantry" on page 224 if you need help getting started.

- Group similar items together in your pantry.

- Keep a notepad in the kitchen to jot down ingredients that need to be replaced.

- Get rid of the equipment and utensils that you never use.

- Use racks, shelves, and bins to store ingredients and equipment neatly.

- Store the utensils you use regularly in a convenient place on your counter so you don't have to dig through drawers to find what you need.

Bourbon-Glazed Beef Tenderloin, page 116

2 Multitask: *do more than one thing at a time.*

"Multitasking" is something most of us do at the office and when we're raising our children, so why not try it when you're cooking? To have everything in the menu ready at the same time, you need to overlap some steps.

For example, for the Bourbon-Glazed Beef Tenderloin menu on page 116, slice the onions and let them cook while you bake the potatoes and prepare the meat.

For the Shrimp Del Sol menu on page 34, you'll need to boil the water for the pasta first. While you're waiting for the water to boil, prepare the ingredients for the salad and the sauce. Then, while the pasta cooks, the sauce can simmer.

Take shortcuts:
use convenience products.

No one has to know. Yes, it would be nice to start everything from scratch, but do you really have that kind of time?

Are convenience products healthful?

Yes, if you make wise selections. Many packaged convenience foods are full of calories, fat, and sodium; even the reduced-calorie, reduced-fat products are often very high in sodium. If you're trying to cut down on sodium, certain products may not be good choices. Read the labels carefully so you know what you're getting.

Which products should I use?

Here's a list of some of the shortcut products we used in our healthful menus:

fresh breads from the bakery: Add some variety to your meals with new flavors and textures of specialty loaves and rolls.

Boboli pizza crusts: Italian cheese-flavored crusts are in the refrigerated bread section of the grocery and come in several sizes.

canned beans: Look for the low-salt versions if you need to reduce your sodium intake.

canned tomato products: Keep tomato sauces, tomato paste, diced tomatoes, and whole tomatoes on hand. Many products come in reduced-sodium versions.

rice and rice blends: A lot of quick-cooking rice blends come with seasoning packets; if you're trying to reduce sodium, omit the seasoning packet, or use only half.

couscous: Flavored varieties are now available.

pasta: Keep a variety of pastas on hand, and you can always make a meal.

salads-in-a-bag: These prewashed salad greens are a big time-saver; just open the bag, and toss with your dressing of choice.

preshredded cheese: Lots of cheeses come in shredded form, so you don't have to get out your grater.

frozen cooked chicken: Bags of cooked chicken are available diced and in strips. The sodium is higher than fresh-cooked chicken, but when you're in a hurry, this product is great for soups, salads, and pasta dishes.

deli roasted chicken: Buy freshly roasted chicken in the deli of the supermarket or packaged roasted chicken in the poultry section. Remove the skin and fat before eating the chicken or using it in recipes.

frozen vegetables: Keep frozen vegetables on hand for when you can't run to the farmers' market for fresh.

vinaigrettes and salad dressings: Check out all of the fat-free and reduced-fat flavors.

hobbies, play with your kids, go for a walk, take a nap, or read a book. The ingredient lists are short, so you don't have to spend a lot of time at the market or in the kitchen gathering ingredients.

There are no complicated cooking procedures to stump you. Some of the recipes don't involve cooking at all—only assembly required.

5 Get fresh: *use seasonal produce.*

When you use fresh fruits and vegetables in your menus, you don't have to do much to make them taste good. Sometimes just pulling them out of your market basket and rinsing is all you need to do. Why not tailor your menus to the seasons and awaken your senses to the pleasures of great-tasting food?

Spring: a time of freshness and rebirth
The spring menus feature foods that say "spring:" asparagus, strawberries, green peas, salmon, and lamb.

Summer: warm days to slow down, take a break, and have some fun
No-stress summer menus show off the best of the garden's bounty: tomatoes, corn, green beans, squash, cucumbers, blackberries, blueberries, peaches, and watermelon.

Autumn: a season of change with increasing activity and anticipation
Brilliant colors and crisp textures mark fall's harvest menus: apples, pears, pumpkins, acorn squash, sweet potatoes, cabbage, and Brussels sprouts.

Winter: the cold months when we seek comfort from the blustery weather and stay close to the warmth of home
Let the cozy menus of winter comfort you with steaming soups, hearty chilis, and "stick-to-your-ribs" fare prepared with hearty root vegetables, robust greens, and tangy citrus fruits.

4 Streamline: *group tasks.*

If you're preparing more than one recipe that calls for chopped or sliced produce, go ahead and do all the ingredient prep at one time. Make separate piles for different recipes.

A perfect plan
Use the step-by-step menu plans to help you get everything done in 30 minutes or less. The menu plans tell you exactly how to get the meal done in the most efficient way so you're in and out of the kitchen in no time. And, if you've got kids, a spouse, or friends who want to pitch in, assign each person a task. You'll get everything done even quicker, plus it will be fun.

More time for fun
All of the menus can be prepared from start to finish in 30 minutes or less so you have time to explore your

Where's the best place to buy produce?

Start with the produce aisles of your local supermarket. Many of the large supermarket chains offer a wide selection of fruits and vegetables from all over the world. If you're looking for interesting varieties and regional specialties, check out farmers' markets, green markets, and roadside stands. When you buy fruits and vegetables from the people who have grown them, you get better flavor, better prices, and perhaps, more information about the products. If you're really industrious, grow your own in your backyard. That's about as fresh as you can get.

What's in season?

Ask the manager of the supermarket produce section or the vendors at the farmers' market what items are at their peak. Although many fruits and vegetables are available year-round, you'll get better flavor and better prices when you buy what's in season.

Celebrate the seasons and explore new varieties and flavors of fresh produce. See what an enjoyable adventure healthy eating can be.

Fresh Strawberries with Orange Custard, page 189

sweets for all seasons

We didn't forget dessert—treat yourself to quick and easy sweets that won't wreck your healthy eating habits. There is an entire chapter of quick and easy desserts suitable for serving with your seasonal menus, and other dessert recipes are included in some of the menu plans. Enjoy any of the following treats with your favorite menus:

Amaretto Strawberries (*page 52*)

Apple Turnovers (*page 206*)

Banana Cream Trifle (*page 210*)

Cherry Poached Pears with
   Dark Chocolate Sauce (*page 193*)

Fresh Strawberries with Orange
   Custard (*page 189*)

Lemon Meringue Cakes (*page 198*)

Melon-Raspberry Compote with Rum (*page 190*)

Raspberry Sorbet with Blueberries (*page 83*)

Strawberry-Topped Cake (*page 23*)

Tropical Fruit Sundaes (*page 194*)

ring

When the daffodils spring from the frozen ground and bits of green bud from the trees, don't you yearn for the sweet flavors of spring? Bring a ruby-red strawberry to your lips; sink your teeth into the plump red fruit; and let the juice run down your fingers. Hear the crisp crunch of your first bite of pencil-thin asparagus. Feel your mouth water as you flake a piece of tender salmon or spoon into a bowl of sweet green peas.

Great for breakfast, brunch, or a midnight supper

Baby Vidalia Onion Frittata
low-fat blueberry muffins
red grapefruit sections

serves 4

Buy chilled fresh grapefruit sections in a jar, and get low-fat muffins
from the bakery at your supermarket.

menu plan

1. *Slice onions, and mince garlic for frittata.*

2. *Prepare frittata.*

3. *Heat muffins in microwave or regular oven while frittata cooks on stovetop.*

4. *Sprinkle cheese on frittata, and broil.*

5. *Serve frittata with muffins and grapefruit sections.*

Baby Vidalia Onion Frittata

1	tablespoon light butter, melted
1	(¾-pound) bunch baby Vidalia onions, thinly sliced with some green tops (about 2 cups), or 1½ cups chopped green onions
1	garlic clove, minced
1	(16-ounce) carton egg substitute
¼	teaspoon salt
¼	teaspoon pepper
⅛	teaspoon hot sauce
¾	cup (3 ounces) shredded reduced-fat sharp Cheddar cheese

Melt butter in a 10-inch ovenproof skillet over medium heat. Add onion and garlic; cook 5 minutes or until tender, stirring occasionally.

Arrange onion mixture evenly in bottom of skillet. Combine egg substitute and next 3 ingredients; pour evenly over onion mixture. Reduce heat to medium-low; cook, uncovered, 8 minutes or until almost set (mixture will still be wet on top).

Preheat broiler.

Broil frittata 3 minutes; sprinkle with cheese, and broil 1 minute or until cheese melts. Let stand 5 minutes before serving. Yield: 4 servings.

Per Serving: Calories 161 (32% from fat) Fat 5.7g (sat 3.4g) Protein 18.7g
Carbohydrate 8.7g Fiber 1.4g Cholesterol 19mg Sodium 494mg
Exchanges: 2 Vegetable, 2 Lean Meat

A blender breakfast for a busy morning

Tropical Berry Smoothie
Blueberry Bagels with Cream Cheese

serves 4

Buy cubed fresh pineapple in the produce section of the supermarket.

menu plan

1. Cube and slice fruit for smoothie.

2. Freeze fruit for smoothie for 15 minutes.

3. While fruit is in freezer, toast bagels, and spread with cream cheese.

4. Blend smoothie.

Tropical Berry Smoothie

1   cup cubed fresh pineapple or 1 (8-ounce) can
        pineapple tidbits in juice, drained
8   large strawberries
1   banana, sliced
⅓   cup orange juice
1   (6-ounce) carton strawberry custard-style yogurt (such
        as Yoplait)
18 ice cubes (about 2 cups)

Place first 3 ingredients on a baking sheet or 15 x 10-inch jelly-roll pan; freeze 15 minutes.

Combine frozen fruit, orange juice, and yogurt in an electric blender. Cover and process until smooth, scraping sides of container occasionally. With blender on, add ice cubes 1 at a time; process until smooth. Yield: 4 (1-cup) servings.

Per Serving: Calories 105 (11% from fat)   Fat 1.3g (sat 0.6g)   Protein 2.4g
Carbohydrate 22.3g   Fiber 1.6g   Cholesterol 4mg   Sodium 24mg
Exchanges: 1 Starch, ½ Fruit

Blueberry Bagels with Cream Cheese

4   (2.8-ounce) blueberry bagels, cut in half and toasted
¼   cup ⅓-less-fat cream cheese

Spread 1½ teaspoons cream cheese on each toasted bagel half. Serve immediately. Yield: 4 servings.

Per Serving: Calories 263 (15% from fat)   Fat 4.3g (sat 2.1g)   Protein 8.9g
Carbohydrate 46.4g   Fiber 2.3g   Cholesterol 9mg   Sodium 412mg
Exchanges: 3 Starch, 1 Fat

pineapples

In Spanish, the name for pineapple is *ananas*, which is derived from a word meaning "excellent fruit." And indeed it is.

varieties   Fresh pineapple is available year-round, but has a peak season from March to July. The two major varieties found in the United States are the Cayenne (from Hawaii) and the Red Spanish (from Florida and Puerto Rico).

selection   Choose pineapples that are slightly soft to the touch and with skins that have no sign of greening. Look for leaves that are crisp and green with no yellow or brown tips. Many stores now have fresh pineapple that has been peeled and cored. Keep fresh pineapple tightly wrapped in the refrigerator for up to 3 days.

Wake up with coffee-flavored pancakes.

Cappuccino Pancakes

veggie breakfast links   orange-passionfruit juice

serves 4

You'll find veggie breakfast links in the frozen food section.

menu plan

1. *Make coffee.*
2. *Prepare Coffee Syrup, and keep warm.*
3. *Prepare pancake batter.*
4. *Cook pancakes.*
5. *Cook breakfast links according to package directions. (Cook links on griddle or skillet with last batch of pancakes.)*

Cappuccino Pancakes

1	cup all-purpose flour
1	teaspoon baking powder
½	teaspoon baking soda
½	teaspoon salt
¼	teaspoon ground cinnamon
1	large egg, lightly beaten
1	(8-ounce) carton coffee low-fat yogurt
¼	cup brewed coffee
¼	cup frozen reduced-calorie whipped topping, thawed

Coffee Syrup

Lightly spoon flour into a dry measuring cup; level with a knife. Combine flour and next 4 ingredients in a medium bowl; make a well in center of mixture. Combine egg, yogurt, and coffee; add to flour mixture, stirring just until dry ingredients are moistened. (Mixture will be thick and lumpy.)

For each pancake, spoon about 3 tablespoons batter onto a hot nonstick griddle or nonstick skillet, spreading slightly. Turn pancakes when tops are covered with bubbles and edges look cooked. Serve immediately with whipped topping and Coffee Syrup.

Yield: 4 servings (serving size: 2 pancakes, 1 tablespoon topping, and 2 tablespoons syrup).

Per Serving: Calories 202 (13% from fat) Fat 2.9g (sat 1.3g) Protein 7.8g Carbohydrate 36.3g Fiber 0.9g Cholesterol 58mg Sodium 636mg **Exchanges:** 2½ Starch

coffee syrup

½	cup reduced-calorie maple syrup
3	tablespoons hot brewed coffee

Combine syrup and coffee. Serve warm.
Yield: ⅔ cup.

Per Tablespoon: Calories 5 (0% from fat) Fat 0.0g (sat 0.0g) Protein 0.0g Carbohydrate 1.5g Fiber 0.0g Cholesterol 0mg Sodium 3mg **Exchange:** Free (up to ¼ cup)

A super-quick, meat-free lunch

Roasted Portobello Sandwiches
baby carrots   frozen seedless red grapes
serves 2

menu plan

1. *Place grapes in a single layer on a baking sheet, and freeze for at least 20 minutes.*

2. *Slice and roast vegetables for sandwiches.*

3. *Toast sandwich buns.*

4. *Assemble sandwiches.*

portobellos

A portobello mushroom is the mature version of a regular brown mushroom. These mushrooms are very large with huge caps and are popular because of their meaty texture and flavor. Select portobellos with a tight underside and light-colored gills. If the gill area appears very dark and spread out, it's a sign of age. Most recipes call for only portobello caps because the stems are very woody.

Roasted Portobello Sandwiches

1	red bell pepper
Cooking spray	
2	(4-inch) portobello caps
2	(½-inch-thick) slices sweet onion
1½	tablespoons balsamic vinegar
2	teaspoons olive oil
2	(2-ounce) onion sandwich buns, halved and toasted
2	(¾-ounce) slices mozzarella cheese
½	cup fresh basil leaves or arugula
1	teaspoon balsamic vinegar

Preheat broiler.

Cut bell pepper in half lengthwise; discard seeds and membranes. Place pepper halves, skin sides up, on a 15 x 10-inch jelly-roll pan coated with cooking spray; flatten with hand. Place mushrooms (gill side down) and onion slices on pan. Combine 1½ tablespoons balsamic vinegar and olive oil, stirring with a whisk. Brush vinegar mixture evenly over mushrooms, onion slices, and pepper halves.

Broil 8 to 9 minutes or until mushroom caps are tender. Remove mushrooms; broil onion and bell pepper 3 additional minutes or until crisp-tender.

Place mushroom caps on bottom halves of buns; carefully place onion and pepper halves over mushroom caps. Place cheese over onion. Broil 1 minute or until cheese begins to melt. Top with basil leaves, and sprinkle each with ½ teaspoon vinegar. Cover with top halves of buns. Yield: 2 servings.

Per Serving: Calories 372 (34% from fat) Fat 13.9g (sat 3.6g) Protein 14.7g Carbohydrate 50.1g Fiber 5.0g Cholesterol 17mg Sodium 463mg
Exchanges: 3 Starch, 1 Vegetable, 1 High-Fat Meat, 1 Fat

Stir-fry a quick veggie meal for lunch or a light supper.

Gingered Snow Pea Stir-Fry
soba noodles   hot green tea   sliced plums

serves 2

Look for the Japanese wheat noodles in Asian markets or
the Asian section of the supermarket.

menu plan

1. Boil water for noodles.

2. Drain and cube tofu; slice carrot; mince garlic; and slice plums.

3. Cook 4 ounces of noodles to get about 2 cups cooked.

4. Stir-fry tofu and vegetables while noodles cook.

5. Prepare tea.

Gingered Snow Pea Stir-Fry

- 1   teaspoon sesame oil
- ½   (12.3-ounce) package extra-firm tofu, drained and cubed
- 2   garlic cloves, minced
- 3   tablespoons ginger-flavored soy sauce, divided (such as House of Tsang)
- 1   cup fat-free, less-sodium chicken broth
- 1½ tablespoons cornstarch
- 1   cup sliced carrot (about 2)
- ½   pound snow peas, trimmed

Heat oil in a wok or large nonstick skillet over medium-high heat until hot. Add tofu and garlic; stir-fry 7 minutes. Add 1 tablespoon soy sauce; stir-fry 2 minutes or until tofu is browned. Remove from pan; set aside.

Combine remaining 2 tablespoons soy sauce, chicken broth, and cornstarch; stir until smooth. Set aside.
Add carrot to pan; stir-fry 5 minutes. Add chicken broth mixture and snow peas; stir-fry 2 minutes. Return tofu mixture to pan; cook until thoroughly heated, stirring gently. Yield: 2 servings.

Per Serving: Calories 236 (29% from fat) Fat 7.6g (sat 1.0g) Protein 13.7g
Carbohydrate 30.7g Fiber 6.2g Cholesterol 0mg Sodium 1169mg
Exchanges: 1 Starch, 3 Vegetable, 1 High-Fat Meat

snow peas

The French name for snow peas means "eat it all," and you can because the entire legume is edible, even the pod. Snow peas are thin and crisp with bright green, almost translucent pods.

selection Snow peas are available year-round with peak seasons in the spring and fall. Select peas that are crisp with brightly colored pods and small seeds. Store the peas in the refrigerator in a plastic bag no longer than 3 days. They start to lose crispness after one day.

preparation You can eat snow peas raw—just pinch off one stem end and pull off the string that runs along one side. If you're cooking snow peas, don't go longer than 1 or 2 minutes, or they'll lose their crunch.

Perfect for a stylish, meat-free meal for guests

Mediterranean Eggplant Provolone
angel hair pasta nests Italian Green Salad

serves 4

Buy angel hair pasta nests in the pasta section of the supermarket,
or use regular angel hair pasta.

menu plan

1. *Boil water for pasta nests.*

2. *Slice eggplant; chop tomatoes, parsley, and basil.*

3. *Prepare tomato mixture.*

4. *Bake eggplant.*

5. *Cook pasta nests according to package directions.*

6. *Prepare salad.*

Mediterranean Eggplant Provolone

2 cups finely chopped plum tomatoes
   (about 4)
2/3 cup chopped fresh parsley
1 1/2 tablespoons chopped fresh basil, divided
2 tablespoons capers, drained
1 tablespoon balsamic vinegar
1/8 teaspoon salt
8 eggplant slices, cut diagonally into 1/2-inch slices
   (about 2 medium)
Cooking spray
4 (1.5-ounce) slices provolone cheese

Preheat oven to 450°.
Combine tomato, parsley, 1 tablespoon basil, capers, vinegar, and salt in a bowl; set aside.

Place eggplant slices on a baking sheet coated with cooking spray; lightly coat eggplant with cooking spray. Bake at 450° for 10 minutes; turn. Bake 2 more minutes or until almost tender. Sprinkle with 1/2 tablespoon basil.
Cut each cheese slice in half; place one cheese slice half on each eggplant slice. Bake 1 minute or until cheese melts. Remove from baking dish with a wide spatula. Place on individual plates; spoon 3/4 cup tomato mixture over each serving.
Yield: 4 servings.

Per Serving: Calories 207 (53% from fat) Fat 12.1g (sat 7.4g) Protein 13.3g
Carbohydrate 13.7g Fiber 4.5g Cholesterol 29mg Sodium 795mg
Exchanges: 3 Vegetable, 1 High-Fat Meat, 1 Fat

Italian Green Salad

1 (10-ounce) package Italian-blend salad greens (about
   6 cups)
1/4 cup fat-free Caesar dressing
Freshly ground black pepper

Divide salad greens evenly among 4 serving plates. Top each serving with 1 tablespoon salad dressing. Sprinkle with freshly ground pepper.
Yield: 4 servings.

Per Serving: Calories 37 (5% from fat) Fat 0.2g (sat 0.0g) Protein 1.4g
Carbohydrate 8.0g Fiber 1.2g Cholesterol 0mg Sodium 191mg
Exchange: 1 Vegetable

a dessert idea: The Café Mocha Granita (page 196) is a refreshing complement to this Mediterranean-style meal. Plan to make it a day ahead.

Crisp asparagus and juicy strawberries in a menu that says "springtime"

Glazed Salmon
Chilled Asparagus with Parmesan
Strawberry-Topped Cake

serves 4

menu plan

1. Prepare asparagus, and let it chill.

2. Microwave glaze for salmon.

3. Broil salmon.

4. Slice strawberries and cake for dessert while salmon is cooking.

5. Assemble dessert just before serving.

a few tips:
cooking fish

1 As fish cooks, its flesh changes from translucent to opaque or solid in appearance. If the fish still has a thin, translucent line when it's flaked, go ahead and remove it from the heat because the residual heat will cook the fish a bit more.

2 A good guide for cooking fish is 10 minutes per inch of thickness. (Measure fish at the thickest part.)

3 To test fish for doneness, pierce the thickest part of the fish with a fork, and twist the fork slightly. The fish should flake easily when it's done.

Glazed Salmon

A fatty fish like salmon doesn't require much basting to keep it moist and tender.

- 3 tablespoons low-sodium soy sauce
- 2 tablespoons brown sugar
- 1 tablespoon honey
- 1 teaspoon bottled minced garlic
- 4 (4-ounce) skinless salmon fillets

Preheat broiler.

Combine first 4 ingredients in a small bowl. Microwave at HIGH 1 minute, stirring after 30 seconds.

Place fish on a broiler pan; brush fish with sugar mixture. Broil 8 minutes or until fish flakes easily when tested with a fork, basting occasionally with remaining sugar mixture. Yield: 4 servings.

Per Serving: Calories 230 (38% from fat) Fat 9.7g (sat 1.7g) Protein 24.2g Carbohydrate 9.0g Fiber 0.0g Cholesterol 77mg Sodium 353mg **Exchanges:** 3 Lean Meat, ½ Starch

Chilled Asparagus with Parmesan

1 pound fresh asparagus
2 tablespoons fresh lemon juice
1 teaspoon Dijon mustard
⅛ teaspoon bottled minced garlic
1 tablespoon preshredded fresh Parmesan cheese

Snap off tough ends of asparagus; arrange spokelike on a 12-inch round glass platter with stems toward outside of platter. Cover with plastic wrap, turning back a small portion of edge to vent. Microwave at HIGH 3 minutes, turning dish once.
While asparagus cooks, combine lemon juice and remaining 3 ingredients.
Drain asparagus, and plunge into ice water until chilled. Drain well and place on serving platter. Pour juice mixture over asparagus, and chill thoroughly. Yield: 4 servings.

Per Serving: Calories 25 (25% from fat) Fat 0.7g (sat 0.3g) Protein 2.2g
Carbohydrate 3.4g Fiber 0.6g Cholesterol 1mg Sodium 72mg
Exchange: 1 Vegetable

Strawberry-Topped Cake

¼ cup strawberry spreadable fruit (such as Polaner's)
2 cups sliced strawberries
4 (1-ounce) slices angel food cake
Grated lemon rind (optional)
Mint sprigs (optional)

Place spreadable fruit in a microwave-safe dish.
Microwave at HIGH 30 seconds or until fruit spread melts. Combine strawberries and spreadable fruit. Spoon evenly over cake slices. Sprinkle with lemon rind, and garnish with mint, if desired.
Yield: 4 servings.

Per Serving: Calories 99 (4% from fat) Fat 0.4g (sat 0.0g) Protein 2.2g
Carbohydrate 25.0g Fiber 1.7g Cholesterol 0mg Sodium 147mg
Exchanges: 1 Starch, 1 Fruit

strawberries

The strawberry is a member of the rose family and has grown wild in Europe and America for centuries.

varieties Not all strawberries are created equal. Certain varieties are known for their vibrant color, others for their sweetness and juiciness. Generally, smaller berries have better flavor than the larger varieties.

storage Pick berries that are bright and shiny, firm and fragrant. Keep strawberries in the refrigerator, but don't wash or hull them. When you're ready to use the berries, rinse them in cold water, and drain well. For the fullest flavor, serve strawberries at room temperature.

A springtime meal in a bowl

Smoked Salmon Pasta Salad
crisp breadsticks   strawberry sorbet

serves 4

menu plan
1. *Boil water for pasta.*
2. *Trim and slice asparagus; cut salmon into strips.*
3. *Cook pasta and asparagus, and drain.*
4. *Combine salad ingredients.*

Smoked Salmon Pasta Salad

  2   cups uncooked farfelle (bow tie pasta)
1½ cups sliced asparagus (about 12 ounces)
  1   (4-ounce) package smoked salmon
1¼ cups grape or cherry tomatoes
 ⅓ cup (1.3 ounces) crumbled feta cheese with basil and
      sun-dried tomatoes
 ½ cup reduced-fat olive oil vinaigrette
 ¼ teaspoon salt
 ¼ teaspoon freshly ground black pepper

Cook pasta in boiling water 7 minutes, omitting salt and fat. Add asparagus; cook 4 more minutes. Drain pasta mixture. Rinse with cold water; drain well.
Cut salmon into ½-inch-wide strips.
Combine pasta mixture, salmon, tomatoes, and remaining ingredients in a large bowl; toss gently. Yield: 4 (1½-cup) servings.

Per Serving: Calories 385 (30% from fat) Fat 12.7g (sat 3.2g) Protein 17.2g
Carbohydrate 53.1g Fiber 3.8g Cholesterol 27mg Sodium 773mg
Exchanges: 3 Starch, 2 Vegetable, 1 Medium-Fat Meat, 1 Fat

asparagus

Asparagus is a member of the lily family, so it's related to onions, leeks, and garlic. The name asparagus is from a Greek word meaning "sprout" or "shoot."

varieties There are two main types of asparagus—green and white (the white is grown underground to keep it from turning green). There's also a purple variety called Viola.

selection Look for firm, bright green (or pale ivory) stalks with tight tips. Although asparagus is best prepared the day you buy it, you can store it in the refrigerator, tightly wrapped in a plastic bag, up to 3 days. Or, store it standing upright in an inch of water, and cover the spears with a plastic bag.

Succulent salmon served over a creamy potato-pea medley

Pan-Seared Salmon
Herbed Potatoes and Peas
French bread **Sorbet Parfaits**
serves 4

menu plan

1. *Prepare parfaits, and freeze until serving time.*

2. *Cook potatoes in microwave.*

3. *Cook salmon.*

4. *Prepare white sauce for potatoes and peas while salmon cooks.*

Pan-Seared Salmon

    4   (4-ounce) salmon fillets
    ¼   teaspoon kosher salt
Dash of pepper
    1   teaspoon olive oil
    1   teaspoon light butter

Sprinkle salmon with salt and pepper. Add oil and butter to a large nonstick skillet; place over medium-high heat until hot. Add salmon, and cook 6 minutes, turning and browning evenly on all sides. Reduce heat to medium, and cook 2 to 3 minutes or just until fish flakes easily when tested with a fork.
Yield: 4 servings.

Per Serving: Calories 146 (35% from fat) Fat 5.6g (sat 1.1g) Protein 22.7g
Carbohydrate 0.0g Fiber 0.0g Cholesterol 61mg Sodium 228mg
Exchanges: 3 Lean Meat

Herbed Potatoes and Peas

    8   small red potatoes, halved
    1   tablespoon light butter
    1½ tablespoons all-purpose flour
    ¾   cup 2% reduced-fat milk
    ¾   cup fat-free, less-sodium chicken broth
    1½ cups frozen petite green peas
    ¼   teaspoon freshly ground black pepper
    2   tablespoons thinly sliced mint or basil

Arrange potato halves in a circle on paper towels in microwave oven. Microwave at HIGH 5 minutes or until tender.
Melt butter in a saucepan over medium heat. Add flour, stirring with a whisk. Gradually add milk and broth, stirring with a whisk. Cook over medium heat until thick, stirring constantly. Add potato and peas; bring to a boil, stirring to coat. Stir in pepper and mint. Yield: 4 servings.

Per Serving: Calories 172 (21% from fat) Fat 4.0g (sat 2.6g) Protein 6.9g
Carbohydrate 26.3g Fiber 3.6g Cholesterol 14mg Sodium 244mg
Exchanges: 1½ Starch, 1 Fat

Sorbet Parfaits

    1   cup raspberry sorbet
    1   cup lemon sorbet
    4   sugar wafers

Spoon ¼ cup raspberry sorbet into each of 4 parfait dishes. Top each with ¼ cup lemon sorbet. Serve each with a wafer. Yield: 4 servings.

Per Serving: Calories 158 (5% from fat) Fat 0.8g (sat 0.2g) Protein 0.1g
Carbohydrate 38.6g Fiber 0.1g Cholesterol 0mg Sodium 5mg
Exchanges: ½ Starch, 2 Fruit

If you've never served mussels, this incredibly flavorful and easy menu is a great way to start.

Mussels with Red Curry
mixed green salad   crusty French bread
Pineapple with Toasted Coconut
serves 2

Use a bag of prewashed salad greens and low-fat vinaigrette for the salad.

menu plan
1. *Boil water for pasta.*

2. *Scrub and debeard mussels.*

3. *Toast coconut over medium-high heat in a nonstick skillet for about 1 minute.*

4. *Prepare pineapple and green salad.*

5. *Cook pasta, and drain.*

6. *Prepare mussel dish.*

chicken broth, and curry paste, stirring well. Bring to a boil, and add mussels. Cover, reduce heat, and simmer 4 minutes or until mussel shells open. Discard any unopened shells.

Divide pasta evenly between 2 shallow bowls; pour broth mixture evenly over pasta, and top evenly with mussels. Sprinkle with chopped parsley, if desired. Yield: 2 servings.

Per Serving: Calories 439 (28% from fat) Fat 13.6g (sat 3.2g) Protein 25.3g Carbohydrate 53.2g Fiber 1.4g Cholesterol 38mg Sodium 654mg **Exchanges:** 3½ Starch, 2 Very Lean Meat, 2 Fat

Mussels with Red Curry

    4   ounces uncooked gemelli (short tube-shaped pasta)
    1   teaspoon olive oil
    2   tablespoons finely chopped shallots
    ½   cup light coconut milk
    ½   cup low-sodium chicken broth
    1   tablespoon red curry paste
   48   mussels (about 2 pounds), scrubbed and debearded
Chopped parsley (optional)

Cook pasta according to package directions, omitting salt and fat; drain.
Heat olive oil in a large skillet over medium heat. Add shallots, and sauté 1 minute. Stir in coconut milk,

Pineapple with Toasted Coconut

Look for fresh pineapple chunks in the produce section of the supermarket, or use drained, canned pineapple chunks packed in juice.

    2   cups pineapple chunks
    1   tablespoon flaked sweetened coconut, toasted

Place 1 cup pineapple in each of 2 dessert dishes. Top evenly with toasted coconut.
Yield: 2 (1-cup) servings.

Per Serving: Calories 99 (16% from fat) Fat 1.8g (sat 1.0g) Protein 0.7g Carbohydrate 22.8g Fiber 2.2g Cholesterol 0mg Sodium 9mg **Exchanges:** 1½ Fruit

a dessert idea: *If you've got a little more time to spend on dessert, try the Banana Cream Trifle on page 210.*

Invite some friends over for a fresh crab cake dinner.

Coastal Crab Cakes
Roasted Asparagus sourdough rolls
Rum-Baked Bananas
serves 6

menu plan

1. *Drain crabmeat and remove shell pieces; chop green onions and parsley.*

2. *Prepare tartar sauce, and let it chill.*

3. *Prepare crab cakes.*

4. *Trim asparagus, and roast.*

5. *Cook crab cakes.*

6. *Assemble banana dessert, and bake while crab cakes cook. Cover and keep warm until serving time.*

Coastal Crab Cakes

Serve these crab cakes with Balsamic Tartar Sauce and fresh lemon wedges. (The analysis does not include the tartar sauce.)

- 1   **pound lump crabmeat, drained and shell pieces removed**
- ½   **cup dry breadcrumbs**
- ½   **cup chopped green onions**
- 2   **tablespoons grated Parmesan cheese**
- 1   **teaspoon dry mustard**
- 1   **large egg, lightly beaten**
- 1   **tablespoon light mayonnaise**
- 1   **tablespoon fat-free milk**
- ¼   **cup all-purpose flour**
- 1   **teaspoon olive oil**

Combine first 5 ingredients in a medium bowl; stir gently. Stir in beaten egg, mayonnaise, and milk.

Shape crabmeat mixture into 6 (3-inch) patties. Dredge patties in flour.
Heat oil in a large nonstick skillet over medium heat. Add patties, and cook 4 minutes on each side or until lightly browned.
Yield: 6 servings.

Per Serving: Calories 214 (24% from fat) Fat 5.6g (sat 1.3g) Protein 20.3g Carbohydrate 27.8g Fiber 1.0g Cholesterol 115mg Sodium 429mg **Exchanges:** 2 Starch, 2 Lean Meat

balsamic tartar sauce

- ¾   **cup light mayonnaise**
- 1   **tablespoon drained capers**
- 1   **tablespoon finely chopped parsley**
- 1   **tablespoon white balsamic vinegar**

Combine all ingredients in small bowl. Cover and chill, or serve immediately. Serve with crab cakes.
Yield: ¾ cup (serving size: 1 tablespoon).

Per Tablespoon: Calories 50 (90% from fat) Fat 5.0g (sat 1.0g) Protein 0.5g Carbohydrate 1.1g Fiber 0.2g Cholesterol 5mg Sodium 176mg **Exchange:** 1 Fat

asparagus: thick or thin?

Slender spears of asparagus are not necessarily younger and more tender than thick spears. The variety of asparagus determines the thickness, so the thick spears are thick when they are young, and the thin ones don't get thicker as they get older. Either variety will work in most recipes; try to buy spears that are all the same size so they'll cook evenly.

Roasted Asparagus

1½ pounds asparagus spears
Olive oil-flavored cooking spray
 ⅛ teaspoon salt

Snap off tough ends of asparagus.
Coat asparagus with cooking spray; place on a baking sheet. Sprinkle with salt. Bake at 450° for 10 minutes or until tender. Yield: 6 servings.

Per Serving: Calories 15 (12% from fat) Fat 0.2g (sat 0.0g) Protein 1.4g
Carbohydrate 2.7g Fiber 1.3g Cholesterol 0mg Sodium 48mg
Exchange: 1 Vegetable

Rum-Baked Bananas

You can substitute ½ cup of pineapple juice for the liqueur and the rum.

   3   large bananas, halved and split lengthwise
   2   tablespoons light butter, melted
   6   tablespoons brown sugar
   ¼   cup banana-flavored liqueur
   ¼   cup white rum
   3   cups vanilla fat-free ice cream

Place banana in an 11 x 7-inch baking dish. Drizzle with butter; sprinkle with brown sugar, liqueur, and rum. Bake at 450° for 6 minutes or until bubbly.
Spoon ½ cup ice cream into each of 6 dessert dishes. Top evenly with baked banana. Yield: 6 servings.

Per Serving: Calories 233 (9% from fat) Fat 2.4g (sat 1.5g) Protein 3.0g
Carbohydrate 51.8g Fiber 1.8g Cholesterol 7mg Sodium 70mg
Exchanges: 2 Starch, 1 Fruit

a few tips:
roasting vegetables

1 Use a heavy roasting pan.

2 Arrange the vegetables in a single layer, completely covering the bottom of the pan.

3 Make sure the vegetables aren't too crowded in the pan so the sides of the pieces will brown.

4 Coat the vegetables with a small amount of fat (oil or cooking spray) so they don't get too dry.

5 Here's a list of some good roasting vegetables:

asparagus	radishes
beets	rutabagas
bell peppers	squash
carrots	sweet potatoes
onions	tomatoes
parsnips	turnips
potatoes	zucchini

Quick, light, and just right for a relaxed dinner

Scallop-Pasta Toss
sourdough rolls   sliced kiwifruit

serves 4

menu plan

1. *Boil water for pasta.*

2. *Prepare sauce for pasta; slice bell pepper; trim peas; mince garlic; and peel and slice kiwifruit.*

3. *Cook pasta; sauté scallops and vegetables.*

4. *Combine pasta, scallops, and vegetables.*

kiwifruit

This odd-looking fruit originally came from New Zealand. It has the same name as a flightless New Zealand bird, perhaps because it looks like a brown egg covered with fine hair. The fruit's flesh is a brilliant green, and it has a ring of tiny black edible seeds in the center.

flavor The sweet-tart flavor of kiwifruit is a bit like that of a strawberry or a pineapple and is an excellent source of vitamin C.

uses Kiwifruit can be halved and scooped out like a melon, or peeled and sliced. Store ripe kiwifruit in the refrigerator up to 3 weeks. Since kiwifruit is grown in both hemispheres, it is generally available year-round.

Scallop-Pasta Toss

Sea scallops are larger than bay scallops and average about 1½ inches in diameter.

- 6 ounces uncooked farfalle (bow tie pasta)
- ¼ cup reduced-fat peanut butter
- 2 tablespoons brown sugar
- 2 tablespoons low-sodium soy sauce
- 2 tablespoons rice wine vinegar
- ½ teaspoon crushed red pepper
- 2 teaspoons vegetable oil
- 1 pound sea scallops
- 1 cup red bell pepper strips
- 2 garlic cloves, minced
- Cooking spray
- 3 cups snow peas, trimmed

Cook pasta according to package directions, omitting salt and fat.

Combine peanut butter and next 4 ingredients, stirring well with a whisk. Set aside.

Heat oil in a large nonstick skillet over high heat until hot. Add scallops; sauté 2 minutes on each side or until browned. Remove from pan.

Coat bell pepper strips and garlic with cooking spray. Place pan over medium-high heat until hot; add bell pepper and garlic. Sauté 2 minutes; add snow peas, and sauté 2 minutes. Return scallops to skillet; add peanut butter mixture. Cook 2 minutes or until thoroughly heated.

Combine drained pasta and scallop mixture in a serving bowl; toss gently. Serve immediately.

Yield: 4 (1¾-cup) servings.

Per Serving: Calories 432 (21% from fat) Fat 10.3g (sat 1.9g) Protein 30.6g
Carbohydrate 53.3g Fiber 4.2g Cholesterol 37mg Sodium 512mg
Exchanges: 3 Starch, 2 Vegetable, 3 Lean Meat

Counter the spiciness of this rich bisque by serving it over Golden Raisin Rice.

Spicy Coconut-Shrimp Bisque
Golden Raisin Rice   pineapple slices

serves 4

Use fresh peeled and cored pineapple from the produce section or canned sliced pineapple in juice. Buy peeled and deveined shrimp at the fish counter.

menu plan

1. Cook rice.
2. Chop onion, bell pepper, and cilantro for bisque; slice pineapple.
3. Prepare bisque.
4. Add remaining ingredients to rice.

Spicy Coconut-Shrimp Bisque

- 4 tablespoons red curry paste
- 2 tablespoons water
- Cooking spray
- 1 pound peeled and deveined medium shrimp
- 1 cup chopped green onions
- 1 cup frozen green peas, thawed
- ½ cup chopped red bell pepper
- 1 (14-ounce) can light coconut milk
- ¼ cup chopped cilantro
- ¼ teaspoon salt

Combine curry paste and water in a small bowl; stir well with a whisk.

Coat a Dutch oven with cooking spray; place over medium heat until hot. Add curry paste mixture and shrimp; cook, uncovered, 4 minutes, stirring frequently. Add onions, peas, and bell pepper; cook 3 minutes or until peas are tender.

Add coconut milk and cilantro; cook 2 minutes or until thoroughly heated. Stir in salt. Remove from heat, cover, and let stand 5 minutes before serving.
Yield: 4 (1¼-cup) servings.

Per Serving: Calories 250 (36% from fat) Fat 10.0g (sat 3.7g) Protein 27.1g Carbohydrate 13.5g Fiber 2.6g Cholesterol 172mg Sodium 538mg **Exchanges:** 1 Starch, 3 Lean Meat

Golden Raisin Rice

- 1 cup uncooked basmati rice
- 2 cups cold water
- 2 tablespoons chopped green onions
- ¼ cup golden raisins
- ¼ teaspoon salt

Combine rice and cold water in a medium saucepan. Bring to a boil; cover, reduce heat, and simmer 15 minutes or until rice is tender and liquid is absorbed.

Remove from heat and let stand, covered, 5 minutes. Stir in onions, raisins, and salt.
Yield: 4 (¾-cup) servings.

Per Serving: Calories 201 (2% from fat) Fat 0.4g (sat 0.1g) Protein 3.7g Carbohydrate 45.4g Fiber 1.1g Cholesterol 0mg Sodium 151mg **Exchanges:** 2 Starch, 1 Fruit

A tangy taste of the tropics

Shrimp Del Sol
Mango Salad crusty French rolls

serves 4

menu plan

1. *Boil water for pasta.*
2. *Chop mango, and slice onion for salad; chop cilantro, and squeeze lime juice for shrimp dish.*
3. *Prepare salad.*
4. *Prepare sauce for shrimp dish.*
5. *Cook pasta while sauce simmers.*
6. *Toss pasta and shrimp mixture.*

mangoes

Mangoes originally came from India, where the mango tree is sacred. Now mangoes are grown in temperate climates all over the world. They grow in a wide variety of shapes from oblong to round and range in size from 6 ounces to 4 pounds.

Store underripe fruit in a paper bag at room temperature. Place ripe mangoes in a plastic bag, and keep in the refrigerator up to 5 days.

Shrimp Del Sol

 1 (14½-ounce) can zesty diced tomatoes seasoned with jalapeño peppers, undrained
 1 (14½-ounce) can no-salt-added diced tomatoes
 2 tablespoons tequila
 1 tablespoon fresh lime juice
 1½ teaspoons ground cumin
 1 pound steamed peeled shrimp with tails
 ¼ cup minced fresh cilantro
 1 (9-ounce) package fresh angel hair pasta, uncooked
 1 teaspoon olive oil

Combine first 5 ingredients in a saucepan. Bring to a boil. Reduce heat; simmer, uncovered, 5 minutes.
Remove tails from shrimp, if desired. Add shrimp and cilantro to tomato mixture; simmer until thoroughly heated. Cook pasta according to package directions using 1 teaspoon oil; drain. Toss shrimp mixture with cooked pasta. Yield: 4 (2-cup) servings.

Per Serving: Calories 347 (9% from fat) Fat 3.3g (sat 0.4g) Protein 32.8g Carbohydrate 45.5g Fiber 3.5g Cholesterol 285mg Sodium 764mg **Exchanges:** 3 Starch, 3 Very Lean Meat

Mango Salad

 1 (10-ounce) package romaine salad
 1 cup refrigerated mango slices, chopped
 ½ cup sliced red onion
 ⅓ cup fat-free balsamic vinaigrette

Combine first 3 ingredients in a bowl. Toss with vinaigrette. Yield: 4 servings.

Per Serving: Calories 52 (3% from fat) Fat 0.2g (sat 0.0g) Protein 1.5g Carbohydrate 11.7g Fiber 1.9g Cholesterol 0mg Sodium 272mg **Exchanges:** 1 Vegetable, ½ Fruit

Most of the ingredients in this shrimp dinner are items that you can keep on hand in your pantry or freezer.

Tomato-Feta Shrimp with Pasta
Cucumber Salad

serves 4

menu plan

1. *Boil water for pasta.*
2. *Slice cucumbers and onion; chop parsley for salad and shrimp dish.*
3. *Prepare salad.*
4. *Cook pasta.*
5. *Prepare tomato-shrimp mixture while pasta cooks.*

Tomato-Feta Shrimp with Pasta

8 ounces uncooked fusilli (short twisted spaghetti)
2 (14½-ounce) cans diced tomatoes with garlic and onion, undrained
½ cup chopped onion
Olive oil-flavored cooking spray
⅓ cup dry white wine
1 tablespoon chopped fresh oregano
¾ pound frozen cooked, peeled, and deveined medium shrimp, thawed
½ cup crumbled feta cheese

Cook pasta according to package directions, omitting salt and fat. Drain.

Drain 1 can diced tomatoes; discard liquid. Combine drained tomatoes with remaining can tomatoes, and set aside.

Place a large nonstick skillet over medium-high heat until hot. Coat onion with cooking spray; add to pan. Sauté 2 minutes or until tender. Add tomatoes, wine, and oregano. Bring to a simmer; cook 5 minutes, stirring frequently.

Stir in shrimp; cook 1 minute or until mixture is thoroughly heated.

Divide pasta among 4 serving plates; top evenly with shrimp mixture. Sprinkle each serving with 2 tablespoons cheese. Yield: 4 servings.

Per Serving: Calories 406 (15% from fat) Fat 6.7g (sat 3.5g) Protein 29.9g
Carbohydrate 55.6g Fiber 2.7g Cholesterol 184mg Sodium 922mg
Exchanges: 3 Starch, 2 Vegetable, 2 Lean Meat

Cucumber Salad

2½ cups sliced cucumber (about 2 medium)
½ cup sliced red onion
¼ cup plain low-fat yogurt
¼ teaspoon salt
2 tablespoons chopped fresh parsley
Lettuce leaves (optional)

Combine first 5 ingredients in a medium bowl; stir gently. Serve on lettuce leaves, if desired.
Yield: 4 servings.

Per Serving: Calories 24 (15% from fat) Fat 0.4g (sat 0.2g) Protein 1.4g
Carbohydrate 4.2g Fiber 0.9g Cholesterol 1mg Sodium 160mg
Exchange: 1 Vegetable

Spice up your life with this south-of-the-border shrimp and salad supper.

Broiled Shrimp
Spicy Poblano Salad baked tortilla chips
Chocolate Ice Cream Sandwiches
serves 4

menu plan

1. *Soften ice cream, and prepare ice cream sandwiches. (You can make the sandwiches ahead of time.)*
2. *Cook couscous for salad.*
3. *Chop chile, tomatoes, and cilantro for salad.*
4. *Combine ingredients for salad.*
5. *Broil shrimp.*

Broiled Shrimp

Olive oil-flavored cooking spray
1 pound large shrimp, peeled and deveined
2 teaspoons bottled minced garlic
¼ teaspoon salt
¼ teaspoon pepper
½ teaspoon ground cumin
2 tablespoons olive oil

Preheat broiler.
Coat a baking sheet with cooking spray. Combine shrimp and remaining 5 ingredients, stirring to coat; place shrimp on baking sheet. Broil 6 to 8 minutes or until shrimp turn pink. Spoon shrimp over Spicy Poblano Salad. Yield: 4 servings.

Per Serving: Calories 185 (44% from fat) Fat 9.0g (sat 1.3g) Protein 23.2g Carbohydrate 1.7g Fiber 0.1g Cholesterol 172mg Sodium 315mg
Exchanges: 3 Lean Meat

Spicy Poblano Salad

1 (6-ounce) package garlic-flavored couscous, uncooked
1 (14.5-ounce) can black beans, rinsed and drained
1 poblano chile, seeded and finely chopped
8 ounces plum tomatoes, chopped
¼ cup chopped cilantro
¼ cup fresh lime juice
1 teaspoon salt-free Mexican seasoning
¼ teaspoon salt
¼ teaspoon black pepper

Prepare couscous according to package directions, omitting oil. Spread couscous on a baking sheet; cool 10 minutes.
Combine black beans and remaining 7 ingredients in a medium bowl. Add couscous; toss gently.
Yield: 4 (1½-cup) servings.

Per Serving: Calories 238 (4% from fat) Fat 1.0g (sat 0.1g) Protein 11.1g Carbohydrate 48.7g Fiber 4.9g Cholesterol 0mg Sodium 312mg
Exchanges: 3 Starch, 1 Vegetable

Chocolate Ice Cream Sandwiches

¾ cup vanilla-chocolate fat-free ice cream, softened
8 chocolate wafers
4 teaspoons fat-free caramel sundae syrup

Spread 3 tablespoons ice cream onto each of 4 wafers; top each with 1 teaspoon caramel and another wafer, pressing gently. Cover and freeze until firm.
Yield: 4 servings.

Per Serving: Calories 91 (22% from fat) Fat 2.2g (sat 0.6g) Protein 1.9g Carbohydrate 16.8g Fiber 0.0g Cholesterol 8mg Sodium 84mg
Exchange: 1 Starch

Enjoy a sophisticated, yet simple, steak dinner.

Shiitake Steak
Steamed Potatoes   Sugar Snap Peas
French rolls
serves 4

menu plan

1. *Wash and quarter potatoes; remove and discard stems from mushrooms. Mince garlic; wash and trim peas.*

2. *Season and broil steak.*

3. *While steak broils, cook potatoes in microwave and mushroom mixture on stovetop.*

4. *Wipe skillet clean, and sauté peas.*

5. *Slice steak.*

Shiitake Steak

1   teaspoon cracked black pepper
1   (1-pound) flank steak (½ inch thick)
Cooking spray
½   pound shiitake mushrooms
½   teaspoon olive oil
⅓   cup chopped green onions
1   tablespoon diced pimento, drained
1   garlic clove, minced
3   tablespoons balsamic vinegar
¼   teaspoon salt

Preheat broiler.
Press pepper into both sides of steak. Place steak on a broiler pan coated with cooking spray. Broil 8 minutes on each side or until steak is done.
Remove and discard stems from mushrooms. Heat oil in a large skillet over medium heat. Add mushroom caps and green onions, and cook 3 minutes, stirring

frequently. Add pimento, garlic, vinegar, and salt. Cook 1 minute.
Cut steak diagonally across grain into thin slices. Spoon mushroom mixture over steak. Yield: 4 servings.

Per Serving: Calories 228 (54% from fat) Fat 13.7g (sat 5.5g) Protein 22.7g Carbohydrate 3.2g Fiber 0.8g Cholesterol 60mg Sodium 221mg
Exchanges: 3 Medium-Fat Meat

wild mushrooms

Wild mushrooms tend to have a stronger flavor than the familiar cultivated white mushrooms. Because so many wild mushrooms are poisonous, it's best to pick them at the supermarket instead of the forest.

A few choices:

chanterelle   trumpet-shaped with a chewy texture and a golden to yellow-orange color. Unlike most wild mushrooms, it has a delicate flavor.

cremini   the brown and fuller-flavored variety of the more common button mushroom.

enoki   an Asian mushroom that grows in clumps. It has long, slender stems and small caps. This mushroom has a crunchy texture and mild flavor.

morel   has an elongated honeycomb cup and a smoky flavor.

shiitake   an Asian mushroom with a floppy, flat cap and a meaty flavor.

Steamed Potatoes

1 pound small red potatoes, quartered
2 tablespoons water
Butter-flavored spray (such as I Can't Believe
      It's Not Butter)
¼ teaspoon salt
¼ teaspoon pepper

Arrange potato quarters in a 1-quart microwave-safe dish. Add water, and cover with heavy-duty plastic wrap. Microwave at HIGH 8 to 10 minutes or until tender. Drain.

Coat potato with butter-flavored spray; sprinkle with salt and pepper. Yield: 4 (¾-cup) servings.

Per Serving: Calories 86 (3% from fat) Fat 0.3g (sat 0.0g) Protein 2.5g
Carbohydrate 18.9g Fiber 2.1g Cholesterol 0mg Sodium 155mg
Exchange: 1 Starch

Sugar Snap Peas

Butter-flavored cooking spray
1 pound sugar snap peas, trimmed
2 teaspoons lemon-pepper seasoning

Coat a large nonstick skillet with cooking spray; place over medium-high heat until hot. Add peas; sauté 3 minutes or until crisp-tender. Coat peas lightly with additional cooking spray, and sprinkle with lemon-pepper seasoning. Yield: 4 servings.

Per Serving: Calories 96 (7% from fat) Fat 0.7g (sat 0.1g) Protein 6.2g
Carbohydrate 17.0g Fiber 3.9g Cholesterol 0mg Sodium 176mg
Exchange: 1 Starch

red potatoes

varieties Round red potatoes are sometimes called boiling potatoes. Small red potatoes are often referred to as "new potatoes," but new potatoes are any variety of young potatoes that haven't had time to convert their sugar fully into starch, so they have a crisp, waxy texture and a thin skin. New potatoes are available in spring and early summer, while round red potatoes are available year-round.

selection Don't buy potatoes with wrinkles, sprouts, or cracks.

storage Store potatoes in a cool, dark, well-ventilated place for up to 2 weeks. Don't keep them in the refrigerator—they'll get very sweet and turn dark when cooked.

a dessert idea: *For a fitting finale, bring out a plate of Lemon Meringue Cakes (page 198).*

A special occasion "just-for-two" springtime menu

Mixed Greens with Raspberry Vinaigrette (page 42)
Broiled Lamb with Rosemary
Parslied Potatoes
hard rolls **Melon Compote (page 42)**
serves 2

menu plan

1. *Trim asparagus; mince garlic. Chop rosemary and parsley. Wash and halve potatoes; slice cucumber and onion.*

2. *Prepare yogurt sauce and wine mixture.*

3. *Broil lamb.*

4. *Cook potatoes in microwave.*

5. *Add asparagus to broiler pan.*

6. *Assemble salad.*

7. *Prepare compote.*

Broiled Lamb with Rosemary

½ pound asparagus
¼ cup plain fat-free yogurt
1 teaspoon Dijon mustard
Butter-flavored cooking spray
¼ teaspoon salt
¼ cup dry red wine
2 small garlic cloves, minced
1 tablespoon chopped fresh rosemary
4 (4-ounce) lamb loin chops, trimmed (1 inch thick)
Freshly ground black pepper

Preheat broiler.
Snap off tough ends of asparagus.
Combine yogurt and mustard; stir well. Set aside.
Coat asparagus with cooking spray. Sprinkle lightly with salt.
Combine wine, garlic, and rosemary.

Place lamb chops on one end of a broiler pan coated with cooking spray. Brush chops with half of wine mixture. Broil 8 minutes. Turn chops, and brush with remaining half of wine mixture. Broil 2 minutes, and add asparagus to pan. Broil 4 to 5 minutes, turning asparagus every 2 minutes, until asparagus is crisp-tender and chops are done. Remove asparagus and chops from pan; sprinkle with freshly ground pepper.
To serve, place half of asparagus and 2 lamb chops on each of two serving plates. Top asparagus with yogurt mixture. Yield: 2 servings.

Per Serving: Calories 296 (36% from fat) Fat 12.0g (sat 4.2g) Protein 37.7g
Carbohydrate 8.4g Fiber 2.4g Cholesterol 108mg Sodium 489mg
Exchanges: 1 Vegetable, 5 Lean Meat

Parslied Potatoes

½ pound small red potatoes, halved
1 tablespoon water
Butter-flavored spray (such as I Can't Believe It's Not Butter)
1½ teaspoons chopped fresh parsley
Freshly ground black pepper

Place potato in a microwave-safe dish. Add water and cover with heavy-duty plastic wrap. Microwave at HIGH 6 to 7 minutes or until tender. Coat with butter-flavored spray, and sprinkle with parsley and pepper. Yield: 2 servings.

Per Serving: Calories 91 (1% from fat) Fat 0.1g (sat 0.0g) Protein 2.7g
Carbohydrate 20.5g Fiber 2.3g Cholesterol 0mg Sodium 9mg
Exchange: 1 Starch

Mixed Greens with Raspberry Vinaigrette

3 cups mixed salad greens
¼ cup sliced cucumber
¼ cup sliced red onion
2 tablespoons fat-free raspberry vinaigrette
Fresh raspberries (optional)

Combine first 3 ingredients. Drizzle with vinaigrette and toss. Garnish with fresh raspberries, if desired. Yield: 2 (1½-cup) servings.

Per Serving: Calories 34 (8% from fat) Fat 0.3g (sat 0.0g) Protein 1.9g
Carbohydrate 7.7g Fiber 2.4g Cholesterol 0mg Sodium 94mg
Exchange: 1 Vegetable

Melon Compote

Buy a container of cubed melon or melon balls in the fresh fruit section of the grocery or from the salad bar.

2 cups honeydew melon or cantaloupe balls or cubes
1 cup ginger ale
Mint sprigs (optional)

Place 1 cup melon balls in each of 2 goblets; add ½ cup ginger ale to each goblet. Garnish with mint sprigs, if desired. Yield: 2 servings.

Per Serving: Calories 81 (1% from fat) Fat 0.1g (sat 0.0g) Protein 0.5g
Carbohydrate 21.8g Fiber 0.7g Cholesterol 0mg Sodium 19mg
Exchange: 1 Fruit

This simple, elegant dessert is a refreshing way to end a classic spring dinner.

Melon Compote

Veal good enough to rival your favorite restaurant's version

Veal Piccata
Squash Sauté   hard rolls
serves 2

menu plan

1. *Boil water for pasta.*

2. *Slice and cook squash, and keep warm.*

3. *Cook pasta.*

4. *Prepare veal recipe.*

Veal Piccata

½ pound veal cutlets
Olive oil-flavored cooking spray
¼ teaspoon salt
¼ teaspoon pepper
¼ cup Italian-seasoned breadcrumbs
2 tablespoons fat-free, less-sodium chicken broth
1 tablespoon dry white wine
1 tablespoon fresh lemon juice
1 tablespoon light butter
2 tablespoons chopped fresh parsley
1½ cups hot cooked angel hair pasta

Place veal between 2 sheets of heavy-duty plastic wrap; flatten to ¼-inch thickness using a meat mallet. Coat veal with cooking spray; sprinkle with salt and pepper. Dredge veal in breadcrumbs.
Heat a large nonstick skillet over medium-high heat; add veal. Cook 1 to 2 minutes on each side or until done. Set veal aside, and keep warm.
Reduce heat; add broth, wine, and lemon juice to skillet. Cook 30 seconds, stirring to loosen browned bits. Remove from heat; add butter and parsley, stirring until butter melts.

Place ¾ cup pasta on each plate; top evenly with veal and sauce. Serve immediately. Yield: 2 servings.

Per Serving: Calories 362 (19% from fat) Fat 7.8g (sat 3.2g) Protein 30.5g Carbohydrate 41.4g Fiber 2.0g Cholesterol 104mg Sodium 866mg
Exchanges: 3 Starch, 3 Lean Meat

Squash Sauté

1 teaspoon light butter
1 zucchini, diagonally sliced
1 small yellow squash, diagonally sliced
1 teaspoon salt-free Greek seasoning

Melt butter in a large nonstick skillet over medium-high heat. Add zucchini and squash; sauté 2 minutes. Add Greek seasoning; sauté 3 additional minutes or until tender. Yield: 2 servings.

Per Serving: Calories 39 (30% from fat) Fat 1.3g (sat 0.7g) Protein 2.3g Carbohydrate 6.5g Fiber 1.7g Cholesterol 3mg Sodium 17mg
Exchange: 1 Vegetable

a few tips:
pounding it out

1 Use a meat mallet (or rolling pin) to tenderize the connective tissue of meat.

2 Place the meat between sheets of heavy-duty plastic wrap or in a large zip-top plastic bag; this makes clean-up easier.

3 Pound the meat to about ¼ inch thick. Not only will the meat be tender, it will cook quickly too.

An attractive arranged salad perfect for a patio luncheon

Asian Citrus Chicken Salad
sesame breadsticks   fruit sorbet

serves 4

Look for crisp sesame breadsticks on the grocery shelves with the crackers and snacks.

menu plan

1. *Prepare dressing.*

2. *Cook chicken.*

3. *Slice oranges and bell pepper while chicken cooks.*

4. *Arrange salads on individual plates.*

ginger

Ginger, or gingerroot, is a plant grown in tropical regions and known for its bumpy root. Its name comes from the Sanskrit word for "horn root." Ginger has a tan skin and flesh that is greenish yellow to ivory. Ginger's peppery, yet sweet flavor has long been a characteristic of Asian and Indian cooking.

The flavor of fresh ginger is very different from that of ground, so ground is not always a good substitute for fresh. Tightly wrap fresh, unpeeled ginger, and keep it in the refrigerator for up to 3 weeks or freeze it for up to 6 months.

Asian Citrus Chicken Salad

⅓ cup honey
2 tablespoons low-sodium soy sauce, divided
⅓ cup raspberry vinegar
2 teaspoons grated peeled fresh ginger
1 tablespoon grated orange rind
⅓ cup fresh orange juice
Cooking spray
4 (4-ounce) skinless, boneless chicken breast halves
4 teaspoons low-sodium soy sauce
8 cups mixed salad greens
3 oranges, peeled and sliced
1 red bell pepper, cut into thin strips

Combine first 6 ingredients in a medium bowl; stir well with a whisk. Set aside.

Coat a large nonstick skillet with cooking spray; place over medium-high heat. Add chicken. Spoon 2 tablespoons orange juice mixture over chicken; cook 5 minutes. Turn chicken, and spoon 2 tablespoons orange juice mixture over chicken. Cook 5 minutes or until done. Remove chicken, and let cool slightly.

Remove skillet from heat. Stir 4 teaspoons soy sauce into drippings in skillet. Set aside. Cut chicken into thin slices; set aside.

Place 2 cups salad greens on each of 4 plates. Arrange orange slices and bell pepper strips over greens. Drizzle 3 tablespoons orange juice mixture over each serving. Arrange sliced chicken over greens. Drizzle each serving with 1 teaspoon of orange juice mixture from pan. Yield: 4 servings.

Per Serving: Calories 300 (6% from fat) Fat 2.0g (sat 0.5g) Protein 30.0g Carbohydrate 42.9g Fiber 6.6g Cholesterol 66mg Sodium 488mg
Exchanges: 1 Starch, 1 Fruit, 2 Vegetable, 3 Very Lean Meat

Celebrate spring with this traditional Mexican dish, and top it with some of your own fresh favorites.

Spicy Chicken Posole
baked tortilla chips
chocolate low-fat ice cream

serves 4

menu plan

1. *Cook bacon and reserve drippings for posole.*

2. *Chop chicken, onion, pepper, and chile for posole.*

3. *Cook chicken.*

4. *Combine posole ingredients, and simmer.*

5. *If you're adding any optional toppings, prepare them while posole simmers.*

Spicy Chicken Posole

A chipotle chile is a dried, smoked jalapeño pepper.

1   bacon slice
1   (7-ounce) can chipotle chiles in adobo sauce
2   (4-ounce) skinless, boneless chicken breast halves, chopped
1   cup chopped onion
1   cup chopped red bell pepper
2   cups fat-free, less-sodium chicken broth
1   (15.5-ounce) can hominy, drained
½   cup (2 ounces) shredded reduced-fat Monterey Jack cheese

Cook bacon in a Dutch oven until crisp; remove bacon, reserving drippings in pan. Reserve bacon for another use.

Remove 1 chipotle chile and 3 tablespoons adobo sauce from can; reserve remaining chiles and sauce for another use. Mince chile, and set aside.

Combine chicken and 3 tablespoons adobo sauce. Heat bacon drippings in pan over medium-high heat until hot. Add chicken, and sauté until chicken is browned. Remove chicken; set aside, and keep warm.

Add onion and pepper to pan; sauté 3 to 4 minutes or until tender. Return chicken to pan; add broth, hominy, and minced chipotle chile. Bring to a boil; reduce heat, and simmer, uncovered, 5 minutes. Top each serving with 2 tablespoons shredded cheese. Yield: 4 servings.

Per Serving: Calories 216 (30% from fat) Fat 7.2g (sat 3.1g) Protein 19.2g Carbohydrate 16.8g Fiber 3.9g Cholesterol 45mg Sodium 955mg **Exchanges:** 1 Starch, 2 Lean Meat

Posole is a thick, hearty soup made with chicken or pork, hominy, and chiles. In the Jalisco region of Mexico, this soup is traditionally served with chopped lettuce, radishes, onions, and fresh cilantro.

You might want to make extra won ton chips—they're great for snacking.

Spring Onion and Chicken Stir-Fry
Bok Choy and Red Pepper Salad
Sesame Won Ton Chips

serves 4

menu plan

1. *Boil water for pasta.*
2. *Slice vegetables for salad.*
3. *Cook pasta.*
4. *Prepare chips while pasta cooks.*
5. *Stir-fry chicken mixture.*
6. *Toss salad.*
7. *Combine pasta and chicken mixture.*

a few tips:
stir-fry basics

Stir-fry and sauté mean the same thing: to cook food quickly in a wok or skillet over high heat while stirring constantly. It's a great low-fat cooking technique because you use little or no oil. To stir-fry successfully, there are a few points to remember:

1 *Cut* all ingredients to approximately the same size and shape so the food will cook evenly.

2 *Slice* foods diagonally to expose more surface area so that the food will cook faster and absorb more flavor.

3 *Heat* the oil or cooking spray in the wok or skillet until it's very hot before you add the food.

4 *Stir* constantly.

Spring Onion and Chicken Stir-Fry

8	ounces uncooked angel hair pasta
2	teaspoons chili oil
4	chicken breast tenders, halved
¼	cup low-sodium chicken broth
1	tablespoon brown sugar
¼	teaspoon salt
2	tablespoons low-sodium soy sauce
1	cup sliced green onions (about 4)
1½	cups fresh bean sprouts

Cook pasta according to package directions, omitting salt and fat. Drain well.

Add oil to a 10-inch nonstick skillet, and place over medium-high heat until hot. Add chicken; stir-fry 5 minutes or until done. Remove chicken from pan; keep warm.

Combine broth and next 3 ingredients, and stir well with a whisk.

Add green onions to pan; stir-fry 1 to 2 minutes or until lightly browned. Return chicken to pan. Stir in broth mixture, drained pasta, and bean sprouts. Yield: 4 (2-cup) servings.

Per Serving: Calories 394 (11% from fat) Fat 4.8g (sat 0.9g) Protein 35.6g Carbohydrate 50.6g Fiber 2.4g Cholesterol 66mg Sodium 479mg
Exchanges: 3 Starch, 1 Vegetable, 4 Lean Meat

Bok Choy and Red Pepper Salad

5   cups sliced bok choy
1   red bell pepper, seeded and cut into thin strips
¼   cup fat-free toasted sesame soy and ginger
      vinaigrette

Combine bok choy and bell pepper in a medium bowl. Pour vinaigrette over bok choy mixture; toss gently. Yield: 4 (1-cup) servings.

Per Serving: Calories 38 (7% from fat)   Fat 0.3g (sat 0.1g)   Protein 1.2g
Carbohydrate 8.0g   Fiber 1.3g   Cholesterol 0mg   Sodium 134mg
Exchange: 1 Vegetable

Sesame Won Ton Chips

Look for fresh won ton wrappers in the produce section of the grocery store.

1   tablespoon sesame seeds
1   large egg white, lightly beaten
1   tablespoon low-sodium soy sauce
½   teaspoon garlic powder
⅛   teaspoon ground ginger
12   fresh or frozen won ton wrappers, thawed
Cooking spray

Place a small skillet over medium-high heat until hot; add sesame seeds, and sauté for 5 to 7 minutes or until seeds are fragrant and golden. Remove from heat, and set aside.
Combine egg white, soy sauce, garlic powder, and ginger in a small bowl.
Cut won ton wrappers in half diagonally, three at a time. Place in a 15 x 10-inch jelly-roll pan coated with cooking spray. Brush egg white mixture over won tons, and sprinkle evenly with sesame seeds.
Bake on lowest oven rack at 375° for 6 to 7 minutes or until crisp and lightly browned. Remove from pan, and cool completely on wire racks.
Yield: 4 servings (serving size: 6 chips).

Per Serving: Calories 92 (17% from fat)   Fat 1.7g (sat 0.2g)   Protein 3.8g
Carbohydrate 15.1g   Fiber 0.1g   Cholesterol 2mg   Sodium 272mg
Exchange: 1 Starch

green onions

Also known as spring onions, green onions are the mild, immature variety of onions that still have their green stalks. Most green onions are small compared to their larger cousins, and they have a fresher, brighter flavor than onions that have been stored for a long period of time and no longer have their greens.

Although similar, green onions and scallions are not the same thing. A green onion has a slightly curved base that looks like it's beginning to turn into a bulb; a true scallion has a straight white base.

You can eat the entire green onion, including the stalk. In fact, green onions are often used to add both color and flavor to a recipe. And if you're using the white bulb part, you don't have to peel it much at all because the skin is thin and translucent.

When you buy green onions, look for crisp, bright greens with no signs of wilting. Keep green onions wrapped in a plastic bag in the refrigerator for up to 2 days.

The spicy, sweet berries are the highlight of this simple supper.

Tarragon Chicken
steamed green beans   whole-wheat rolls
Marinated Strawberries
serves 4

menu plan

1. *Slice strawberries, and marinate.*

2. *Steam a 16-ounce package of frozen green beans in microwave according to package directions.*

3. *Prepare chicken while beans cook.*

Marinated Strawberries

Tarragon Chicken

Cooking spray
- 4   (4-ounce) skinless, boneless chicken breast halves
- ¼   teaspoon salt
- ¼   teaspoon pepper
- ½   cup low-fat sour cream
- 2   tablespoons honey mustard
- 1   teaspoon dried tarragon

Coat a nonstick skillet with cooking spray; place over medium-high heat until hot. Sprinkle chicken with salt and pepper. Add chicken to pan; cook 5 minutes on each side or until done. Transfer to a platter; keep warm.

Stir sour cream, mustard, and tarragon into pan; cook until thoroughly heated. Spoon over chicken. Yield: 4 servings.

Per Serving: Calories 170 (16% from fat) Fat 3.1g (sat 1.4g) Protein 27.2g Carbohydrate 4.2g Fiber 0.0g Cholesterol 71mg Sodium 263mg **Exchange:** 4 Very Lean Meat

Marinated Strawberries

- 2   tablespoons fresh lime juice
- 2   tablespoons honey
- ½   teaspoon olive oil
- ½   teaspoon cracked black pepper
- 1   quart strawberries, cut into thick slices
Grated lime rind (optional)

Combine first 4 ingredients; stir with a whisk. Add strawberries, and toss. Cover and chill. Sprinkle with lime rind, if desired. Yield: 4 (¾-cup) servings.

Per Serving: Calories 174 (7% from fat) Fat 1.0g (sat 0.1g) Protein 0.8g Carbohydrate 17.5g Fiber 2.7g Cholesterol 0mg Sodium 2mg **Exchange:** 1 Fruit

Toss together a satisfying pasta meal and simple salad—just add bread.

Chicken-Asparagus Pasta
Spinach Salad whole-wheat rolls

serves 2

menu plan

1. *Boil water for pasta.*

2. *Trim asparagus, and slice onion for salad.*

3. *Cook pasta; add asparagus.*

4. *Cook chicken and combine olive oil mixture while pasta cooks.*

5. *Toss salad.*

6. *Combine ingredients for pasta dish.*

Chicken-Asparagus Pasta

    4   quarts water
    4   ounces uncooked linguine
    ½   pound asparagus
Garlic-flavored cooking spray
    2   (4-ounce) skinless, boneless chicken breast halves
    1   tablespoon olive oil
    ¼   teaspoon crushed red pepper
    ¼   teaspoon salt
    ⅛   teaspoon ground black pepper
    2   garlic cloves, minced
    3   tablespoons preshredded fresh Parmesan cheese

Bring water to a boil; add pasta, and cook 6 minutes.
Snap off tough ends of asparagus.
Add asparagus to pasta and water; cook 2 minutes. Drain, reserving ¼ cup cooking liquid.
Cook chicken in a grill pan coated with cooking spray 6 to 7 minutes on each side or until done. Cool chicken slightly. Cut chicken into strips.
Combine 1 tablespoon olive oil and next 4 ingredients in a small bowl.

Combine pasta mixture and olive oil mixture. Add sliced chicken, cheese, and reserved liquid; toss well. Yield: 2 (1½-cup) servings.

Per Serving: Calories 471 (26% from fat) Fat 13.8g (sat 3.7g) Protein 38.3g Carbohydrate 46.6g Fiber 2.8g Cholesterol 78mg Sodium 530mg Exchanges: 3 Starch, 4 Lean Meat

Spinach Salad

Use a bag of prewashed torn spinach, and save remaining spinach for another salad.

    3   cups torn spinach
    ¼   cup sliced red onion
    ½   cup grape or cherry tomatoes
    2   tablespoons fat-free balsamic vinaigrette
    ½   cup plain croutons

Combine first 3 ingredients in a large bowl. Add vinaigrette, and toss. Top with croutons.
Yield: 2 (2-cup) servings.

Per Serving: Calories 116 (23% from fat) Fat 2.9g (sat 0.1g) Protein 4.5g Carbohydrate 18.8g Fiber 5.2g Cholesterol 0mg Sodium 431mg Exchanges: 1 Starch, 1 Vegetable, ½ Fat

grape tomatoes

Grape tomatoes are similar to cherry tomatoes, but they're slightly smaller in diameter and have a more elongated shape, similar to that of a grape. The skin is thin and crisp; the flavor is sweet and juicy.

Sheer luxury, without a lot of fuss

Chicken with Dijon Cream Sauce
Hearts of Palm Salad
French rolls   **Amaretto Strawberries**

serves 4

menu plan

1. *Cook chicken.*

2. *Assemble salad.*

3. *Make sauce for chicken.*

4. *Prepare strawberries.*

Chicken with Dijon Cream Sauce

  4   (4-ounce) skinless, boneless chicken breast halves
Cooking spray
1½ teaspoons lemon-pepper seasoning
 ⅓ cup fat-free, less-sodium chicken broth
1½ tablespoons Dijon mustard
 ⅓ cup fat-free half-and-half or fat-free evaporated milk

Coat chicken with cooking spray. Sprinkle both sides of chicken with seasoning. Place a large nonstick skillet over medium-high heat until hot. Add chicken to pan, and cook 4 minutes on each side or until browned. Remove chicken from pan; set aside, and keep warm.
Add broth to pan, stirring to loosen browned bits. Combine mustard and half-and-half; add to pan. Reduce heat, and simmer 6 minutes or until sauce is slightly thick. Spoon sauce over chicken. Yield: 4 servings.

Per Serving: Calories 150 (12% from fat) Fat 2.0g (sat 0.4g) Protein 26.3g Carbohydrate 3.0g Fiber 0.0g Cholesterol 66mg Sodium 440mg **Exchanges:** 4 Very Lean Meat

Hearts of Palm Salad

  1   (14-ounce) can hearts of palm, drained and chopped
  6   cups mixed salad greens
 ¼ cup reduced-fat olive oil vinaigrette

Arrange hearts of palm evenly over salad greens. Drizzle with vinaigrette. Yield: 4 (1½-cup) servings.

Per Serving: Calories 55 (57% from fat) Fat 3.5g (sat 0.3g) Protein 2.3g Carbohydrate 5.5g Fiber 5.1g Cholesterol 0mg Sodium 390mg **Exchanges:** 1 Vegetable, ½ Fat

Amaretto Strawberries

  2   cups vanilla low-fat yogurt
  2   cups sliced strawberries
 ¼ cup amaretto (almond-flavored liqueur)

Spoon ½ cup yogurt into each of 4 dessert dishes. Top each serving with ½ cup strawberries; drizzle 1 tablespoon liqueur over each. Yield: 4 (1-cup) servings.

Per Serving: Calories 171 (9% from fat) Fat 1.8g (sat 1.0g) Protein 6.1g Carbohydrate 26.2g Fiber 2.0g Cholesterol 6mg Sodium 76mg **Exchanges:** 2 Starch

spring produce

Vegetables	Fruits	Herbs
Artichokes	Bananas	Chives
Arugula	Blood Oranges	Dill
Asparagus	Coconuts	Garlic Chives
Avocados	Grapefruit	Lemon Grass
Baby Leeks	Kiwifruit	Mint
Beets	Lemons	Parsley
Belgian Endive	Limes	Thyme
Broccoli Rabe	Mangoes	
Cauliflower	Navel Oranges	
Dandelion Greens	Papayas	
Green Onions	Passionfruit	
Kale	Pineapple	
Lettuce	Strawberries	
Mushrooms	Tangerines	
Radishes	Valencia Oranges	
Red Potatoes		
Rhubarb		
Snap Beans		
Snow Peas		
Spinach		
Sugar Snap Peas		
Sweet Onions		
Swiss Chard		

Strawberries

Artichokes

Mint

Sugar Snap Peas

Papayas

Chives

Snow Peas

Sweet Onions

Although many produce items are available year-round, this chart lists those that are at their peak during this season. Check with farmers' markets in your area for regional varieties.

sum

From the garden to the plate, with few steps in between, is when summer tastes its best. Biting into a thick, juicy tomato sandwich. Grinning with blackberry-stained hands and mouth, holding a half-full bucket. Nibbling on plump, tender kernels from a freshly shucked ear of Silver Queen corn. Putting your whole mouth into a slice of sweet watermelon and spitting out the seeds. Sweet summer memories.

mer

Cool off with a summer-style soup and sandwich lunch.

Chilled Honeydew Soup
Sourdough Tomato Grills
serves 4

Buy cubed melon in the fresh produce section of the grocery store.

menu plan

1. *Prepare and chill soup.*

2. *Slice tomatoes, and prepare mayonnaise mixture for sandwiches.*

3. *Cook sandwiches.*

Chilled Honeydew Soup

5   cups cubed peeled honeydew melon (about ½ medium)
½   cup orange juice
¼   cup sweet white wine
2   tablespoons fresh lime juice
1   tablespoon honey
1   teaspoon grated lime rind

Place melon in a food processor; process until smooth, scraping down sides of bowl occasionally. Transfer melon to a large bowl.

Stir in orange juice and next 3 ingredients. Cover and chill at least 15 minutes. Garnish with grated lime rind. Yield: 4 (1-cup) servings.

Per Serving: Calories 108 (2% from fat) Fat 0.2g (sat 0.1g) Protein 1.2g Carbohydrate 25.9g Fiber 1.2g Cholesterol 0mg Sodium 21mg
Exchanges: 1½ Fruit

Sourdough Tomato Grills

If you've got a griddle, you can cook all four sandwiches at one time.

⅓   cup light mayonnaise
2   tablespoons stone-ground mustard
¼   cup (1 ounce) shredded reduced-fat Cheddar cheese
8   (1.15-ounce) slices sourdough bread
8   slices tomato
Freshly ground pepper
Olive oil-flavored cooking spray

Combine first 3 ingredients. Spread mayonnaise mixture on 1 side of each bread slice. Top each of 4 slices with 2 tomato slices, and sprinkle with pepper. Top with remaining bread slices. Coat sandwiches with cooking spray.

Place a large nonstick skillet over medium-high heat until hot. Add sandwiches, 2 at a time, and cook 3 minutes on each side or until lightly browned. Serve immediately. Yield: 4 servings.

Per Serving: Calories 270 (34% from fat) Fat 10.2g (sat 2.1g) Protein 9.0g Carbohydrate 36.2g Fiber 1.9g Cholesterol 11mg Sodium 678mg
Exchanges: 2 Starch, 1 Vegetable, 1 Lean Meat, 1 Fat

tomatoes

Is it a vegetable or a fruit? Who cares when it tastes so good in the summertime? Botanically speaking, a tomato is classified as a fruit since it's formed from a fertilized flower and has seeds. But in terms of meal planning, we tend to use it as a vegetable.

Although tomatoes are available year-round, they are best in the summer. If you've eaten winter tomatoes, you know that they lack color and are mealy.

varieties Dozens of varieties are available, and they range widely in size, shape, and color. A few common types are:

Beefsteak: large, bright red, and slightly elliptical

Globe: medium-sized, firm and juicy

Plum: also called the Italian plum; egg-shaped; comes in red and yellow

Green: popular for frying, they are red tomatoes that are picked before they're fully ripe, so they're not as sweet as red.

Cherry: about 1 inch in diameter; come in red and yellow; bright color, very sweet

selection You'll get the best flavor if you pick your own from the vine, or buy vine-ripened tomatoes, which are available in specialty produce markets. Supermarkets usually have tomatoes that have been picked green and ripened in special warming rooms. Choose firm, well-shaped tomatoes that are fragrant and have richly colored skin. They should be heavy for their size and blemish-free.

storage Don't store tomatoes in the refrigerator because cold temperatures make their flesh pulpy and ruins the flavor.

A simple pasta lunch with a refreshing fruit soup for dessert

Pasta with Beans and Spinach
Broiled Tomato Halves   Chilled Peach Soup

serves 4

It's quicker to use frozen peaches for the soup, but if you've
got fresh on hand, the flavor will be even better!

menu plan

1. *Boil water for pasta; place beans and
spinach in a colander.*

2. *Make and chill soup.*

3. *Cook pasta.*

4. *Chop basil, mince garlic, and halve tomatoes.*

5. *Top tomato halves with breadcrumbs.*

6. *Combine ingredients for pasta dish, and let stand.*

7. *Broil tomatoes.*

Pasta with Beans and Spinach

6	ounces (about 1½ cups) uncooked gemelli (short tube-shaped pasta) or farfalle (bow tie pasta)
1	(15-ounce) can cannellini beans or other white beans
4	cups torn spinach
2	tablespoons extra-virgin olive oil
2	tablespoons white balsamic vinegar
1	tablespoon chopped fresh or 1 teaspoon dried basil
1	garlic clove, minced
¼	teaspoon salt
½	cup (2 ounces) preshredded fresh Parmesan cheese
½	teaspoon freshly ground pepper

Cook pasta according to package directions, omitting
salt and fat.
Place beans in a colander; place spinach on top of
beans. Set aside.

Combine olive oil and next 4 ingredients in a small bowl.
When pasta is done, remove ¼ cup pasta water from
pan; set aside. Pour remaining pasta water and pasta
over spinach and beans in colander. Stir ¼ cup
reserved pasta water into reserved olive oil mixture.
Drain pasta mixture well; place in a large bowl. Pour
olive oil mixture over pasta mixture; toss well. Sprinkle
with Parmesan cheese and pepper; toss well. Let stand
5 minutes; serve warm.
Yield: 4 (1¼-cup) servings.

Per Serving: Calories 371 (28% from fat) Fat 11.7g (sat 3.4g) Protein 17.9g
Carbohydrate 48.7g Fiber 7.3g Cholesterol 10mg Sodium 754mg
Exchanges: 3 Starch, 1 Vegetable, 1 Medium-Fat Meat, 1 Fat

Broiled Tomato Halves

2	teaspoons Dijon mustard
2	tomatoes, halved
¼	cup Italian-seasoned breadcrumbs
	Olive oil-flavored cooking spray

Preheat broiler.
Spread ½ teaspoon mustard on each tomato half; top
each with 1 tablespoon breadcrumbs. Coat breadcrumbs with cooking spray.
Place tomatoes on a rack in a broiler pan; broil 2 to 4
minutes or until lightly browned. Yield: 4 servings.

Per Serving: Calories 44 (14% from fat) Fat 0.7g (sat 0.1g) Protein 1.6g
Carbohydrate 8.2g Fiber 0.7g Cholesterol 0mg Sodium 279mg
Exchange: 1 Vegetable

Chilled Peach Soup

Chilled Peach Soup

1¾ cups frozen sliced peaches

1¼ cups peach nectar, divided

¾ cup vanilla low-fat yogurt

1 tablespoon sifted powdered sugar

Mint sprig (optional)

Place peaches and ¼ cup peach nectar in a food processor, and process until smooth. Add 1 cup peach nectar, yogurt, and sugar; process until blended. Cover and chill at least 15 minutes. Garnish with mint, if desired. Yield: 4 (¾-cup) servings.

Per Serving: Calories 110 (6% from fat)   Fat 0.7g (sat 0.4g)   Protein 2.7g
Carbohydrate 24.9g   Fiber 1.3g   Cholesterol 2mg   Sodium 34mg
Exchanges: ½ Starch, 1 Fruit

This fresh-from-the-garden stew is a meal in a bowl.

Summer Vegetable Stew
Parmesan Polenta Rounds   Roasted Plums
serves 4

menu plan

1. *Trim and mince fennel; halve carrots; cut beans; pit and slice plums.*

2. *Prepare stew.*

3. *While stew cooks, bake polenta rounds.*

4. *Roast plums.*

Summer Vegetable Stew

1	fennel bulb with stalks (about ½ pound)
1	tablespoon olive oil
3	cups low-sodium chicken broth
1	(14½-ounce) can Italian-seasoned diced tomatoes
1½	cups baby carrots, halved lengthwise
1½	cups green beans, cut into 2-inch pieces (about ½ pound)
2	tablespoons fresh thyme leaves
½	teaspoon freshly ground pepper
1	cup fresh or frozen green peas

Parmesan Polenta Rounds
½ cup (2 ounces) crumbled goat cheese

Rinse fennel thoroughly; trim and reserve fronds. Mince fronds, reserving 1 tablespoon. Trim tough outer leaves and discard. Cut bulb in half lengthwise, and discard core. Cut bulb crosswise into ¼-inch slices; set aside.

Heat olive oil in a Dutch oven over medium heat; add fennel slices, and sauté 5 minutes. Stir in broth and next 5 ingredients; bring to a boil over high heat. Cover, reduce heat, and simmer 15 minutes. Stir in peas and reserved fennel fronds; cover and simmer 2 minutes.

Ladle 1¼ cups stew into each of 4 bowls; top with Parmesan Polenta Rounds, and sprinkle evenly with cheese. Yield: 4 servings.

Per Serving: Calories 309 (29% from fat) Fat 10.0g (sat 4.0g) Protein 13.9g Carbohydrate 41.1g Fiber 8.9g Cholesterol 15mg Sodium 756mg **Exchanges:** 2 Starch, 2 Vegetable, 1 High-Fat Meat

Parmesan Polenta Rounds

1	(16-ounce) tube of polenta

Olive oil-flavored cooking spray

4	teaspoons grated Parmesan cheese

Preheat oven to 450°.
Cut polenta evenly into eight slices. Coat both sides with cooking spray; place on a baking sheet. Sprinkle evenly with cheese. Bake at 450° for 10 minutes.
Yield: 4 servings (serving size: 2 slices).

Per Serving: Calories 89 (7% from fat) Fat 0.7g (sat 0.3g) Protein 2.7g Carbohydrate 16.1g Fiber 2.0g Cholesterol 1mg Sodium 229mg **Exchange:** 1 Starch

Roasted Plums

2	pounds plums, pitted and sliced
3	tablespoons brown sugar
½	cup frozen reduced-calorie whipped topping, thawed

Preheat oven to 475°.
Combine plum slices and brown sugar; toss. Spread on a 15 x 10-inch jelly-roll pan. Bake, uncovered, at 475° for 12 minutes or until thoroughly heated. Remove; cool slightly. Serve warm with whipped topping.
Yield: 4 servings.

Per Serving: Calories 153 (13% from fat) Fat 2.3g (sat 0.8g) Protein 1.8g Carbohydrate 34.4g Fiber 4.1g Cholesterol 0mg Sodium 9mg **Exchanges:** 2 Fruit, ½ Fat

No need to heat up the kitchen with this easy grilled meal.

Cajun Catfish
Grilled Vegetables (page 64)
Peach-Gingersnap Dessert (page 64)
serves 4

menu plan

1. *Cut vegetables.*

2. *Peel and slice peaches, and crush gingersnaps for dessert.*

3. *Grill fish and vegetables.*

4. *Assemble dessert just before serving.*

a few tips:
good grilling

1 Don't open the grill lid too often. Open the lid only when basting, turning, or at the recommended final cooking time.

2 Use a grilling basket for delicate fish or small pieces of vegetables.

3 Don't turn the food frequently. The rule of thumb is to only turn the food once, halfway through grilling time. This helps seal in the juices and prevents the food from sticking and falling apart.

4 Don't use a barbecue or meat fork to turn meat. This pierces the meat and releases juices and flavor. Use long-handled tongs for turning and removing food from the grill.

Cajun Catfish

Grill the lemon slices 1 to 2 minutes on each side or until lightly browned.

 4   teaspoons Cajun seasoning
 4   (4-ounce) farm-raised catfish fillets (½ to 1 inch thick)
Cooking spray
 4   teaspoons fresh lemon juice
Grilled lemon slices (optional)

Prepare grill.

Sprinkle Cajun seasoning on both sides of fillets; lightly coat fish with cooking spray. Arrange fish in a wire grilling basket coated with cooking spray. Place basket on grill rack; cover and grill 5 minutes. Turn grill basket over; drizzle lemon juice over fish. Cover and grill 5 minutes or until fish flakes easily when tested with a fork. Serve with grilled lemon slices, if desired. Yield: 4 servings.

Per Serving: Calories 137 (34% from fat) Fat 5.1g (sat 1.1g) Protein 20.8g Carbohydrate 1.6g Fiber 0.3g Cholesterol 66mg Sodium 546mg
Exchanges: 3 Very Lean Meat

▶

Grilled Vegetables

1   tablespoon olive oil
2   zucchini, halved lengthwise
2   yellow squash, halved lengthwise
1   large red onion, cut into 4 slices
¼   teaspoon salt
¼   teaspoon pepper
Cooking spray

Prepare grill.
Drizzle oil evenly over vegetables; sprinkle with salt and pepper.
Place vegetables on grill rack coated with cooking spray. Grill zucchini and squash 2 minutes on each side or until tender. Grill onion, uncovered, 5 minutes on each side or until tender.
Yield: 4 servings (serving size: 1 slice zucchini, 1 slice squash, and 1 slice onion).

Per Serving: Calories 76 (42% from fat) Fat 3.9g (sat 0.5g) Protein 2.2g Carbohydrate 9.8g Fiber 2.5g Cholesterol 0mg Sodium 152mg
Exchanges: 2 Vegetable, 1 Fat

Peach-Gingersnap Dessert

6   gingersnaps
4   peaches
2   cups vanilla fat-free ice cream

Place gingersnaps in a small zip-top plastic bag; crush with a rolling pin.
Peel peaches. Slice each peach, and place in a dessert dish. Top each serving with ½ cup ice cream. Sprinkle crushed gingersnaps evenly over ice cream.
Yield: 4 servings.

Per Serving: Calories 181 (7% from fat) Fat 1.5g (sat 0.4g) Protein 3.2g Carbohydrate 38.7g Fiber 2.0g Cholesterol 3mg Sodium 52mg
Exchanges: 1½ Starch, 1 Fruit

peaches

origin Peaches originally came from China, and then through Europe by way of Persia, so they used to be known as *Persian apples.*

varieties There are two categories of peaches: *freestone,* in which the pit falls easily away from the flesh, and *clingstone,* where the fruit adheres to the pit. Freestone peaches are what you'll usually find in the market, with the peak season being May to October.

selection Look for intensely fragrant peaches that give slightly when you press on the fruit with your palm. Check for soft spots because peaches bruise very easily. The soft, velvety skin should not be wrinkled or dry.

storage Store ripe peaches in the refrigerator in a plastic bag for up to 5 days. Their flavor is better when they're brought to room temperature. To peel the fuzzy skin before eating, place the peach in boiling water for about 30 seconds. Plunge it into ice cold water; the skin will peel right off.

summer produce

Vegetables	Fruits	Herbs
Avocados	Apricots	Basil
Beets	Blackberries	Bay Leaves
Bell Peppers	Blueberries	Borage
Cabbage	Boysenberries	Chives
Carrots	Cantaloupe	Cilantro
Celery	Casaba Melons	Dill
Chili Peppers	Cherries	Lavender
Collards	Crenshaw Melons	Lemon Balm
Corn	Figs	Marjoram
Cucumbers	Grapes	Mint
Eggplant	Guava	Oregano
Frisée	Honeydew Melons	Rosemary
Green Beans	Mangoes	Sage
Jícama	Nectarines	Summer Savory
Kale	Papayas	Tarragon
Lima Beans	Peaches	Thyme
Okra	Plums	
Pattypan Squash	Raspberries	
Peas	Watermelon	
Radicchio		
Radishes		
Tomatoes		
Turnips		
Yellow Squash		
Zucchini		

Bell Peppers · Cantaloupe · Corn · Cucumbers · Plums

Okra · Blueberries · Oregano · Honeydew Melons · Zucchini

Although many produce items are available year-round, this chart lists those that are at their peak during this season. Check with farmers' markets in your area for regional varieties.

Take your palate on a tropical vacation with these sun-kissed flavors.

Curried Mahimahi
Green Onion Rice Steamed Snow Peas (page 68)
Icy Tropical Fruit Float (page 68)

serves 4

menu plan

1. *Cook rice.*

2. *Slice carambola, and freeze fruit for float.*

3. *Slice and chop onions for fish and rice; trim peas.*

4. *Cook fish.*

5. *While fish is cooking, steam snow peas in microwave.*

6. *Make floats.*

Curried Mahimahi

1   tablespoon all-purpose flour
1   teaspoon curry powder
¼   teaspoon salt
⅛   teaspoon pepper
4   (4-ounce) mahimahi fillets (about ¾ inch thick)
2   teaspoons vegetable oil
⅓   cup hot mango chutney
2   tablespoons raisins
2   tablespoons flaked sweetened coconut
1   tablespoon hot water
¼   cup sliced green onions (about 1)

Combine first 4 ingredients in a shallow bowl; dredge one side of each fillet in flour mixture. Heat oil in a nonstick skillet over medium-high heat until hot. Add fish, floured side down, and cook 3 minutes on each side or until fish flakes easily when tested with a fork. **Combine** chutney and next 3 ingredients. Serve fish immediately with chutney mixture. Sprinkle each serving with green onions. Yield: 4 servings.

Per Serving: Calories 162 (27% from fat) Fat 4.8g (sat 1.7g) Protein 22.0g Carbohydrate 7.3g Fiber 0.7g Cholesterol 54mg Sodium 248mg **Exchanges:** ½ Starch, 3 Very Lean Meat

Green Onion Rice

1   cup uncooked basmati rice
2   cups water
¼   teaspoon salt
3   tablespoons chopped green onions (about 1 small)

Combine first 3 ingredients in a medium saucepan; bring to a boil. Cover; reduce heat, and simmer 20 minutes or until water is absorbed and rice is tender. Remove from heat and let stand 5 minutes. Add green onions, and fluff with a fork. Yield: 4 (¾-cup) servings.

Per Serving: Calories 170 (2% from fat) Fat 0.3g (sat 0.1g) Protein 3.4g Carbohydrate 37.3g Fiber 0.7g Cholesterol 0mg Sodium 150mg **Exchanges:** 2 Starch

▶

Steamed Snow Peas

1 pound snow peas, trimmed
2 tablespoons water
1 tablespoon light butter
¼ teaspoon salt

Place snow peas and water in a microwave-safe dish. Cover and microwave at HIGH 3 minutes or until crisp-tender, rotating dish a half-turn after 1½ minutes. Drain. Add light butter and salt; toss well. Yield: 4 servings.

Per Serving: Calories 60 (26% from fat) Fat 1.7g (sat 1.0g) Protein 3.2g
Carbohydrate 8.6g Fiber 2.9g Cholesterol 5mg Sodium 169mg
Exchanges: 2 Vegetable

Icy Tropical Fruit Float

The carambola and grapes will not freeze solid, but they become icy, making this a refreshing hot weather dessert.

1 carambola (star fruit), cut crosswise into thin slices
24 seedless red grapes
1 cup pineapple sherbet
1 cup gingerale, chilled

Divide carambola and grapes evenly among 4 tall glasses. Place in freezer until ready to serve.
To serve, spoon ¼ cup sherbet on top of fruit in each glass. Pour ¼ cup gingerale over each serving, and serve immediately. Yield: 4 servings.

Per Serving: Calories 108 (6% from fat) Fat 0.7g (sat 0.3g) Protein 0.8g
Carbohydrate 26.4g Fiber 0.5g Cholesterol 0mg Sodium 20mg
Exchanges: ½ Starch, 1 Fruit

carambola

Also known as *star fruit*, this fruit has a star shape when it's cut crosswise. Carambolas are 3 to 5 inches long and have five ribs that run the length of the fruit. It has a thin, yellow skin that doesn't have to be peeled before you eat it.

The flavor ranges from sweet to sweet-tart. Usually, the farther apart the ribs, the sweeter the fruit.

Keep ripe fruit tightly wrapped in a plastic bag in the refrigerator for up to a week. This tropical fruit is available from the end of the summer to midwinter.

Refreshing and flavorful—perfect for a summer dinner

Grilled Mahimahi   Minted Couscous
Tropical Fruit with Mango Sauce

serves 4

menu plan

1. *Grate lime or lemon, and squeeze juice for marinade; crush garlic.*

2. *Shred lettuce; chop cucumber and mint; peel and slice fruit for dessert.*

3. *Marinate fish; prepare couscous while fish is marinating.*

4. *Grill fish.*

5. *Prepare fruit dessert.*

Grilled Mahimahi

 2 tablespoons fresh lime or lemon juice
 2 tablespoons olive oil
 1 tablespoon honey
 2 garlic cloves, crushed
 ½ teaspoon salt
 ½ teaspoon ground cumin
 ½ teaspoon freshly ground pepper
 4 (4-ounce) mahimahi fillets
Cooking spray
 2 cups shredded romaine lettuce

Prepare grill.
Combine first 7 ingredients in a zip-top plastic bag. Add fish; turn to coat. Let stand 10 minutes. Remove fish from bag. Pour marinade into a saucepan; bring to a boil and cook 1 minute.
Place fish on grill rack coated with cooking spray; cover and grill 4 minutes on each side or until fish flakes easily when tested with a fork.
Place ½ cup lettuce on each plate; top with fish. Spoon marinade over fish. Yield: 4 servings.

Per Serving: Calories 190 (40% from fat) Fat 8.4g (sat 1.3g) Protein 21.9g
Carbohydrate 6.3g Fiber 0.5g Cholesterol 60mg Sodium 389mg
Exchanges: 1 Vegetable, 3 Lean Meat

Minted Couscous

 1 (5.9-ounce) package toasted pine nut couscous mix
1¼ cups finely chopped cucumber (about 1 medium)
 ¼ cup chopped fresh mint
 1 teaspoon grated lime or lemon rind

Prepare couscous according to package directions, omitting fat. Let couscous stand 5 minutes, and stir in cucumber, mint, and rind. Yield: 4 (1-cup) servings.

Per Serving: Calories 156 (12% from fat) Fat 2.0g (sat 0.4g) Protein 5.6g
Carbohydrate 31.3g Fiber 1.8g Cholesterol 0mg Sodium 339mg
Exchanges: 2 Starch

Tropical Fruit with Mango Sauce

 1 large banana, sliced
 2 tablespoons plus 1 teaspoon pineapple juice, divided
 1 large mango, peeled and sliced
 2 tablespoons sugar
 4 (½-inch-thick) slices pineapple
 4 kiwifruit, peeled and sliced
 ½ cup vanilla low-fat yogurt

Toss banana with 1 teaspoon pineapple juice; set aside.
Place mango, sugar, and remaining 2 tablespoons pineapple juice in a blender; process until smooth.
Spoon 3 tablespoons sauce onto each plate; arrange fruit over sauce. Top each with 2 tablespoons yogurt. Yield: 4 servings.

Per Serving: Calories 185 (6% from fat) Fat 1.2g (sat 0.4g) Protein 2.9g
Carbohydrate 44.5g Fiber 4.5g Cholesterol 1mg Sodium 24mg
Exchanges: 1 Starch, 2 Fruit

A fresh and flavorful patio dinner for two

Red Snapper
Sliced Tomato Salad   Grilled Chili-Cheese Corn
Fresh Melon Medley
serves 2

Buy cubed watermelon and cantaloupe from the grocery store
salad bar or in containers from the produce section.

menu plan

1. *Prepare tomato salad; cover and chill.*

2. *Prepare melon salad; cover and chill.*

3. *Prepare butter mixture; prepare corn.*

4. *Prepare fish.*

5. *Grill fish and corn together.*

Red Snapper

2 (4-ounce) red snapper fillets
2 tablespoons fat-free balsamic vinaigrette
¼ teaspoon salt
¼ teaspoon pepper
Cooking spray

Prepare grill.
Brush fish evenly with vinaigrette; sprinkle with salt
and pepper.
Place fish, skin side down, on grill rack coated with
cooking spray. Cover and grill 4 to 5 minutes on each
side or until fish flakes easily when tested with a fork.
Yield: 2 servings.

Per Serving: Calories 130 (13% from fat) Fat 1.9g (sat 0.3g) Protein 23.3g
Carbohydrate 3.2g Fiber 0.1g Cholesterol 42mg Sodium 566mg
Exchanges: 3 Very Lean Meat

Sliced Tomato Salad

2 tablespoons lemon juice
1 tablespoon balsamic vinegar
1 large tomato, sliced
¼ teaspoon freshly ground pepper
4 teaspoons chopped fresh basil

Combine lemon juice and vinegar. Sprinkle tomato
slices evenly with lemon juice mixture, pepper, and
basil. Yield: 2 servings.

Per Serving: Calories 21 (13% from fat) Fat 0.3g (sat 0.0g) Protein 0.8g
Carbohydrate 5.1g Fiber 1.0g Cholesterol 0mg Sodium 7mg
Exchange: 1 Vegetable

Grilled Chili-Cheese Corn

2 tablespoons preshredded fresh Parmesan cheese
1 tablespoon light butter, softened
2¼ teaspoons chili powder
2 ears fresh corn
Cooking spray

Prepare grill.
Combine first 3 ingredients in a small bowl.
Remove husks and silks from corn; spread butter mixture evenly on corn. Place corn on grill rack coated
with cooking spray. Cover and grill 10 minutes, turing
occasionally. Cut kernels from ears of corn.
Yield: 2 servings.

Per Serving: Calories 134 (44% from fat) Fat 6.6g (sat 2.7g) Protein 5.5g
Carbohydrate 17.1g Fiber 3.5g Cholesterol 15mg Sodium 192mg
Exchanges: 1 Starch, 1 Fat

Fresh Melon Medley

Fresh Melon Medley

1 teaspoon grated orange rind
¼ cup fresh orange juice
¼ cup pineapple juice
1 tablespoon white rum
1 tablespoon honey
2 cups cubed seeded watermelon
1 cup cubed cantaloupe
Orange rind strips (optional)

Combine first 5 ingredients in a small saucepan. Bring to a boil; reduce heat, and simmer, uncovered, 1 minute.
Combine melon cubes in a medium bowl; add orange juice mixture, and toss gently. Cover and chill. Garnish with orange rind strips, if desired.
Yield: 2 (1½-cup) servings.

Per Serving: Calories 168 (5% from fat) Fat 1.0g (sat 0.1g) Protein 2.1g Carbohydrate 35.6g Fiber 1.6g Cholesterol 0mg Sodium 11mg
Exchanges: ½ Starch, 2 Fruit

Add an artful touch to your dinner with the rice triangles.

Curried Snapper with Pineapple Salsa
Pressed Rice Triangles   tomato slices

serves 2

menu plan

1. *Cook rice.*

2. *Prepare pineapple salsa, and slice tomatoes.*

3. *Make rice triangles.*

4. *Cook fish.*

Curried Snapper with Pineapple Salsa

1½ cups diced pineapple
 3 tablespoons chopped green onions (about 1)
 1 small jalapeño pepper, seeded and minced
 1 tablespoon fresh lime juice
 ½ teaspoon cornstarch
 ½ teaspoon salt
 ½ teaspoon curry powder
 2 (4-ounce) red snapper fillets, cut in half crosswise
 2 teaspoons olive oil
Cooking spray
Cilantro sprigs (optional)
Lime slices (optional)

Combine first 4 ingredients in a medium bowl, and set aside.
Combine cornstarch, salt, and curry powder in a small bowl; rub cornstarch mixture evenly over fish.
Heat oil in a large nonstick skillet coated with cooking spray over medium-high heat. Add fish, and cook 3 minutes; turn and cook 2 to 3 minutes or until fish flakes easily when tested with a fork. To serve, spoon pineapple mixture evenly over fish. If desired, garnish with cilantro and lime slices. Yield: 2 servings.

Per Serving: Calories 236 (27% from fat) Fat 7.1g (sat 0.1g) Protein 24.2g
Carbohydrate 20.0g Fiber 2.2g Cholesterol 42mg Sodium 663mg
Exchanges: 1 Fruit, 3 Lean Meat

Pressed Rice Triangles

 1 cup water
 ¼ teaspoon salt
 ½ cup uncooked short-grain rice
Cooking spray

Combine water and salt in a small saucepan; bring to a boil. Add rice; cover, reduce heat, and simmer 20 minutes or until rice is tender and liquid is absorbed.
Press rice firmly into a 6 x 3-inch loafpan coated with cooking spray, using the back of a wet spoon. Let stand 5 minutes; invert onto a cutting board and cut into 2 squares. Cut each square into 2 triangles. Yield: 2 servings (serving size: 2 triangles).

Per Serving: Calories 182 (3% from fat) Fat 0.6g (sat 0.1g) Protein 3.3g
Carbohydrate 39.6g Fiber 0.7g Cholesterol 0mg Sodium 294mg
Exchanges: 2½ Starch

a few tips:
sticky rice

1 *Use* short-grain rice for the rice triangles because the fat, round grains have a higher starch content than long- or medium-grain rice.

2 *Cooked* short-grain rice is very moist and sticky. It's the preferred type of rice in the Orient because it's easy to eat with chopsticks.

3 *Varieties* of short-grain rice include *pearl rice*, Italian *arborio*, and Japanese *mochi*.

The broiled fish with vegetables is practically a meal in itself.

Broiled Tilapia with Vegetables
Parslied Potato Wedges   Balsamic Mixed Greens
foccacia or other bread

serves 4

If tilapia is not available, you can use another delicate white fish
like flounder, sole, or orange roughy.

menu plan

1. *Slice potatoes; cut squash and onion; chop parsley.*

2. *Steam potatoes. Broil vegetables while potatoes cook.*

3. *Prepare salad.*

4. *Broil fish.*

Broiled Tilapia with Vegetables

2   yellow squash, cut into ½-inch cubes
2   cups grape or cherry tomatoes
2   small onions, peeled, cut into eighths
     and separated
Cooking spray
¼   teaspoon salt
4   (4-ounce) tilapia or other white fish fillets
1   teaspoon Old Bay seasoning
2   teaspoons olive oil
1   tablespoon fresh lime juice
Lime wedges (optional)

Preheat broiler.
Place squash, tomatoes, and onion on a baking sheet coated with cooking spray; coat vegetables lightly with cooking spray, and sprinkle with salt. Broil 10 minutes, stirring once. Transfer vegetables to a bowl; cover and set aside.
Spray pan with cooking spray. Place fish (flattest side down) on pan; coat fish lightly with cooking spray. Broil 3 minutes; turn, coat other side of fish with cooking spray, and sprinkle with seasoning. Broil 2 to 3 minutes or until fish flakes easily when tested with a fork.
Drizzle olive oil and lime juice over fish and vegetables. Garnish with lime wedges, if desired.
Yield: 4 servings.

Per Serving: Calories 210 (18% from fat) Fat 4.2g (sat 0.7g) Protein 25.1g Carbohydrate 19.1g Fiber 4.6g Cholesterol 42mg Sodium 384mg
Exchanges: 3 Vegetable, 3 Very Lean Meat

Old Bay seasoning: *a seasoning blend often used on seafood. Its main ingredients are celery salt, dry mustard, red and black pepper, cloves, allspice, ginger, cinnamon, and paprika.*

Parslied Potato Wedges

1 pound small red potatoes, cut into wedges
1 cup water
2 tablespoons chopped fresh parsley
Butter-flavored spray (such as I Can't Believe It's
    Not Butter)

Place potato and water in a saucepan; cover and bring to boil. Reduce heat and simmer, covered, 10 to 15 minutes or until tender. Drain; stir in parsley, and coat lightly with butter-flavored spray. Yield: 4 servings.

Per Serving: Calories 85 (1% from fat) Fat 0.1g (sat 0.0g) Protein 2.6g Carbohydrate 18.9g Fiber 2.1g Cholesterol 0mg Sodium 9mg Exchange: 1 Starch

Balsamic Mixed Greens

4 cups gourmet salad greens
2 tablespoons fat-free balsamic vinaigrette
1 ounce crumbled feta cheese with basil and sun-dried
    tomatoes
Freshly ground pepper (optional)

Toss salad greens with dressing; top with crumbled feta cheese and pepper, if desired. Yield: 4 (1-cup) servings.

Per Serving: Calories 34 (42% from fat) Fat 1.6g (sat 1.1g) Protein 1.9g Carbohydrate 3.1g Fiber 1.0g Cholesterol 6mg Sodium 184mg Exchange: 1 Vegetable

a dessert idea: *Spoon into a dish of Fresh Berries with Ginger Cream (page 189).*

yellow squash

selection Yellow squash is in the summer squash family—squash with thin, edible skins and soft seeds. Other varieties of summer squash are zucchini and pattypan. Whether you buy straight-neck or crookneck, yellow squash should be firm, smooth-skinned, and small in size. (The larger the squash, the less tender it is.) The skin should be shiny and bright yellow. Be sure to look at the stem; if it's hard, dry, shriveled, or dark, the squash is not fresh.

storage Store yellow squash in a plastic bag with holes in the refrigerator for no more than 3 to 5 days. You don't need to peel the squash before you cook it—just cut off the ends.

preparation Yellow squash is tender and doesn't require a long cooking time. Since it contains a lot of water, the best cooking methods are those that will dry out the squash a bit, such as sautéing and grilling.

nutrients Yellow squash is a good source of vitamin A, vitamin C, and niacin. Since you eat the skin and the seeds, it's also a source of fiber. As with all fresh vegetables, squash is low in fat and sodium.

A crisp, cool lunch for a sultry summer day

Fresh Tuna-Bean Salad
crusty French baguettes   cantaloupe wedges
Frosty Cappuccino
serves 4

menu plan

1. *Make and chill coffee for dessert beverage.*

2. *Trim beans; chop dill and onion; halve tomatoes; slice cantaloupe.*

3. *Broil tuna, and cut into pieces.*

4. *Cook green beans.*

5. *Assemble salad.*

6. *Prepare dessert beverage.*

Fresh Tuna-Bean Salad

  4 teaspoons olive oil, divided
  1 tablespoon Dijon mustard, divided
  1 (12-ounce) tuna steak (about 1 inch thick)
  2 cups green beans, trimmed (about ½ pound)
  6 tablespoons white wine vinegar
  2 tablespoons chopped fresh dill
  ¼ teaspoon salt
  ½ teaspoon freshly ground pepper
  ¼ cup chopped red onion
  2 cups halved cherry tomatoes
  1 (16-ounce) can cannellini beans or other white beans, rinsed and drained
  1 head Bibb lettuce, separated into leaves

Preheat broiler.
Combine 2 teaspoons oil and 1 teaspoon mustard; brush evenly over fish. Broil fish 3 minutes on each side or until fish flakes easily when tested with a fork. Cut fish into 1-inch pieces; set aside.

Place green beans in a saucepan; add water to cover. Bring to a boil, and cook, uncovered, 3 to 4 minutes or until crisp-tender; drain.
Combine vinegar, remaining 2 teaspoons mustard, dill, salt, and pepper. Add 2 teaspoons oil, stirring well with a whisk.
Combine green beans, onion, tomato, and tuna in a small bowl; toss gently. Combine 1 tablespoon vinegar mixture and cannellini beans. Arrange lettuce on a serving platter. Arrange bean mixture over lettuce, and top with tuna mixture. Drizzle remaining vinegar mixture over salad. Yield: 4 servings (serving size: ½ cup cannellini beans and 1¼ cups tuna mixture).

Per Serving: Calories 272 (31% from fat) Fat 9.4g (sat 1.8g) Protein 25.9g Carbohydrate 20.1g Fiber 6.5g Cholesterol 33mg Sodium 593mg
Exchanges: 1 Starch, 1 Vegetable, 3 Lean Meat

Frosty Cappuccino

  2 cups vanilla fat-free ice cream, softened
  3 cups chilled strong brewed coffee, divided
  2 tablespoons sugar
  1 teaspoon unsweetened cocoa
  1 teaspoon ground cinnamon

Combine ice cream, 1 cup coffee, and sugar in a blender. Process just until smooth. Stir in remaining 2 cups coffee. Serve over crushed ice in chilled glasses or mugs. Sprinkle evenly with cocoa and cinnamon. Serve immediately. Yield: 4 (1¼-cup) servings.

Per Serving: Calories 131 (1% from fat) Fat 0.1g (sat 0.0g) Protein 2.3g Carbohydrate 29.6g Fiber 0.1g Cholesterol 0mg Sodium 44mg
Exchanges: 2 Starch

A seafood supper with Asian simplicity

Sesame Tuna with Cucumber Salad
Asian-Style Pasta   fresh orange sections

serves 4

Chinese noodles and black sesame seeds are found at Asian markets. If they
aren't available, use vermicelli and regular sesame seeds.

menu plan

1. *Boil water for noodles.*

2. *Cut cucumber; slice onions and pepper;
grate ginger; peel and section 2 oranges.*

3. *Cook noodles.*

4. *Marinate cucumbers.*

5. *Prepare pasta dish.*

6. *Grill tuna.*

Sesame Tuna with Cucumber Salad

1	English (seedless) cucumber
¼	cup rice wine vinegar
1	tablespoon grated peeled fresh ginger
1	teaspoon sugar
4	(4-ounce) tuna steaks (1 inch thick)
1	tablespoon reduced-sodium soy sauce
1½	teaspoons sesame seeds
1½	teaspoons black sesame seeds
	Cooking spray

Prepare grill.

Cut cucumber lengthwise into long strips with a
vegetable peeler. Combine vinegar, ginger, and sugar;
toss with cucumber. Set aside.

Brush both sides of fish with soy sauce. Sprinkle
sesame seeds over one side of fish, pressing gently
to coat.

Place fish on grill rack coated with cooking spray;
cover and grill 4 to 5 minutes on each side or until
fish flakes easily when tested with a fork.
Yield: 4 servings.

Per Serving: Calories 200 (32% from fat) Fat 7.0g (sat 1.6g) Protein 27.8g
Carbohydrate 5.0g Fiber 1.2g Cholesterol 43mg Sodium 169mg
Exchanges: 1 Vegetable, 4 Lean Meat

Asian-Style Pasta

4	ounces uncooked Chinese-style noodles
¼	cup sliced green onions (about 1)
1	red bell pepper, thinly sliced
2	tablespoons rice wine vinegar
2	tablespoons water
2	tablespoons reduced-fat peanut butter
2	tablespoons grated peeled fresh ginger
¼	teaspoon salt
¼	teaspoon crushed red pepper

Cook pasta according to package directions, omitting
salt and fat. Drain pasta; transfer to a large bowl.
Add green onions and red bell pepper; set aside, and
cool slightly.

Combine vinegar and remaining 5 ingredients; stir
well. Add vinegar mixture to pasta mixture, stirring
well. Serve at room temperature.
Yield: 4 (¾-cup) servings.

Per Serving: Calories 163 (20% from fat) Fat 3.6g (sat 0.7g) Protein 6.0g
Carbohydrate 27.0g Fiber 1.7g Cholesterol 0mg Sodium 214mg
Exchanges: 2 Starch, ½ Fat

Summer corn and sweet fruit are perfect partners for the flavorful grilled tuna.

Grilled Teriyaki Tuna
Summer Corn and Rice Salad
Tropical Gingered Fruit

serves 4

Low-sodium soy sauce and fresh parsley are good substitutes for the teriyaki sauce and the cilantro.

menu plan

1. *Thaw corn, and cook rice for salad.*

2. *Chop cilantro, cucumber, and basil; grate ginger; slice banana.*

3. *Prepare salad.*

4. *Grill tuna, and prepare mayonnaise mixture.*

5. *Prepare fruit syrup; combine with fruit.*

Grilled Teriyaki Tuna

- ¼ cup light mayonnaise
- 1 teaspoon low-sodium teriyaki sauce
- 1 tablespoon chopped fresh cilantro
- 4 (4-ounce) tuna steaks (¾ inch thick)
- Olive oil-flavored cooking spray
- ¼ teaspoon salt
- ½ teaspoon pepper

Prepare grill.
Combine first 3 ingredients; set aside.
Coat fish with cooking spray; sprinkle with salt and pepper. Place fish on grill rack coated with cooking spray; cover and grill 5 minutes on each side or to desired degree of doneness. Serve with mayonnaise mixture. Yield: 4 servings (serving size: 1 tuna steak and 1 tablespoon mayonnaise mixture).

Per Serving: Calories 216 (45% from fat) Fat 10.7g (sat 2.4g) Protein 26.6g Carbohydrate 1.3g Fiber 0.1g Cholesterol 48mg Sodium 352mg
Exchanges: 4 Lean Meat

Summer Corn and Rice Salad

- 2 teaspoons sesame oil
- 1⅓ cups frozen shoepeg white corn, thawed
- 1½ cups cooked instant rice (such as Success Rice)
- 1 cup chopped cucumber (about 1 medium)
- ⅓ cup reduced-fat olive oil vinaigrette
- ½ cup thinly sliced fresh basil
- Large basil leaves (optional)

Heat oil in a large nonstick skillet over medium-high heat. Add corn; sauté 3 minutes or until lightly browned. Transfer to a bowl; stir in rice and next 3 ingredients. Serve on large basil leaves, if desired.
Yield: 4 (1-cup) servings.

Per Serving: Calories 190 (31% from fat) Fat 6.6g (sat 0.7g) Protein 3.3g Carbohydrate 31.6g Fiber 2.0g Cholesterol 0mg Sodium 163mg
Exchanges: 2 Starch, 1 Fat

a few tips:
storing fresh herbs

1 To store fresh herbs, wrap the stems in a soaking wet paper towel, keeping the herb foliage dry. Place the wrapped herbs in a zip-top plastic bag, seal with air inside, and store in the refrigerator.

2 Or, place the stem ends in a glass with two inches of water, cover the foliage loosely with a plastic bag, and store in the refrigerator.

Tropical Gingered Fruit

Use canned pineapple chunks in juice or buy fresh cubes in the produce section of the grocery store.

½ cup sugar
½ cup hot water, divided
2 tablespoons lime juice
1 tablespoon grated peeled fresh ginger
2 cups pineapple cubes
2 bananas halved lengthwise, and cut
   into 2-inch pieces

Combine sugar and 1 tablespoon water in a large skillet; place over medium heat. Cook 5 minutes or until sugar mixture is golden, stirring frequently.

Add remaining water, lime juice, and ginger; bring to a boil. Reduce heat, and simmer, uncovered, until sugar dissolves, stirring occasionally.

Remove sugar mixture from heat. Add pineapple and banana; toss well. Yield: 4 (1-cup) servings.

Per Serving: Calories 261 (4% from fat) Fat 1.2g (sat 0.2g) Protein 1.5g
Carbohydrate 66.7g Fiber 4.0g Cholesterol 0mg Sodium 3mg
Exchanges: 1 Starch, 3 Fruit

corn

varieties The two most popular varieties of corn are yellow corn and white corn. (The shoepeg corn used in the salad is one variety of white corn.) Yellow corn has larger, fuller-flavored kernels; white corn is smaller and sweeter.

flavor The peak season for fresh corn is May through September. The natural sugar in corn starts to turn to starch as soon as the corn is picked, so if you want sweet corn, it's important to buy fresh corn as soon after it's picked as possible.

Frozen corn is often a good choice, as it's frozen soon after it is picked and keeps the sweet, "just-picked" flavor.

selection If you're buying fresh corn, look for husks that are tightly closed and stems that are green and moist instead of woody. There should be a lot of golden brown silk coming out of the corn, and the corn should feel plump through the husk. Check the ripeness of the corn by looking at the kernels; if there is a lot of space between the rows and the kernels are small, the corn is not ripe. Overripe corn will have dimpled or wrinkled kernels.

The soup is cold, but the spice is hot.

Chipotle Gazpacho with Shrimp
sourdough bread Blackberries with Cream

serves 4

menu plan

1. *Cook, peel, and chop shrimp.*

2. *Chop tomato, bell pepper, and cucumber.*

3. *Prepare soup, and chill.*

4. *Prepare dessert.*

Chipotle Gazpacho with Shrimp

This chilled soup is spicy hot. If you want a milder soup, use regular vegetable juice instead of picante-flavored vegetable juice.

> 2   cups chopped tomato (about 2 large)
> 1   cup chopped green bell pepper (about 1)
> ¾   cup chopped peeled cucumber (about ½ large)
> ¼   cup finely chopped onion
> 1   (11.5-ounce) can picante-flavored vegetable juice
> 1   canned chipotle chile
> 1   pound shrimp, cooked, peeled, and coarsely chopped
> ¼   teaspoon salt
> ⅛   teaspoon ground black pepper

Combine first 6 ingredients in a large bowl. Place half of mixture in a food processor, and process until smooth. Add pureed mixture to remaining tomato mixture. Stir in shrimp, salt, and pepper. Cover and chill 15 minutes. Yield: 4 (1½-cup) servings.

Per Serving: Calories 174 (13% from fat) Fat 2.5g (sat 0.5g) Protein 24.9g
Carbohydrate 12.3g Fiber 2.6g Cholesterol 172mg Sodium 598mg
Exchanges: 2 Vegetable, 3 Very Lean Meat

Blackberries with Cream

> ½   cup low-fat sour cream
> 1   tablespoon brown sugar
> ⅛   teaspoon vanilla extract
> 3   cups blackberries

Combine sour cream, sugar, and vanilla. To serve, spoon sour cream mixture evenly over berries.
Yield: 4 (¾-cup) servings.

Per Serving: Calories 105 (33% from fat) Fat 4.0g (sat 2.3g) Protein 1.6g
Carbohydrate 17.1g Fiber 5.6g Cholesterol 11mg Sodium 13mg
Exchanges: 1 Fruit, 1 Fat

blackberries

Blackberries, also called "brambles," grow on thornbushes and are the largest type of wild berries. The berries are purplish-black and range in size from ½ to 1 inch long.

Blackberries are generally available from May through August. Buy plump berries with deep color and no hull. If the hulls are still attached, the berries are not mature, and they will be tart.

Although fresh from the bush is best, you can refrigerate blackberries in a single layer, lightly covered, for 1 to 2 days.

Savor the flavors of the Mediterranean with a simple supper.

Orange-Basil Grilled Shrimp
Mediterranean Pasta   Easy Caesar Salad
serves 4

Fresh pasta (found in the refrigerated section of the grocery store) cooks in about half the time of dry pasta.

menu plan

1. Boil water for pasta.

2. Slice and mince basil; chop tomato.

3. Prepare shrimp skewers.

4. Grill shrimp.

5. Cook pasta.

6. Prepare pasta dish; toss salad.

Orange-Basil Grilled Shrimp

    3   tablespoons thawed orange juice concentrate
    2   tablespoons minced fresh basil
    2   tablespoons lemon juice
    2   tablespoons olive oil
   32   unpeeled jumbo shrimp (about 2 pounds)
   Cooking spray

Prepare grill.
Combine first 4 ingredients in a small bowl.
Peel and devein shrimp, leaving tails intact. Thread 4 shrimp onto each of 8 (10-inch) skewers; brush with half of orange juice mixture.
Place skewers on grill rack coated with cooking spray; grill 5 minutes on each side, basting with remaining orange juice mixture.
Yield: 4 servings (serving size: 2 skewers).

Per Serving: Calories 265 (34% from fat)   Fat 9.9g (sat 1.5g)   Protein 34.9g Carbohydrate 7.3g   Fiber 0.1g   Cholesterol 259mg   Sodium 252mg
Exchanges: ½ Fruit, 5 Lean Meat

Mediterranean Pasta

   ½   cup thinly sliced fresh basil
    1   tablespoon olive oil
    2   teaspoons balsamic vinegar
   ½   teaspoon freshly ground pepper
   ¼   teaspoon salt
    1   (9-ounce) package fresh angel hair pasta
   ½   cup chopped plum tomato

Combine first 5 ingredients in a medium bowl.
Cook pasta according to package directions, omitting salt and fat; drain well. Add pasta and tomato to basil mixture; toss gently. Yield: 4 (¾-cup) servings.

Per Serving: Calories 273 (15% from fat)   Fat 4.5g (sat 0.6g)   Protein 8.5g Carbohydrate 49.0g   Fiber 1.8g   Cholesterol 0mg   Sodium 153mg
Exchanges: 3 Starch, 1 Fat

Easy Caesar Salad

    1   (10-ounce) package romaine salad
   ¼   cup fat-free Caesar dressing

Combine lettuce and dressing; toss well.
Yield: 4 (1-cup) servings.

Per Serving: Calories 26 (3% from fat)   Fat 0.1g (sat 0.0g)   Protein 1.1g Carbohydrate 4.7g   Fiber 1.2g   Cholesterol 0mg   Sodium 81mg
Exchange: 1 Vegetable

a dessert idea: Serve Café Mocha Granita (page 196) in chilled wine glasses.

This zesty grilled shrimp menu is great for a festive dinner on the deck.

Grilled Shrimp with Tomato Relish
Romaine Salad with Peppers
Raspberry Sorbet with Blueberries

serves 4

You can buy peeled and deveined shrimp at the fish counter in the supermarket.

menu plan

1. *Chop ingredients for tomato relish.*

2. *Cube bread, shred lettuce, and chop bell pepper for salad.*

3. *Prepare shrimp skewers, and grill.*

4. *Prepare salad.*

5. *Prepare dessert just before serving.*

a few tips:
buying shrimp

1 Shrimp come in all sizes, small to jumbo, and the number of shrimp per pound for the different sizes will vary, depending on the market in your area.

2 Fresh raw shrimp will vary in color from light gray to pink. The color is an indication of the type of water the shrimp came from, not the quality.

3 The flesh should feel firm and slippery, and the shrimp should have a mild, almost sweet smell. If you smell an odor of ammonia, the shrimp is probably not fresh.

Grilled Shrimp with Tomato Relish

1 pound peeled and deveined jumbo shrimp
3 tablespoons lemon juice
1 tablespoon olive oil
1 teaspoon bottled minced garlic
2 cups diced seeded tomato (about 2 medium)
2 tablespoons chopped fresh parsley
2 tablespoons sliced ripe olives
¼ teaspoon pepper
¼ teaspoon salt
Cooking spray

Prepare grill.
Thread shrimp evenly onto 4 skewers. Combine lemon juice, oil, and garlic. Pour half of lemon juice mixture over shrimp; set remaining mixture aside.
Combine tomato and next 4 ingredients; add reserved juice mixture, stirring well.
Place shrimp on grill rack coated with cooking spray; cover and grill 3 minutes on each side or until done. Serve shrimp over tomato mixture.
Yield: 4 servings.

Per Serving: Calories 179 (32% from fat) Fat 6.3g (sat 0.1g) Protein 23.9g Carbohydrate 6.4g Fiber 1.2g Cholesterol 172mg Sodium 366mg
Exchanges: 1 Vegetable, 3 Lean Meat

Romaine Salad with Peppers

2 (1-ounce) slices Italian bread (¾ inch thick)
⅓ cup fat-free red wine vinaigrette
½ teaspoon dried oregano
⅛ teaspoon black pepper
2 cups shredded romaine lettuce
½ cup chopped yellow bell pepper (about ½ large)
1 ounce crumbled feta cheese with peppercorns

Preheat oven to 400°.
Cut bread into cubes. Arrange bread cubes in a single layer on a baking pan. Bake at 400° for 10 minutes.
Combine vinaigrette, oregano, and black pepper.
Combine lettuce, yellow pepper, and feta cheese. Add bread cubes and vinaigrette mixture, and toss.
Yield: 4 (1-cup) servings.

Per Serving: Calories 85 (19% from fat) Fat 1.8g (sat 1.1g) Protein 3.4g Carbohydrate 13.9g Fiber 1.6g Cholesterol 6mg Sodium 558mg
Exchange: 1 Starch

Raspberry Sorbet with Blueberries

2 cups raspberry sorbet
2 cups blueberries

Spoon ½ cup sorbet into each of 4 dessert dishes. Top each serving with ½ cup blueberries.
Yield: 4 (1-cup) servings.

Per Serving: Calories 161 (2% from fat) Fat 0.3g (sat 0.0g) Protein 0.5g Carbohydrate 40.3g Fiber 4.0g Cholesterol 0mg Sodium 4mg
Exchanges: 1½ Starch, 1 Fruit

blueberries

Small, round, smooth-skinned blueberries are at their peak from June through the middle of summer. Although blueberries grow wild in many parts of the country, the wild berries are usually smaller and have a more intense flavor than cultivated berries.

selection Pick indigo-blue berries with a silvery frost. Look for firm berries, discarding those that are shriveled and moldy. Try to select berries that are uniform in size.

storage Don't wash blueberries until you're ready to use them. Store them in the refrigerator in a single layer, if possible, in a moisture-proof container for up to 5 days.

a dessert idea: *You can also use your fresh blueberries in the Blueberry Cream Cheese Pie on page 205.*

Super-easy paella with orzo instead of rice

Pasta Paella
hard rolls   nectarine slices

serves 4

menu plan

1. *Boil water for orzo.*

2. *Peel and devein shrimp; slice onion.*

3. *Cook orzo.*

4. *Cook sausage and shrimp mixture.*

5. *Complete paella.*

6. *Peel and slice nectarines.*

nectarines

Nectarines are in the peach family and are noted for their smooth, fuzz-free skins. The flesh is sweet and juicy—like nectar.

selection Nectarines are at their peak in July and August. Look for fragrant, brightly colored fruit, and avoid those that are hard or overly green.

storage Let underripe nectarines ripen at room temperature for 1 to 2 days; refrigerate ripe fruit and eat within 5 days.

Pasta Paella

  6   cups water
  ⅛ teaspoon saffron threads
1½ cups (about 8 ounces) uncooked orzo (rice-shaped pasta)
Olive oil-flavored cooking spray
  1   cup sliced lite kielbasa sausage (about 4 ounces)
  1   (14.5-ounce) can Mexican-flavored stewed tomatoes
  1   pound large shrimp, peeled and deveined
  1   cup frozen green peas, thawed
  ¼ cup sliced green onions (about 1)

Combine water and saffron threads in a Dutch oven; bring to a boil. Add orzo, and cook according to package directions, omitting salt and fat; drain.

Coat a large saucepan with cooking spray; place over medium heat until hot. Add sausage; sauté 3 minutes. Add tomatoes, and bring to a simmer. Add shrimp; cook 3 to 5 minutes or until shrimp turn pink. Add peas and green onions; simmer 2 minutes. Add cooked orzo, and toss gently. Yield: 4 servings.

Per Serving: Calories 440 (12% from fat) Fat 5.9g (sat 1.8g) Protein 37.4g Carbohydrate 57.4g Fiber 3.7g Cholesterol 187mg Sodium 776mg
Exchanges: 3 Starch, 2 Vegetable, 3 Lean Meat

a dessert idea: *Use fresh nectarines to make Nectarine Melba Sundaes (page 194).*

Add margaritas to the menu if you're feeling festive.

Grilled Beef Fajita Salad
Frozen Yogurt with Raspberry Sauce
serves 4

menu plan

1. *Thaw frozen raspberries.*

2. *Remove husks and silks from corn; slice peppers and onion.*

3. *Prepare raspberry sauce; cover and chill until serving time.*

4. *Grill beef and vegetables.*

5. *Prepare salad.*

6. *Wrap tortillas in foil for grilling.*

Grilled Beef Fajita Salad

The sodium is a little high in this salad because of the dressing and the tortillas. If you need to reduce sodium, use a low-sodium dressing, and leave off the tortillas.

2   large ears fresh corn
¾   cup fat-free red wine vinaigrette
5½ teaspoons salt-free Mexican seasoning, divided
12 ounces boneless top sirloin steak
Cooking spray
2   large yellow or red bell peppers, each cut into 6 wedges
4   (½-inch-thick) slices red onion
4   (8-inch) flour tortillas
1   (10-ounce) package romaine salad

Prepare grill.
Remove and discard husks and silks from corn; set aside. Combine red wine vinaigrette and 2½ teaspoons Mexican seasoning. Stir well; set aside.
Rub remaining 1 tablespoon Mexican seasoning on steak. Place steak, pepper, onion, and corn on grill

rack coated with cooking spray. Cover; grill 6 minutes on each side or to desired degree of doneness. Remove steak, pepper, and onion from grill, and keep warm.
Place foil-wrapped tortillas on grill with corn, and grill 3 minutes or until corn is lightly browned.
Cut steak diagonally across grain into ¼-inch-thick slices. Cut kernels from ears of corn.
Toss lettuce with vinaigrette mixture, and divide evenly among 4 plates. Top evenly with steak slices and vegetables. Serve with warm tortillas.
Yield: 4 servings.

Per Serving: Calories 424 (20% from fat) Fat 9.4g (sat 2.5g) Protein 28.5g Carbohydrate 59.0g Fiber 7.4g Cholesterol 57mg Sodium 1155mg
Exchanges: 3 Starch, 2 Vegetable, 2 Medium-Fat Meat

Frozen Yogurt with Raspberry Sauce

1   (12-ounce) package frozen raspberries in light syrup, thawed
3   tablespoons sugar
1   teaspoon lemon juice
2   cups vanilla low-fat frozen yogurt

Place raspberries, sugar, and lemon juice in a blender; process until smooth. If desired, press through a sieve over a bowl, discarding solids. To serve, spoon sauce over frozen yogurt.
Yield: 4 servings (serving size: ¼ cup sauce and ½ cup yogurt).

Per Serving: Calories 203 (8% from fat) Fat 1.7g (sat 1.1g) Protein 3.0g Carbohydrate 46.1g Fiber 3.7g Cholesterol 8mg Sodium 29mg
Exchanges: 1 Starch, 2 Fruit

Not your usual burger.

Middle Eastern Lamb Burgers
Red Pepper Hummus fresh vegetables
serves 2

Serve the hummus with precut vegetables from the produce section of the grocery.

menu plan

1. *Make hummus.*

2. *Combine ingredients for lamb patties.*

3. *Cook lamb patties.*

4. *If desired, slice tomato and onion while burgers cook.*

5. *Assemble sandwiches.*

Middle Eastern Lamb Burgers

    3   tablespoons regular oats
    1   tablespoon cold water
   ¾   teaspoon ground cumin
   ½   teaspoon salt
   ¼   teaspoon ground red pepper
   ½   pound lean ground lamb
Cooking spray
    2   (6-inch) pitas
Spinach leaves
    2   tablespoons plain fat-free yogurt
Sliced tomato (optional)
Sliced onion (optional)
Mango chutney (optional)

Combine first 5 ingredients in a food processor or blender; process until mixture forms a paste. Stir paste into lamb, mixing well; shape into 2 (1-inch-thick) patties.

Place a large nonstick skillet over medium-high heat until hot. Add lamb patties; cook, covered, 3 to 4 minutes on each side or to desired degree of doneness. Remove from skillet; drain on paper towels.

Cut a 1-inch slice off the top of each pita, and open pocket. (Discard tops.) Line pitas with spinach leaves; top with lamb patties. Top each with 1 tablespoon yogurt, and, if desired, sliced tomato, sliced onion, and chutney. Yield: 2 servings.

Per Serving: Calories 397 (23% from fat) Fat 10.2g (sat 3.2g) Protein 33.6g Carbohydrate 40.9g Fiber 2.6g Cholesterol 81mg Sodium 998mg
Exchanges: 3 Starch, 3 Lean Meat

Red Pepper Hummus

    1   (7-ounce) bottle roasted red peppers, drained
    1   (15-ounce) can chickpeas (garbanzo beans), drained
    1   garlic clove
    1   teaspoon ground coriander
   ½   teaspoon ground red pepper
   ¼   teaspoon salt

Combine all ingredients in a food processor; process until smooth. Serve hummus with fresh vegetables (such as broccoli and cauliflower florets, celery sticks, or baby carrots). Store in an airtight container in refrigerator up to one week. Yield: 1½ cups.

Per Tablespoon: Calories 22 (16% from fat) Fat 0.4g (sat 0.0g) Protein 1.1g Carbohydrate 3.8g Fiber 0.5g Cholesterol 0mg Sodium 49mg
Exchange: Free (up to 3 tablespoons)

Invite another couple over for an intimate Italian dinner.

Carbonara Primavera
mixed greens with red wine vinaigrette   ## Parmesan Garlic Bread

serves 4

Purchase the broccoli florets and the red bell pepper pieces
from the salad bar at the grocery store.

menu plan

1. *Boil water for pasta.*

2. *Cook bacon in microwave.*

3. *Cook pasta and vegetables.*

4. *Prepare cheese mixture; spread on bread.*

5. *Make sauce for pasta.*

6. *Prepare salad.*

7. *Broil bread.*

Carbonara Primavera

    8   ounces uncooked spaghetti
    3   quarts boiling water
1½   cups broccoli florets
1½   cups red bell pepper pieces
    3   slices lower-sodium bacon (such as Hormel)
2½   tablespoons all-purpose flour
    1   cup low-sodium chicken broth
    1   cup 2% reduced-fat milk
 ⅓   cup (1.3-ounces) garlic-flavored shredded cheese
        blend or preshredded fresh Parmesan cheese
 ½   teaspoon salt
 ¾   teaspoon freshly ground black pepper

Cook pasta in boiling water 7 minutes; add vegetables, and cook 2 minutes or until pasta is done and vegetables are tender.

Arrange bacon on a microwave-safe plate, and cover with paper towels. Microwave at HIGH 3 minutes or until done; drain and crumble bacon.

Place flour in a saucepan; gradually add broth and milk, stirring with a whisk until blended. Cook over medium heat, until thickened and bubbly, stirring constantly. Stir in cheese, salt, and black pepper.

Combine pasta mixture and sauce mixture; toss to combine. Top with crumbled bacon.

Yield: 4 (1½-cup) servings.

Per Serving: Calories 352 (20% from fat) Fat 7.8g (sat 3.4g) Protein 16.9g Carbohydrate 53.9g Fiber 3.2g Cholesterol 17mg Sodium 591mg **Exchanges:** 3 Starch, 2 Vegetable

Parmesan Garlic Bread

1½   tablespoons yogurt-based spread, softened (such as
        Brummel and Brown)
    2   tablespoons preshredded fresh Parmesan cheese
    1   garlic clove, pressed
    2   teaspoons minced fresh oregano
    1   (6-inch) French sandwich roll, cut into 4 slices

Preheat broiler.

Combine first 4 ingredients; spread evenly on one side of bread slices.

Reassemble loaf, and place on a baking sheet. Broil 1½ minutes or until crisp and golden. Serve immediately. Yield: 4 servings.

Per Serving: Calories 92 (34% from fat) Fat 3.5g (sat 1.1g) Protein 3.3g Carbohydrate 11.9g Fiber 0.8g Cholesterol 2mg Sodium 209mg **Exchanges:** 1 Starch, ½ Fat

a dessert idea: *Delight your friends with creamy Mocha Pudding (page 209).*

Try a grilled chicken salad with fruit when you need a light dinner.

Grilled Chicken-Apricot Salad
baguette slices
Lemon Sorbet with Blackberries
serves 4

menu plan

1. *Prepare blackberry mixture, and chill.*

2. *Slice apricots, and chill; slice bell pepper.*

3. *Prepare apricot purée.*

4. *Flatten chicken; grill chicken and green onions.*

5. *Assemble salad.*

6. *Spoon blackberry mixture over sorbet just before serving.*

Grilled Chicken-Apricot Salad

6   apricots, divided
⅓   cup apricot preserves
¼   cup white wine vinegar
1½ tablespoons olive oil
¾   teaspoon salt, divided
4   (4-ounce) skinless, boneless chicken breast halves
¼   teaspoon black pepper
Cooking spray
8   green onions
6   cups gourmet salad greens
1   cup red bell pepper slices (about 1 medium)

Prepare grill.

Cut apricots in half, and remove pits. Cut 8 halves into slices; cover slices, and chill.

Place 4 apricot halves, preserves, vinegar, oil, and ½ teaspoon salt in a blender, and process until smooth. Reserve ¾ cup apricot purée for salad dressing. Set ½ cup apricot purée aside as a basting sauce.

Place chicken between 2 sheets of heavy-duty plastic wrap, and pound to ½-inch thickness, using a meat mallet or rolling pin. Sprinkle chicken with ¼ teaspoon salt and black pepper.

Place chicken and green onions on grill rack coated with cooking spray; cover and grill chicken 10 minutes or until done, turning and basting frequently with ½ cup apricot purée. Remove green onions after 6 minutes or when tender. Cut chicken crosswise into strips.

Combine salad greens, red bell pepper slices, and reserved apricot slices in a large bowl. Drizzle with reserved ¾ cup apricot purée; toss gently. To serve, arrange chicken strips over salad mixture. Top with green onions. Yield: 4 servings.

Per Serving: Calories 297 (27% from fat) Fat 8.8g (sat 1.6g) Protein 28.4g Carbohydrate 26.5g Fiber 3.1g Cholesterol 72mg Sodium 521mg
Exchanges: 1 Fruit, 2 Vegetable, 3 Lean Meat

Lemon Sorbet with Blackberries

1   cup blackberries
1   tablespoon sugar
2   cups lemon sorbet

Combine blackberries and sugar in a bowl, stirring gently. Cover and chill.

Spoon ½ cup sorbet into each of 4 dessert dishes. Top each with ¼ cup berry mixture. Serve immediately. Yield: 4 servings.

Per Serving: Calories 166 (1% from fat) Fat 0.1g (sat 0.0g) Protein 0.2g Carbohydrate 41.6g Fiber 1.4g Cholesterol 0mg Sodium 0mg
Exchanges: 1 Starch, 2 Fruit

Mozzarella-Tomato Salad

Featuring summer's best stuff: corn, tomatoes, and melon

Oriental Chicken and Corn Soup
Mozzarella-Tomato Salad
fresh watermelon
serves 4

menu plan

1. *Mince garlic, grate ginger, and slice onions for soup.*

2. *Remove husks and silks from corn; cut kernels from cob.*

3. *Slice tomatoes, prepare salad, and chill.*

4. *Slice watermelon.*

5. *Cook soup.*

Oriental Chicken and Corn Soup

Use frozen thawed corn kernels if fresh corn is not available.

½ pound skinless, boneless chicken breast halves, cut into ⅛-inch-thick strips
4 cups plus 2 tablespoons fat-free, less-sodium chicken broth, divided
1½ teaspoons dark sesame oil, divided
3 tablespoons cornstarch, divided
2 garlic cloves, minced
1 tablespoon grated peeled fresh ginger
1½ cups fresh corn kernels (about 2 ears)
¼ cup water
1 large egg, lightly beaten
2 tablespoons sliced green onions

Combine chicken, 2 tablespoons chicken broth, ½ teaspoon sesame oil, and 1 tablespoon cornstarch in a medium bowl.

Heat ½ teaspoon sesame oil in a large nonstick skillet over high heat; add garlic and ginger, and sauté 10 seconds. Add chicken mixture, and sauté 2 minutes. Add 4 cups broth; cover and bring to boil. Add corn; reduce heat, and simmer 10 minutes.

Combine 2 tablespoons cornstarch and water; add to soup, and stir until mixture comes to a boil. Slowly pour beaten egg into boiling soup; stir about 30 seconds or until thin strands are formed. Stir in ½ teaspoon sesame oil. Sprinkle with green onions.

Yield: 4 (1½-cup) servings.

Per Serving: Calories 194 (20% from fat) Fat 4.4g (sat 0.9g) Protein 17.2g Carbohydrate 19.0g Fiber 1.9g Cholesterol 88mg Sodium 702mg **Exchanges:** 1 Starch, 2 Lean Meat

Mozzarella-Tomato Salad

2 large red tomatoes, each cut into 4 slices
6 (1-ounce) slices part-skim mozzarella cheese, each cut in half
12 large basil leaves
2 large yellow tomatoes, each cut into 4 slices
3 tablespoons fat-free balsamic vinaigrette
1 teaspoon freshly ground pepper

Stack 4 tomato slices, 3 cheese slices, and 3 basil leaves in each of 4 stacks, alternating tomato, cheese, and basil. Drizzle stacks evenly with vinaigrette. Cover and chill. Sprinkle with pepper before serving.

Yield: 4 servings.

Per Serving: Calories 165 (43% from fat) Fat 7.9g (sat 4.7g) Protein 14.0g Carbohydrate 11.4g Fiber 1.9g Cholesterol 23mg Sodium 407mg **Exchanges:** 2 Vegetable, 1 High-Fat Meat

Fill up at lunch with this fresh garden sandwich.

Roasted Chicken Sandwiches
fresh red bell pepper strips
Peaches and Cream
serves 4

If foccacia is not available in the deli or bakery, use a 10-ounce Italian bread shell (such as Boboli).

menu plan

1. *Prepare peach mixture for dessert, and chill until serving time.*

2. *Shred zucchini, slice tomato, and skin chicken for sandwiches. Slice 1 large red bell pepper.*

3. *Cook zucchini mixture for sandwiches.*

4. *Broil bread, and assemble sandwiches.*

Roasted Chicken Sandwiches

If you need to reduce the sodium, use 8 (1-ounce) slices of French bread instead of the foccacia.

2½ cups shredded zucchini (about 3 medium)
Olive oil-flavored cooking spray
 1 (4.4-ounce) container light spiced Gournay cheese product (about ½ cup)
 3 tablespoons grated Parmesan cheese
 3 tablespoons light mayonnaise
 1 (10-ounce) foccacia (from deli), quartered
 1 large tomato, thinly sliced
 2 (5-ounce) roasted chicken breast halves, skinned and sliced
 ½ teaspoon freshly ground pepper

Preheat broiler.
Press zucchini between paper towels until barely moist. Coat a large nonstick skillet with cooking spray; place over medium heat until hot. Add zucchini, and sauté 2

minutes. Transfer to a medium bowl. Stir in Gournay cheese, Parmesan cheese, and mayonnaise.
Cut each bread quarter in half horizontally. Place on a baking sheet, cut sides up. Broil 3 minutes. Spread zucchini mixture evenly on bread; broil 3 minutes or until hot and lightly browned.
Top 4 pieces of bread evenly with tomato, chicken, and pepper; cover with remaining bread pieces.
Yield: 4 servings.

Per Serving: Calories 411 (30% from fat) Fat 13.9g (sat 5.0g) Protein 37.5g
Carbohydrate 34.3g Fiber 1.4g Cholesterol 80mg Sodium 1083mg
Exchanges: 2 Starch, 1 Vegetable, 4 Lean Meat

Peaches and Cream

 4 ripe peaches, peeled and pitted
 2 tablespoons low-sugar peach preserves, melted
 1 tablespoon sugar
 ¼ teaspoon vanilla extract
 1 tablespoon amaretto (optional)
 2 cups vanilla low-fat ice cream

Cut peaches into ½-inch cubes over a bowl, reserving juice. Mash half of peaches with a fork; add juice, preserves, next 2 ingredients, and amaretto, if desired. Stir in remaining cubed peaches. Cover and chill.
Spoon ½ cup ice cream into each of 4 dessert dishes; top each evenly with peach mixture. Yield: 4 servings.

Per Serving: Calories 170 (11% from fat) Fat 2.1g (sat 1.0g) Protein 3.7g
Carbohydrate 35.8g Fiber 3.0g Cholesterol 5mg Sodium 58mg
Exchanges: 1 Starch, 1 Fruit, ½ Fat

Pack a pita in your brown bag lunch.

Mediterranean Chicken Pitas
Minted Cantaloupe
serves 2

If you can't find the crumbled feta cheese with basil and tomatoes, use any feta—flavored or plain. The Greek seasoning adds plenty of flavor.

menu plan

1. *Prepare cantaloupe dish, and chill.*

2. *Chop chicken and cucumber; slice tomato.*

3. *Prepare chicken mixture for sandwiches.*

4. *Assemble sandwiches.*

Mediterranean Chicken Pitas

To soften pita bread, wrap it in a moist towel, and microwave at HIGH for 30 seconds or until soft.

- 1 cup chopped roasted skinless, boneless chicken breast (about 3 ounces)
- ¼ cup chopped peeled cucumber (about ½ small)
- 1 tablespoon crumbled feta cheese with basil and sun-dried tomatoes
- ⅓ cup light mayonnaise
- ½ teaspoon salt-free Greek seasoning
- 6 large spinach leaves
- 2 (8-inch) pitas
- 1 plum tomato, sliced

Combine first 5 ingredients.
Place 3 spinach leaves on one-half of each pita. Top spinach evenly with chicken mixture. Fold pitas over filling. Secure with wooden picks, if desired. Serve with sliced tomato. Yield: 2 servings.

Per Serving: Calories 400 (33% from fat) Fat 14.5g (sat 3.6g) Protein 27.4g Carbohydrate 37.7g Fiber 2.0g Cholesterol 72mg Sodium 682mg
Exchanges: 2 Starch, 2 Vegetable, 2 Medium-Fat Meat, 1 Fat

Minted Cantaloupe

Look for fresh cantaloupe cubes on the deli salad bar, or substitute frozen cantaloupe balls.

- ⅓ cup white grape juice
- 2 teaspoons finely chopped fresh mint
- 2 cups fresh cantaloupe cubes or balls

Combine grape juice and mint. Pour over cantaloupe. Cover and chill. Yield: 2 (1-cup) servings.

Per Serving: Calories 82 (4% from fat) Fat 0.4g (sat 0.1g) Protein 1.4g Carbohydrate 20.2g Fiber 1.2g Cholesterol 0mg Sodium 16mg
Exchanges: 1½ Fruit

cantaloupe

American cantaloupes are really *muskmelons*. True cantaloupes, named for a castle in Italy, are not exported from Europe. The American melons have raised netting over a smooth grayish-beige skin. The pale orange flesh of a ripe melon is very sweet and juicy.

Choose melons that are heavy for their size and have a sweet, fruity fragrance. They should yield slightly to pressure at the end opposite the stem. Avoid cantaloupes with soft spots.

Store unripe cantaloupes at room temperature and ripe ones in the refrigerator. If you're keeping cantaloupe in the refrigerator for more than 2 days, wrap it in plastic wrap so it won't absorb other food odors.

No need to heat up the kitchen with this grilled dinner.

Chicken with Onion and Pepper
onion rolls   Melon with Strawberry Sauce
serves 4

menu plan

1. *Prepare marinade; marinate chicken.*

2. *Quarter bell pepper; slice onion; slice strawberries.*

3. *Cube melon; prepare strawberry sauce.*

4. *Grill chicken and pepper.*

5. *Spoon sauce over melon just before serving.*

Chicken with Onion and Pepper

½ cup low-sodium soy sauce
2   tablespoons honey
2   tablespoons red wine vinegar
½ teaspoon hot sauce
½ teaspoon garlic powder
4   (4-ounce) skinless, boneless chicken breast halves
1   green bell pepper, quartered
1   large sweet or red onion, cut into 4 (½-inch-thick) slices
Cooking spray

Combine first 5 ingredients; pour half of mixture over chicken. Cover and marinate 10 minutes. Set aside remaining soy sauce mixture.
Place chicken, pepper, and onion on grill rack coated with cooking spray. Cover and grill chicken 5 to 6 minutes on each side or until done, basting with reserved soy sauce mixture. Remove chicken, and grill vegetables 2 additional minutes or until desired tenderness, basting with reserved soy sauce mixture. Yield: 4 servings.

Per Serving: Calories 226 (14% from fat) Fat 3.5g (sat 0.9g) Protein 27.7g Carbohydrate 17.6g Fiber 2.0g Cholesterol 72mg Sodium 849mg
Exchanges: 1 Starch, 1 Vegetable, 3 Very Lean Meat

Melon with Strawberry Sauce

Get watermelon cubes from the grocery store salad bar or in the produce section.

4   cups cubed seeded watermelon
1½ cups sliced strawberries
3   tablespoons orange juice
2   tablespoons sugar

Place 1 cup melon in each of 4 dessert dishes.
Combine strawberries, orange juice, and sugar in a food processor or blender; process until smooth. To serve, spoon sauce evenly over melon. Yield: 4 servings.

Per Serving: Calories 90 (8% from fat) Fat 0.8g (sat 0.1g) Protein 1.3g Carbohydrate 21.2g Fiber 1.9g Cholesterol 0mg Sodium 4mg
Exchanges: ½ Starch, 1 Fruit

watermelon

To pick a ripe watermelon, use the thump test. Slap the side of the melon with your hand—if you hear a hollow thump, the melon is probably ripe. The rind should be dull instead of shiny and should just barely yield to pressure.

Better than take-out Thai—and possibly quicker!

Spicy Noodles with Chicken
Asian Slaw
lemon sherbet   fresh plum slices

serves 2

Somen (Japanese whole-wheat noodles) are available in
Asian markets and the Asian food section of the supermarket.

menu plan

1. *Boil water for noodles; thaw chicken.*

2. *Chop onions; trim peas; slice cabbage,
pepper, and onions for slaw.*

3. *Cook noodles, and slice plums.*

4. *Prepare slaw.*

5. *Cook chicken mixture.*

napa cabbage

Napa, or Chinese cabbage, is an elongated
cabbage with crinkly, cream-colored leaves
with green tips and thick veins. The loosely
packed leaves are thin, crisp, and have a
delicate flavor.

Spicy Noodles with Chicken

*If you need to reduce the sodium in this recipe, use 1½
cups fresh cooked chicken instead of the frozen.*

    4 ounces somen (whole-wheat noodles) or
          angel hair pasta, uncooked
    2 teaspoons dark sesame oil
    3 green onions, chopped
    6 ounces frozen chicken strips, thawed (about 1½ cups)
 1½ cups snow peas, trimmed
    1 tablespoon salt-free Thai seasoning
          (such as The Spice Hunter)
    2 tablespoons hoisin sauce

Cook noodles according to package directions, omitting
salt and fat; drain.

Heat oil in a large nonstick skillet over medium-high
heat until hot. Add green onions, and sauté just until tender. Stir in chicken and remaining 3 ingredients. Cook
until thoroughly heated, stirring constantly.

Combine noodles and chicken mixture, tossing well.
Yield: 2 (2¼-cup) servings.

Per Serving: Calories 430 (19% from fat) Fat 9.2g (sat 1.5g) Protein 33.5g
Carbohydrate 51.6g Fiber 3.0g Cholesterol 73mg Sodium 1161mg
Exchanges: 3 Starch, 1 Vegetable, 3 Lean Meat

hoisin how-tos

Look for hoisin sauce in the Asian section of the supermarket or in an Asian market.

Hoisin sauce is high in sodium. If you need to reduce the sodium in your diet, you can make your own hoisin sauce.

Hoisin sauce: Mix 3 tablespoons brown sugar, 3 tablespoons low-sodium soy sauce, and ¼ teaspoon garlic powder to make about ¼ cup sauce.

Asian Slaw

  2 **cups thinly sliced napa (Chinese) cabbage**
 ⅓ **cup thinly sliced red bell pepper**
  2 **tablespoons sliced green onions**
  1 **tablespoon rice vinegar**
1½ **teaspoons hoisin sauce**
 ¼ **teaspoon dark sesame oil**

Combine first 3 ingredients in a bowl.
Combine vinegar, hoisin sauce, and oil. Pour vinegar mixture over cabbage mixture; toss well. Serve immediately, or cover and chill. Yield: 2 (1-cup) servings.

Per Serving: Calories 32 (25% from fat) Fat 0.9g (sat 0.1g) Protein 1.0g
Carbohydrate 5.6g Fiber 1.7g Cholesterol 0mg Sodium 76mg
Exchange: 1 Vegetable

plums

Plums are a pitted fruit and in the same family as peaches, apricots, and nectarines.

varieties Hundreds of plum varieties are grown all over the world. They are either oval or round and usually range in size from 1 to 3 inches in diameter. Plums can be red, yellow, green, purple, or blue, depending on the variety. The flavors vary from extremely sweet to tart.

selection Buy plums that are plump and well colored for their variety. If the fruit yields to gentle pressure, it's ripe and ready to eat. If the plum is still slightly firm, let it ripen at room temperature in a loosely closed paper bag.

storage Store very firm plums at room temperature until they're slightly soft. Refrigerate ripe plums in a plastic bag for up to 4 days.

Use your grill to get the best flavor from the sausage, vegetables, and even the bread.

Garden Sausage Grill with Couscous
Grilled Flatbread cantaloupe wedges

serves 4

menu plan

1. *Prepare marinade; slice sausage; cut up vegetables; chop basil; slice cantaloupe.*

2. *Marinate vegetables.*

3. *Prepare couscous, and let stand while grilling sausage and vegetables.*

4. *Prepare pizza crust dough, and place on grill after removing sausage and vegetables.*

Garden Sausage Grill with Couscous

2 tablespoons balsamic vinegar
1 tablespoon brown sugar
1 tablespoon olive oil
⅛ teaspoon black pepper
1 large red bell pepper, cut into 1-inch strips
1 small eggplant, cut into ½-inch slices
1 (5.8-ounce) package roasted garlic and
    olive oil couscous
Cooking spray
¾ pound turkey kielbasa

Prepare grill.
Combine first 4 ingredients in a large bowl. Add pepper strips and eggplant slices; toss gently to coat.
Prepare couscous according to package directions, and set aside.
Remove vegetables from bowl, reserving marinade. Place pepper strips, eggplant, and sausage on grill rack coated with cooking spray; cover and grill 3 minutes. Baste vegetables with reserved marinade; turn vegetables and sausage. Grill 3 minutes; remove sausage and pepper strips, and return pepper strips to

bowl. Baste eggplant, and grill 4 minutes, basting and turning eggplant after 2 minutes. Remove eggplant from grill, and add to pepper strips.
Add remaining marinade to vegetables; toss to coat. Cut sausage into 4 equal portions. Serve sausage and vegetables with couscous. Yield: 4 servings.

Per Serving: Calories 347 (31% from fat) Fat 11.8g (sat 4.3g) Protein 18.4g Carbohydrate 43.5g Fiber 4.4g Cholesterol 45mg Sodium 909mg **Exchanges:** 2 Starch, 2 Vegetable, 1 High-Fat Meat, 1 Fat

Grilled Flatbread

1 (10-ounce) can refrigerated pizza crust dough
Olive oil-flavored cooking spray
1 tablespoon olive oil
2 tablespoons preshredded fresh Parmesan cheese
2 tablespoons chopped fresh basil

Prepare grill.
Unroll pizza dough. Coat both sides with cooking spray, and place dough on a large baking sheet. Brush dough with olive oil.
Combine cheese and basil in a small bowl.
Remove dough from baking sheet, and place on grill rack coated with cooking spray. Grill 2 minutes or until bottom is lightly browned. Turn dough over, and sprinkle evenly with cheese mixture; grill 2 minutes or until lightly browned and crisp. Remove bread from grill, and cut into 8 pieces. Store extra bread in a zip-top plastic bag or an airtight container. Yield: 8 servings.

Per Serving: Calories 116 (27% from fat) Fat 3.5g (sat 1.0g) Protein 3.8g Carbohydrate 16.9g Fiber 0.5g Cholesterol 2mg Sodium 265mg **Exchanges:** 1 Starch, 1 Fat

autu

umn

When the air turns cool and the trees blaze with color, fill up your basket, and taste the harvest. Crisp, crunchy apples in every shade of red, gold, and green. Sweet, tender pears. Earthy, meaty mushrooms. Buttery acorn squash roasted with a touch of brown sugar and cinnamon. Toasted pumpkin seeds. Sweet carrots, fennel, leeks, and turnips all simmering in a savory stew. Come and join the feast.

Fill up at lunchtime with this crunchy, satisfying salad.

Grains and Greens Salad
sliced apples   warm pita bread
mint iced tea

serves 4

Look for mint-flavored tea bags at the grocery, or add fresh mint when steeping your tea. Use about 1 cup of mint leaves for every 6 cups of water.

menu plan

1. *Bring liquids to a boil for couscous.*

2. *Prepare couscous.*

3. *While couscous stands, slice apples and chop peanuts.*

4. *Heat pita bread in oven for about 5 minutes.*

5. *Arrange salad while bread is warming.*

Grains and Greens Salad

1   (15-ounce) can lentil and carrots soup (such as Health Valley)
½   cup water
1   (6.1-ounce) package tomato lentil couscous mix
4   cups gourmet salad greens
¼   cup fat-free balsamic vinaigrette
¼   cup (1 ounce) crumbled garlic-flavored feta cheese
¼   cup chopped unsalted peanuts

Combine soup, water, and seasoning packet from couscous mix in a medium saucepan; bring to a boil. Stir in couscous. Remove from heat; cover and let stand 5 minutes or until liquid is absorbed. Fluff with a fork.
Combine salad greens and vinaigrette; toss gently. Place 1 cup greens on each of 4 plates. Spoon ¾ cup couscous mixture over each serving; sprinkle evenly with crumbled feta cheese and peanuts.
Yield: 4 servings.

Per Serving: Calories 285 (21% from fat) Fat 6.5g (sat 1.7g) Protein 15.3g Carbohydrate 50.3g Fiber 9.0g Cholesterol 6mg Sodium 882mg
Exchanges: 3 Starch, 1 Vegetable, 1 Fat

A light lunch with savory rustic flavors

Tuscan White Bean Salad
whole-grain rolls
low-fat apple-cinnamon bars

serves 3

Look for low-fat fruit bars in the snack section of the grocery store.

menu plan

1. *Rinse and drain beans, mince garlic, and chop parsley for salad.*

2. *Grill tomatoes.*

3. *Combine salad ingredients.*

plum tomatoes

Plum tomatoes are available almost all year and are great for cooking because of their firm texture.

They have an oblong shape and come in red and yellow. When you're yearning for fresh tomatoes after the summer, plum tomatoes are what you need.

Tuscan White Bean Salad

If you want to serve the salad on lettuce leaves, romaine or Bibb is a good choice for fall.

  6 plum tomatoes
Olive oil-flavored cooking spray
  2 large garlic cloves, minced
  1 (19-ounce) can cannellini beans, rinsed and drained
  ⅓ cup thinly sliced red onion
  ¼ cup coarsely chopped flat-leaf parsley
  ¼ cup fat-free balsamic vinaigrette
  ¼ cup (1 ounce) preshredded fresh Parmesan cheese
Romaine lettuce leaves (optional)

Prepare grill.
Cut tomatoes in half vertically; coat with cooking spray. Place tomato and garlic in a zip-top plastic bag; shake to coat tomato.
Place tomato on grill rack coated with cooking spray; grill, covered, 3 minutes, turning once. (Tomato should be slightly charred, but not mushy.)
Combine beans and next 3 ingredients; toss well.
Gently fold tomato into bean mixture; sprinkle with cheese. Serve on romaine lettuce leaves, if desired. Yield: 3 (1-cup) servings.

Per Serving: Calories 237 (13% from fat) Fat 3.5g (sat 1.7g) Protein 15.0g Carbohydrate 38.3g Fiber 5.8g Cholesterol 6mg Sodium 849mg
Exchanges: 2 Starch, 2 Vegetable, 1 Lean Meat

No chopping required in this meat-free, "dump and cook" chili.

Vegetarian Chili
Poppy Seed Coleslaw
cornbread

serves 6

To reduce the sodium in the chili, use 2 cans of
low-sodium kidney beans instead of the regular beans.

menu plan

1. *Prepare cornbread from mix following
low-fat package directions.*

2. *Prepare chili.*

3. *Prepare coleslaw while cornbread bakes
and chili cooks.*

Vegetarian Chili

Cooking spray
 1 cup frozen chopped onion
 1 (12-ounce) package frozen burger-style vegetable
    protein crumbles
 2 (14½-ounce) cans chili-style tomatoes, undrained
 1 (16-ounce) can dark red kidney beans, rinsed and
    drained
 1 (15-ounce) can ranch-style beans, undrained
 1 cup water
 1 tablespoon chili powder
 ½ teaspoon ground cumin
Low-fat sour cream (optional)
Crushed low-fat tortilla chips (optional)
Shredded reduced-fat Cheddar cheese (optional)

Coat a Dutch oven with cooking spray; heat over
medium-high heat until hot. Add onion; sauté 5 minutes. Stir in vegetable protein crumbles and next 6
ingredients; bring to a boil. Cover, reduce heat, and
simmer 15 minutes, stirring occasionally. Serve with
toppings, if desired. Yield: 6 (1⅓-cup) servings.

Per Serving: Calories 241 (15% from fat) Fat 4.0g (sat 0.1g) Protein 17.9g
Carbohydrate 33.4g Fiber 10.7g Cholesterol 0mg Sodium 999mg
Exchanges: 2 Starch, 1 Vegetable, 1 Lean Meat

Poppy Seed Coleslaw

 1 (16-ounce) package coleslaw
 1 red bell pepper, chopped
 1 celery stalk, thinly sliced
 ¾ cup light coleslaw dressing (such as Marzetti's)
 1 teaspoon poppy seeds

Combine all ingredients in a bowl, tossing gently.
Cover and chill. Yield: 6 (1-cup) servings.

Per Serving: Calories 125 (53% from fat) Fat 7.4g (sat 1.1g) Protein 1.2g
Carbohydrate 15.1g Fiber 2.2g Cholesterol 25mg Sodium 400mg
Exchanges: 3 Vegetable, 1 Fat

A simple meal featuring two traditional New England favorites: hearty chowder and a creamy coffee beverage

Chunky Two-Potato Clam Chowder
Coffee Smoothie   oyster crackers

serves 4

menu plan

1. *Set ice cream out to soften for smoothie.*

2. *Microwave potatoes for chowder.*

3. *Cook bacon for chowder while potatoes cook.*

4. *Prepare chowder.*

5. *Make smoothie.*

Chunky Two-Potato Clam Chowder

1 Yukon Gold potato (about 8 ounces), coarsely chopped
1 sweet potato, peeled and coarsely chopped
2 reduced-sodium bacon slices
2 (6½-ounce) cans chopped clams, undrained
1 (14½-ounce) can no-salt-added stewed tomatoes, undrained
2 garlic cloves, crushed
¼ teaspoon dried thyme
¼ teaspoon salt

Place chopped potato in an 11 x 7-inch microwave-safe dish; microwave at HIGH 5 minutes, rotating dish a half-turn after 2½ minutes.
Cook bacon in a small Dutch oven until crisp; remove bacon, reserving drippings in pan. Crumble bacon, and set aside.
Drain clams, reserving juice. Set clams aside. Add clam juice, potato, stewed tomatoes, and remaining 3 ingredients to pan; bring to a boil. Cover, reduce heat, and simmer 5 minutes. Stir in clams, and simmer 5 minutes.
Ladle soup into individual bowls. Top each serving with crumbled bacon. Yield: 4 (1-cup) servings.

Per Serving: 164 Calories (6% from fat) Fat 1.1g (sat 0.4g) Protein 9.6g Carbohydrate 28.1g Fiber 3.7g Cholesterol 18.4mg Sodium 592mg **Exchanges:** 2 Starch

Coffee Smoothie

Vary this recipe with your favorite flavored coffee mix.

½ cup strong brewed coffee
2 tablespoons instant Kahlúa-flavored coffee mix (such as General Mills' International Coffee Kahlúa Café)
1 tablespoon Kahlúa (coffee-flavored liqueur)
4½ cups vanilla fat-free ice cream, softened

Combine coffee, coffee mix, and liqueur in a 1-cup glass measure. Microwave at HIGH 30 seconds; stir until coffee mix dissolves.
Combine coffee mixture and ice cream in a blender; process until smooth. Serve immediately. Yield: 4 (1-cup) servings.

Per Serving: Calories 242 (0% from fat) Fat 0.1g (sat 0.0g) Protein 4.6g Carbohydrate 51.8g Fiber 0.0g Cholesterol 0mg Sodium 94mg **Exchanges:** 3 Starch

Coffee Smoothie

This stew is a quick and easy version of cioppino—an Italian-style fish stew.

Shrimp and Tomato Stew
Sweet-and-Sour Spinach Salad
soft breadsticks

serves 2

menu plan

1. *Combine spinach salad ingredients, and chill.*

2. *Prepare stew.*

3. *Toast breadsticks in oven for about 5 minutes while stew is simmering. Drizzle dressing over salad.*

Shrimp and Tomato Stew

Buy peeled and deveined shrimp in the seafood section of your grocery store.

1 (14½-ounce) can no-salt-added stewed tomatoes, undrained
1 (14½-ounce) can fat-free, less-sodium chicken broth
½ teaspoon hot sauce
1 teaspoon dried Italian seasoning
½ pound large shrimp, peeled and deveined

Combine first 4 ingredients in a large saucepan; bring to a boil. Reduce heat, and simmer, uncovered, 5 minutes. Add shrimp, and simmer 5 minutes or until shrimp turn pink. Yield: 2 (1-cup) servings.

Per Serving: Calories 199 (9% from fat) Fat 2.1g (sat 0.4g) Protein 25.8g Carbohydrate 17.0g Fiber 1.1g Cholesterol 172mg Sodium 382mg **Exchanges:** 1 Starch, 3 Very Lean Meat

Sweet-and-Sour Spinach Salad

3 cups torn spinach
½ cup sliced mushrooms
½ small red onion, sliced
3 tablespoons oil-free sweet-and-sour dressing (such as Old Dutch)

Combine first 3 ingredients, and toss well. Drizzle with sweet-and-sour dressing. Yield: 2 (1½-cup) servings.

Per Serving: Calories 83 (5% from fat) Fat 0.5g (sat 0.1g) Protein 3.6g Carbohydrate 18.1g Fiber 4.9g Cholesterol 0mg Sodium 339mg **Exchanges:** 1 Starch, 1 Vegetable

spinach

Select spinach with crisp, dark leaves and no yellow spots. If you're buying a bunch of spinach, you'll need to wash it and trim off the stems. The fresh spinach in bags has already been washed, but you still may need to trim a few stems.

This chunky chili will have you coming back for more.

Chipotle-Corn Chili
low-fat tortilla chips   **Caramel Sundaes**

serves 4

The chipotle salsa adds a smoky, sweet flavor to the chili,
but you can use any type of chunky salsa.

menu plan

1. *Brown meat for chili.*

2. *Toast pumpkinseeds, if desired, in a nonstick skillet over medium heat for about 3 minutes or until lightly browned.*

3. *Cook chili.*

4. *Prepare sundaes just before serving.*

Chipotle-Corn Chili

The coarsely ground chili meat contributes to the texture of this hearty chili. Ask the meat market to grind it for you if it's not available in packaged form.

  1   **pound coarsely ground round chili meat**
  ¼   **teaspoon pepper**
Cooking spray
1¾   **cups whole-kernel corn**
  1   **(14½-ounce) can no-salt-added diced tomatoes, undrained**
1½   **cups bottled thick 'n' chunky chipotle salsa**
  ¾   **cup (3 ounces) preshredded reduced-fat Mexican blend cheese (such as Sargento)**
  2   **tablespoons unsalted pumpkinseeds, toasted (optional)**

Combine meat and pepper in a small Dutch oven coated with cooking spray. Cook over medium-high heat 10 minutes or until browned, stirring to crumble. Drain, if necessary.
Reduce heat to medium; add corn, and cook, uncovered, 3 minutes, stirring occasionally. Add diced tomatoes and salsa; cook, uncovered, 5 minutes, stirring occasionally. Ladle into each of 4 soup bowls. Top each serving with 3 tablespoons cheese and, if desired, pumpkinseeds. Yield: 4 (1¼-cup) servings.

Per Serving: Calories 334 (38% from fat) Fat 14.2g (sat 6.4g) Protein 31.6g Carbohydrate 22.5g Fiber 2.9g Cholesterol 49mg Sodium 942mg
Exchanges: 1½ Starch, 4 Lean Meat

Caramel Sundaes

  2   **cups vanilla low-fat ice cream**
  8   **teaspoons caramel fat-free apple dip (such as Marzetti's)**

Scoop ½ cup ice cream into each of 4 serving bowls. Top each serving with 2 teaspoons apple dip. Serve sundaes immediately. Yield: 4 (½-cup) servings.

Per Serving: Calories 150 (12% from fat) Fat 2.0g (sat 1.0g) Protein 3.3g Carbohydrate 28.0g Fiber 1.0g Cholesterol 5mg Sodium 85mg
Exchanges: 2 Starch

pumpkinseeds

Pumpkinseeds, or *pepitas*, are a popular ingredient in Mexican cooking. You can buy them in a variety of forms: salted, unsalted, roasted, raw, with or without hulls. With the white hull removed, they are medium-dark green and have a delicious flavor.

Look for pumpkinseeds in health food stores, Mexican markets, and supermarkets.

Enjoy a quick Mexican-style meal before you take a siesta.

Beefy Jícama Wraps
Black Beans with Sour Cream
Citrus Salad

serves 2

menu plan

1. *Prepare lettuce; peel and slice orange for salad.*

2. *Peel and slice vegetables for wraps.*

3. *Cook meat mixture for wraps.*

4. *Heat black beans in microwave.*

5. *Heat tortillas, and assemble wraps.*

6. *Toss salad.*

Beefy Jícama Wraps

½ **pound lean boneless sirloin steak**
½ **teaspoon vegetable oil**
¼ **teaspoon salt**
¼ **teaspoon pepper**
1 **cup (¼-inch) julienne-cut peeled jícama**
   (about 1 small jícama)
½ **cup sliced red onion**
1 **tablespoon fresh lime juice**
½ **teaspoon chili powder**
2 **(8-inch) flour tortillas**
¼ **cup picante sauce**

Cut steak across grain into very thin strips. Heat oil in a large nonstick skillet over medium-high heat. Add meat; sprinkle with salt and pepper. Cook 5 minutes or until meat is browned, turning occasionally.
Add jícama, onion, lime juice, and chili powder; cook 2 minutes, stirring frequently.
Wrap tortillas in heavy-duty plastic wrap. Microwave at HIGH 30 seconds or until warm. Spoon half of mixture down center of each tortilla. Roll up; serve immediately with picante sauce. Yield: 2 servings.

Per Serving: Calories 312 (27% from fat) Fat 9.3g (sat 2.7g) Protein 27.9g Carbohydrate 27.8g Fiber 4.6g Cholesterol 69mg Sodium 858mg **Exchanges:** 2 Starch, 3 Lean Meat

Black Beans with Sour Cream

1 **cup drained canned black beans**
2 **tablespoons low-fat sour cream**

Place beans in a small microwave-safe bowl; cover. Microwave at HIGH 2 minutes or until thoroughly heated, stirring after 1 minute. Dollop each serving with 1 tablespoon sour cream.
Yield: 2 (½-cup) servings.

Per Serving: Calories 150 (15% from fat) Fat 2.5g (sat 1.3g) Protein 9.2g Carbohydrate 24.1g Fiber 4.2g Cholesterol 6mg Sodium 276mg **Exchanges:** 2 Starch

Citrus Salad

2 **cups torn Bibb lettuce**
1 **orange, peeled and sliced**
1½ **tablespoons reduced-fat olive oil vinaigrette**

Combine all ingredients in a medium bowl; toss well. Yield: 2 (1-cup) servings.

Per Serving: 61 Calories (37% from fat) Fat 2.5g (sat 0.2g) Protein 1.3g Carbohydrate 10.2g Fiber 3.3g Cholesterol 0mg Sodium 93mg **Exchanges:** ½ Fruit, 1 Vegetable, ½ Fat

autumn produce

Vegetables	Fruits	Herbs
Belgian Endive	Apples	Bay Leaves
Broccoli	Cranberries	Parsley
Brussels Sprouts	Grapes	Rosemary
Cabbage	Mission Figs	Sage
Cauliflower	Pears	Thyme
Eggplant	Persimmons	
Escarole	Pomegranates	
Fennel	Quinces	
Frisée		
Leeks		
Mushrooms		
Parsnips		
Pumpkins		
Red Bell Peppers		
Red Potatoes		
Rutabagas		
Shallots		
Sweet Potatoes		
Winter Squash		
Yukon Gold Potatoes		

Rosemary

Red Grapes

Pears

Pumpkin

Bell Peppers

Shiitake Mushrooms

Sage

Eggplant

Although many produce items are available year-round, this chart lists those that are at their peak during this season. Check with farmers' markets in your area for regional varieties.

This high-flavor meal is one of our Test Kitchens staff's top picks.

Bourbon-Glazed Beef Tenderloin
Roasted Rosemary Potatoes   Caramelized Sweet Onions
mixed green salad with fat-free vinaigrette
serves 4

menu plan

1. *Slice onions and begin cooking to caramelize.*

2. *Mince rosemary, and roast potatoes while onions are cooking.*

3. *Prepare bourbon mixture for steaks.*

4. *When onions and potatoes have been cooking for about 15 minutes, cook steaks.*

5. *Toss a bag of mixed salad greens with fat-free vinaigrette.*

Bourbon-Glazed Beef Tenderloin

  6 tablespoons bourbon
  ¼ cup reduced-sodium soy sauce
  3 tablespoons dark brown sugar
  3 tablespoons balsamic vinegar
  2 tablespoons low-sodium Worcestershire sauce
  4 (4-ounce) beef tenderloin steaks, trimmed (about 1 inch thick)
Cooking spray

Combine first 5 ingredients in a small bowl. Place steaks in a shallow dish, and spoon ¼ cup bourbon mixture over steaks. Set remaining bourbon mixture aside. Turn steaks to coat evenly.
Coat a large skillet with cooking spray; place over high heat until hot. Add steaks to pan; reduce heat to medium-high. Cook 3 minutes on each side or to desired degree of doneness. Remove steaks from pan; keep warm.
Increase heat to high; add reserved bourbon mixture to pan. Bring to a boil, scraping pan to loosen browned bits; simmer 1 minute or until sauce is reduced to ¼ cup. To serve, spoon sauce over steaks. Yield: 4 servings (serving size: 1 steak and 1 tablespoon sauce).

Per Serving: 218 Calories (31% from fat) Fat 7.5g (sat 3.0g) Protein 24.1g Carbohydrate 12.3g Fiber 0.0g Cholesterol 70mg Sodium 441mg **Exchanges:** 1 Starch, 3 Lean Meat

Roasted Rosemary Potatoes

Olive oil-flavored cooking spray
  1 (1¼-pound) package new potato wedges (such as Simply Potatoes)
  2 teaspoons minced fresh rosemary
  ¼ teaspoon salt

Preheat oven to 500°.
Coat a roasting pan with cooking spray. Spread potato wedges evenly in pan. Coat potatoes with cooking spray; sprinkle with rosemary and salt. Bake at 500° for 20 minutes. Yield 4 (¾-cup) servings.

Per Serving: Calories 92 (4% from fat) Fat 0.4g (sat 0.1g) Protein 3.5g Carbohydrate 17.9g Fiber 3.7g Cholesterol 0mg Sodium 296mg **Exchange:** 1 Starch

a dessert idea: *Go the extra mile and make creamy Mocha Pudding (page 209) for your menu finale.*

Caramelized Sweet Onions

If onions begin to burn, add 1 tablespoon of water, stir well, and continue cooking.

2   large Vidalia or other sweet onions, sliced
2   tablespoons olive oil
¼   teaspoon salt

Place a large nonstick skillet over high heat until hot. Add onion and oil; reduce heat to medium, and cook 25 minutes or until onion is caramelized, stirring often. Stir in salt. Yield: 4 (¼-cup) servings.

Per Serving: Calories 127 (50% from fat)   Fat 7.0g (sat 0.1g)   Protein 2.1g   Carbohydrate 15.3g   Fiber 3.3g   Cholesterol 0mg   Sodium 152mg
Exchanges: 1 Starch, 1 Fat

A homestyle pot roast dinner in a matter of minutes

Beef in Roasted Pepper Gravy
Steamed Green Beans
Caramel-Apple Crumble

serves 8

menu plan

1. *Boil water for noodles.*

2. *Chop peppers and parsley for beef dish.*

3. *Cook beef dish while noodles cook.*

4. *Steam beans in microwave.*

5. *Cook apples in microwave.*

6. *Spoon apple mixture over ice cream just before serving dessert.*

a few tips:
precooked pot roast

Now you can enjoy a pot roast meal without spending hours in the kitchen.

1 Look for refrigerated fully cooked pot roasts in the meat department of your grocery store. They vary in weight, but are usually 2 to 2½ pounds.

2 The roasts are fully cooked and ready to eat. All you have to do is heat them up on the stovetop or in the microwave.

3 There is no more fat than in a regular roast, but the sodium is higher because of the preservatives. You probably won't need to add any salt.

Beef in Roasted Pepper Gravy

1   (12-ounce) package medium egg noodles, uncooked
1   (2¼ to 2½-pound) package refrigerated fully cooked beef pot roast with gravy
1   (14½-ounce) can diced tomatoes with onion and garlic, undrained
1   cup frozen small white onions
1   (7-ounce) bottle roasted red bell peppers, drained and chopped
½   teaspoon black pepper
½   cup chopped fresh parsley

Cook noodles according to package directions, omitting salt and fat.

Remove pot roast from package, reserving gravy; add gravy to a 4-quart Dutch oven. Add tomatoes, onions, roasted bell pepper, and black pepper to gravy. Bring gravy mixture to a boil; cover, reduce heat, and simmer 10 minutes.

Cut pot roast into 2-inch pieces. Add to gravy mixture; cover and cook 5 additional minutes.

Drain noodles; toss with parsley. Serve beef mixture over noodles.

Yield: 8 servings (serving size: ¾ cup meat mixture and about 1 cup noodles).

Per Serving: Calories 391 (19% from fat) Fat 8.1g (sat 2.9g) Protein 38.2g Carbohydrate 40.1g Fiber 1.8g Cholesterol 121mg Sodium 647mg
Exchanges: 2 Starch, 2 Vegetable, 4 Lean Meat

Steamed Green Beans

2 (16-ounce) packages frozen cut green beans
2 teaspoons extra-virgin olive oil
½ teaspoon salt
½ teaspoon pepper

Cook beans in microwave according to package directions; drain. Toss with olive oil, salt, and pepper.
Yield: 8 (¾-cup) servings.

Per Serving: Calories 44 (29% from fat) Fat 1.4g (sat 0.2g) Protein 1.9g
Carbohydrate 7.6g Fiber 2.9g Cholesterol 0mg Sodium 161mg
Exchanges: 1½ Vegetable

Caramel-Apple Crumble

2 (20-ounce) cans sliced apples, drained
½ teaspoon ground cinnamon
⅓ cup fat-free caramel ice cream topping
4 cups low-fat caramel-praline crunch ice cream
4 shortbread cookies, crumbled

Place sliced apples in an 8-inch square baking dish.
Sprinkle with cinnamon; drizzle with caramel topping. Cover with plastic wrap, and vent; microwave at
HIGH 12 minutes, rotating dish every 4 minutes. Let
stand to cool.
Spoon ½ cup ice cream into each of 8 dessert dishes;
top each serving with ½ cup apple mixture. Sprinkle
crumbled cookies evenly over apple mixture.
Yield: 8 servings.

Per Serving: Calories 267 (13% from fat) Fat 3.8g (sat 1.0g) Protein 4.1g
Carbohydrate 53.4g Fiber 2.6g Cholesterol 6mg Sodium 134mg
Exchanges: 2 Starch, 1½ Fruit, 1 Fat

fresh, frozen, or canned?

Depending on where you live, some fresh fruits
and vegetables will not be available during certain seasons. But you still have the convenient
option of using frozen or canned products.
Although you won't get the variety of shapes
and colors that you get with fresh produce,
sometimes the processed form of the food actually has more nutrients than the fresh version.

frozen If frozen foods are stored under
proper conditions, they might contain slightly
more nutrients than their fresh counterparts
that have been picked, shipped, and stored in a
warehouse. However, there might be some vitamin loss if the food is blanched before freezing.

Plain frozen vegetables (those without sauces
and seasonings) generally don't have added
flavorings or preservatives, so the sodium and
fat content is about the same as fresh. Frozen
fruits often have sugar or syrup added; look for
packages of unsweetened fruit if you want the
product that most closely resembles fresh.

canned Canned fruits have less fiber than
fresh fruits with the skin, and those that are
canned in syrup have more calories than fresh.
The sodium content of canned products is
higher than that of fresh because salt is added
during canning. The heat from the canning
process destroys water-soluble vitamins like
vitamin C, and both vitamins and minerals leak
into the water and are lost when the product is
drained.

Maple-glazed pork and nutty sweet potatoes, m-m-m-m!

Maple-Glazed Pork Chops
Nutty Sweet Potato Patties   Braised Cabbage and Bacon
whole-grain rolls

serves 4

Look for the precooked sweet potato patties in the frozen
vegetable section of the grocery store.

menu plan

1. *Toast pecans; dredge potato patties, and bake.*
2. *Chop cabbage, and prepare cabbage dish.*
3. *Cook pork chops.*

Maple-Glazed Pork Chops

  4 (4-ounce) boneless center-cut loin pork chops,
      trimmed
 ½ teaspoon dried thyme
 ¼ teaspoon salt
 ¼ teaspoon pepper
  2 teaspoons vegetable oil
  2 tablespoons red wine vinegar
  2 tablespoons maple or maple-flavored syrup

Sprinkle pork chops evenly with thyme, salt, and
pepper. Heat vegetable oil in a large skillet over
medium-high heat. Add pork; cook 2 to 3 minutes on
each side or until browned.
Remove pork from pan; set aside. Add vinegar to pan,
scraping pan to loosen browned bits. Add syrup, and
bring to a boil. Cook 1 minute, stirring constantly.
Return chops to pan, and cook 2 minutes.
Yield: 4 servings.

Per Serving: Calories 192 (38% from fat) Fat 8.1g (sat 2.3g) Protein 21.6g
Carbohydrate 7.5g Fiber 0.2g Cholesterol 59mg Sodium 191mg
Exchanges: ½ Starch, 3 Lean Meat

Nutty Sweet Potato Patties

*Toast pecans in a small skillet over medium-high heat 2
minutes or until lightly browned, stirring often.*

  1 large egg white, lightly beaten
  1 (16-ounce) package precooked sweet potato patties
  2 teaspoons sugar
 ¼ teaspoon pepper
 ⅓ cup toasted wheat germ
Cooking spray
  2 tablespoons chopped pecans, toasted
  2 teaspoons light butter, melted

Preheat oven to 425°.
Place egg white in a shallow bowl. Dip each sweet
potato patty in egg white, and sprinkle with sugar and
pepper; dredge in wheat germ.
Place patties on a baking sheet lightly coated with
cooking spray. Bake at 425° for 14 minutes. Sprinkle
with pecans; drizzle melted butter over pecans. Serve
immediately. Yield: 4 servings (serving size: 2 patties).

Per Serving: Calories 215 (20% from fat) Fat 4.7g (sat 1.1g) Protein 4.1g
Carbohydrate 37.7g Fiber 3.5g Cholesterol 3mg Sodium 196mg
Exchanges: 2½ Starch, 1 Fat

Braised Cabbage and Bacon

2   reduced-fat bacon slices
1   small green cabbage (about 1¾ pounds),
       coarsely chopped
¼   teaspoon salt
¼   teaspoon pepper
¼   cup water

Cook bacon in a Dutch oven over medium-high heat until crisp. Remove bacon from pan, reserving drippings in pan. Crumble bacon, and set aside.

Add chopped cabbage to bacon drippings in pan; sauté 2 minutes.

Add salt, pepper, and water; cover and cook 7 minutes or until cabbage is crisp-tender. Uncover, and cook 5 minutes, stirring occasionally. To serve, sprinkle cabbage with crumbled bacon.

Yield: 4 (¾-cup) servings.

Per Serving: Calories 55 (26% from fat)   Fat 1.6g (sat 0.4g)   Protein 3.2g
Carbohydrate 8.6g   Fiber 4.4g   Cholesterol 3mg   Sodium 234mg
Exchanges: 2 Vegetable

It's great to grill out when the air starts turning crisp and cool.

Turkish Pork with Figs
Mediterranean Bulgur Salad
pita bread   red grapes

serves 4

menu plan

1. *Boil water; soak figs and bulgur.*

2. *Quarter onions; marinate pork and onions.*

3. *Dice tomato, and chop parsley for bulgur salad.*

4. *Grill pork.*

5. *Drain bulgur; toss with other salad ingredients.*

Turkish Pork with Figs

1   cup boiling water
12   whole dried figs
2   tablespoons brown sugar
2   tablespoons salt-free Moroccan rub (such as
        The Spice Hunter)
2   tablespoons balsamic vinegar
2   teaspoons olive oil
4   (4-ounce) boneless center-cut loin pork chops (about
        ½ inch thick)
1   red onion, quartered
Cooking spray

Prepare grill.

Pour boiling water over figs in a small bowl. Cover and let stand 5 minutes.

Combine brown sugar and next 3 ingredients in a large heavy-duty, zip-top plastic bag. Add pork chops and onion; seal bag and toss gently. Set aside.

Drain figs; place on 2 (8-inch) metal or wooden skewers. Remove pork chops and onion from bag,

discarding marinade. Place pork chops, onion, and fig skewers on grill rack coated with cooking spray; grill, covered, 12 minutes or until pork chops are done, turning once. Yield: 4 servings.

Per Serving: Calories 321 (35% from fat) Fat 12.5g (sat 4.1g) Protein 23.6g Carbohydrate 29.9g Fiber 5.7g Cholesterol 73mg Sodium 62mg **Exchanges:** 1 Starch, 1 Fruit, 3 Lean Meat

Mediterranean Bulgur Salad

1   cup boiling water
¾   cup uncooked bulgur
1   (6-ounce) jar marinated artichoke hearts, undrained
1   cup diced plum tomato (about 2 tomatoes)
2   tablespoons chopped fresh parsley
⅛   teaspoon salt
⅛   teaspoon pepper
2   tablespoons crumbled feta cheese with garlic and
        herbs

Pour boiling water over bulgur in a medium bowl; cover and let stand 20 minutes.

Drain marinated artichoke hearts, reserving 2 table-spoons marinade.

Chop artichoke hearts. Combine reserved marinade, artichoke hearts, tomato, parsley, salt, and pepper.

Drain bulgur. Add to tomato mixture; toss gently. Sprinkle with cheese. Serve at room temperature or chilled. Yield: 4 (¾-cup) servings.

Per Serving: Calories 122 (10% from fat) Fat 1.3g (sat 0.6g) Protein 5.1g Carbohydrate 25.1g Fiber 5.6g Cholesterol 3mg Sodium 281mg **Exchanges:** 1 Starch, 1 Vegetable

Capture the flavor of fall with this sweet and savory pork dinner.

Sage Pork with Pear Chutney
Walnut Rice   steamed broccoli

serves 4

menu plan

1. *Chop pears, grate rind, and squeeze juice for pear mixture.*

2. *Start simmering pear mixture.*

3. *Cook rice.*

4. *Steam broccoli.*

5. *Rub pork with herb mixture, and cook.*

Sage Pork with Pear Chutney

2   firm ripe pears, chopped
¾   cup dried cherries
2   navel oranges
1   teaspoon grated peeled fresh ginger
¼   teaspoon ground cinnamon
2   teaspoons chopped fresh sage or
      ¾ teaspoon rubbed sage
¼   teaspoon salt
¼   teaspoon pepper
4   (4-ounce) boneless center-cut loin pork chops,
      trimmed (½ inch thick)
Cooking spray
Fresh sage leaves (optional)

Combine pear and cherries in a 1½-quart saucepan. Grate 1 teaspoon rind from one orange; add rind to pear mixture.

Squeeze juice from both oranges; combine orange juice, ginger, and cinnamon. Add to pear mixture. Bring mixture to a boil; reduce heat, and simmer, uncovered, 4 minutes or until pear is crisp-tender; stirring often. Remove from heat; let stand 10 minutes.

Combine chopped sage, salt, and pepper in a small bowl. Rub both sides of pork with sage mixture. Coat a large nonstick skillet with cooking spray; place over medium-high heat until hot. Add pork; cook 4 minutes on each side or until browned. Serve pork with pear mixture. Garnish with sage leaves, if desired. Yield: 4 servings (serving size: 1 pork chop and about ½ cup pear mixture).

Per Serving: Calories 349 (20% from fat) Fat 7.7g (sat 2.7g) Protein 28.0g Carbohydrate 40.6g Fiber 5.0g Cholesterol 73mg Sodium 203mg **Exchanges:** 3 Fruit, 3 Lean Meat

Walnut Rice

1   (6.2-ounce) package fast-cooking recipe long-grain
      and wild rice (such as Uncle Ben's)
2   cups fat-free, less-sodium chicken broth
3   tablespoons chopped walnuts
2   green onions chopped
1   tablespoon yogurt-based spread (such as Brummel
      and Brown)

Cook rice according to package directions, using chicken broth instead of water, omitting fat, and using only 2 tablespoons of seasoning mix.

Combine cooked rice, walnuts, green onions, and yogurt spread. Yield: 4 (1-cup) servings.

Per Serving: Calories 212 (24% from fat) Fat 5.7g (sat 1.0g) Protein 7.0g Carbohydrate 34.1g Fiber 1.4g Cholesterol 0mg Sodium 912mg **Exchanges:** 2 Starch, 1 Fat

A down-home dinner to remember

Spicy-Sweet Pork Medallions
Tangy Slaw Corn-on-the Cob
Cinnamon Apples

serves 4

menu plan

1. *Boil water for corn.*

2. *Prepare slaw; chill.*

3. *Cook corn.*

4. *Mix cinnamon mixture; microwave apples.*

5. *Slice pork, and cook.*

Spicy-Sweet Pork Medallions

1   (1-pound) pork tenderloin
¼   teaspoon salt
¼   teaspoon ground white pepper
¼   teaspoon ground red pepper
½   cup water
¼   cup honey

Cut pork diagonally across grain into 8 (½-inch-thick) slices. Sprinkle with salt and peppers.
Place a large nonstick skillet over medium-high heat until hot. Add pork, and cook 3 minutes on each side or until browned; set aside. Add water to pan, scraping pan to loosen browned bits; simmer 1 minute. Add honey, and cook over medium heat 4 minutes or until glaze is thickened. Return pork to pan and simmer 2 minutes, turning once.
Yield: 4 servings.

Per Serving: Calories 192 (13% from fat) Fat 2.8g (sat 1.0g) Protein 23.9g
Carbohydrate 17.6g Fiber 0.0g Cholesterol 74mg Sodium 203mg
Exchanges: 1 Starch, 3 Very Lean Meat

a few tips:
pork tenderloins

1 Look for pork tenderloin with moist, firm flesh and deep pink skin—not gray or red. Packaged tenderloins usually come two to a package, so check the total weight printed on the label.

2 Tenderloins are very lean, so when you're trimming the fat off, be careful not to cut into the meat. Pull the fat away from the meat with your fingers, and use a sharp knife to cut it away.

3 The thin, translucent membrane that covers the tenderloin tends to shrink when heated and can cause the meat to cook unevenly, so you need to remove the membrane. Use the sharp tip of a knife to get under the membrane, and pull it away from the meat with your fingers.

4 Since pork tenderloin has a mild flavor, it's best to season it before cooking.

5 Don't cook the pork until it's gray; it's done if the meat is pale pink and the juices run clear. (The recommended safe temperature for cooked pork is 160°.)

Tangy Slaw

¼ cup creamy mustard blend (such as Dijonnaise)
3 tablespoons sugar
2 tablespoons cider vinegar
1 tablespoon apple cider
2 tablespoons sweet pickle relish
1 (7-ounce) package shredded cabbage

Combine first 4 ingredients; stir well with a whisk. Combine pickle relish and cabbage in a bowl; pour dressing over slaw, and toss gently. Cover and chill. Yield: 4 (½-cup) servings.

Per Serving: Calories 76 (1% from fat) Fat 0.1g (sat 0.0g) Protein 0.6g Carbohydrate 18.6g Fiber 1.2g Cholesterol 0mg Sodium 281mg **Exchanges:** 1 Starch, 1 Vegetable

cabbage

varieties The cabbage we normally think of comes in round heads which are either pale to dark green (see photo) or dark purplish-red. The leaves of common cabbages are tightly packed; Savoy cabbage has looser leaves and is better to use when you need to peel away individual leaves.

selection Buy cabbage that's heavy and has shiny leaves with no sign of yellowing or any dark patches. As a time-saver, you can also purchase bags of prewashed, preshredded cabbage in the produce section of the grocery store.

Corn-on-the-Cob

If you don't have the yogurt-based spread, you can use light butter or reduced-calorie margarine.

4 (6-inch) ears frozen corn
4 teaspoons yogurt-based spread (such as Brummel and Brown)
½ teaspoon salt
½ teaspoon pepper

Cook corn according to package directions. Spread yogurt spread over warm corn, and sprinkle with salt and pepper. Yield: 4 servings.

Per Serving: Calories 73 (27% from fat) Fat 2.2g (sat 0.0g) Protein 1.9g Carbohydrate 14.0g Fiber 1.6g Cholesterol 0mg Sodium 326mg **Exchange:** 1 Starch

Cinnamon Apples

2 (16-ounce) cans sliced apples, drained
¼ cup packed brown sugar
1½ teaspoons ground cinnamon

Place apple in a 2-quart microwave-safe dish. Add brown sugar and cinnamon, and stir gently. Cover with heavy-duty plastic wrap and vent. Microwave at HIGH 10 minutes or until apple is tender; stir well before serving. Yield: 4 (1-cup) servings.

Per Serving: Calories 154 (0% from fat) Fat 0.0g (sat 0.0g) Protein 0.0g Carbohydrate 38.1g Fiber 4.2g Cholesterol 0mg Sodium 46mg **Exchanges:** 1 Starch, 1½ Fruit

Easy weeknight fare

Fried Rice with Ham and Peas
Sugar Snap Peas with Basil
orange sections

serves 2

menu plan

1. *Cook rice using 1 bag of boil-in-bag rice or use leftover rice.*

2. *Chill rice about 5 to 10 minutes.*

3. *Section oranges, slice onions, dice ham, chop basil, and trim peas.*

4. *Prepare fried rice.*

5. *Cook peas in microwave.*

Fried Rice with Ham and Peas

2 teaspoons dark sesame oil
½ cup frozen green peas
½ cup sliced green onions (about 2 onions)
1¼ cups long-grain cooked rice, chilled
½ cup diced, low-sodium cooked ham
1 large egg, lightly beaten
2 tablespoons low-sodium soy sauce
1 tablespoon water

Heat oil in a large nonstick skillet. Add peas and onions; sauté 3 minutes or until tender. Add rice and ham; cook until thoroughly heated. Push rice mixture to the sides of the pan, forming a well in the center.
Add egg to well and cook until set, stirring occasionally. Stir rice mixture into egg mixture. Stir in soy sauce and water. Yield: 2 (1-cup) servings.

Per Serving: Calories 310 (28% from fat) Fat 9.5g (sat 2.2g) Protein 15.9g
Carbohydrate 38.1g Fiber 2.9g Cholesterol 131mg Sodium 802mg
Exchanges: 2 Starch, 1 Vegetable, 1 Medium-Fat Meat, 1 Fat

Sugar Snap Peas with Basil

½ pound sugar snap peas, trimmed
2 tablespoons orange juice
2 teaspoons light butter, melted
1 tablespoon finely chopped fresh basil

Combine all ingredients in a 1½-quart casserole, stirring gently. Cover with heavy-duty plastic wrap, and vent. Microwave at HIGH 2 minutes or until peas are crisp-tender, stirring after 1 minute.
Yield: 2 (1-cup) servings.

Per Serving: Calories 72 (29% from fat) Fat 2.3g (sat 1.4g) Protein 3.4g
Carbohydrate 10.3g Fiber 3.0g Cholesterol 7mg Sodium 28mg
Exchanges: 2 Vegetable, ½ Fat

a few tips:
fried rice

1 For the best fried rice, start with leftover rice.

2 If you don't have leftover rice, prepare boil-in-bag rice or another quick-cooking rice, and let it chill while you prepare the other ingredients.

3 Use your imagination, and stir in any combination of chopped chicken, meat, and vegetables—whatever you've got in the fridge!

Ham and sweet potatoes are a great combo for a satisfying supper.

Skillet Ham
Lemon-Tarragon Beans   Whipped Sweet Potatoes

serves 4

menu plan

1. *Trim beans; peel and cube potatoes.*

2. *Cook sweet potatoes.*

3. *Microwave beans while sweet potatoes cook.*

4. *Cook ham, and keep warm.*

5. *Whip potatoes.*

6. *Toss beans with lemon juice and herbs.*

Skillet Ham

2   tablespoons maple syrup
2   teaspoons light butter
1   (¾-pound) slice lean ham, cut into 4 pieces

Combine syrup and butter in a large nonstick skillet; place over medium-high heat until butter melts. Add ham; cook 2 minutes on each side or until glazed and thoroughly heated. Yield: 4 servings.

Per Serving: Calories 135 (37% from fat) Fat 5.5g (sat 2.2g) Protein 15.2g Carbohydrate 7.0g Fiber 0.0g Cholesterol 48mg Sodium 883mg
Exchanges: ½ Starch, 2 Lean Meat

Lemon-Tarragon Beans

1   pound green beans, trimmed
¼   cup water
2   teaspoons fresh lemon juice
1   teaspoon chopped fresh tarragon
¼   teaspoon salt

Combine beans and water in a microwave-safe dish; cover, and microwave at HIGH 6 minutes or until tender. Drain. Toss with lemon juice, tarragon, and salt. Yield: 4 servings.

Per Serving: Calories 39 (7% from fat) Fat 0.3g (sat 0.1g) Protein 2.1g Carbohydrate 8.8g Fiber 3.1g Cholesterol 0mg Sodium 149mg
Exchange: 1 Vegetable

Whipped Sweet Potatoes

1   pound sweet potatoes, peeled and cut into 1-inch cubes (about 2 potatoes)
1   (5-ounce) can fat-free evaporated milk
¼   cup maple syrup
¼   teaspoon ground cinnamon or apple-pie spice
½   teaspoon vanilla extract
¼   teaspoon salt
1   tablespoon light butter

Steam sweet potato, covered, 10 minutes or until tender, and drain.
Return sweet potato to pan. Beat at medium speed of a mixer until smooth. Add milk and next 4 ingredients; beat well. Place pan over medium-low heat; add butter, stirring until butter melts. Yield: 4 (½-cup) servings.

Per Serving: Calories 193 (8% from fat) Fat 1.8g (sat 1.1g) Protein 4.3g Carbohydrate 40.6g Fiber 1.7g Cholesterol 8mg Sodium 226mg
Exchanges: 2½ Starch

a dessert idea: *Apple Cider Applesauce (page 186) is a great ending for this meal.*

An easy lunch for a crisp, fall day.

Roasted Chicken and Pear Salad
sourdough rolls
Cinnamon Ice Cream
serves 4

menu plan

1. *Set out ice cream to soften.*

2. *Slice pears, shred chicken, and toast walnuts for salad.*

3. *Arrange salads.*

4. *Stir cinnamon into ice cream.*

5. *Refreeze ice cream just before serving the salad.*

a few tips:
deli chicken

Using roasted chicken from the grocery store deli is a great way to save time when you need cooked chicken in a hurry. You can buy a whole chicken (they're usually about 1½ or 2 pounds) or chicken breasts.

Deli-roasted chickens are roasted with the skin, so you'll need to remove the skin and fat. And these chickens contain a good bit of sodium from the seasoning on the skin. When you remove the skin, you get rid of some of the seasoning, but some of the flavor and salt was absorbed into the meat as the chicken roasted. As with any poultry product, the breast meat is lower in fat than the dark meat.

Roasted Chicken and Pear Salad

5 cups gourmet salad greens
½ cup reduced-fat walnut raspberry vinaigrette, divided
2 ripe pears, cored and thinly sliced
1½ cups shredded roasted chicken breast
2 ounces Gorgonzola cheese, crumbled
3 tablespoons chopped walnuts, toasted

Combine salad greens and ¼ cup vinaigrette in a medium bowl; toss well. Arrange salad greens evenly on each of 4 plates.

Arrange pear and chicken evenly over greens. Sprinkle each evenly with cheese and walnuts. Drizzle 1 tablespoon dressing over each salad. Yield: 4 servings.

Per Serving: Calories 291 (44% from fat) Fat 14.2g (sat 3.3g) Protein 19.3g
Carbohydrate 23.2g Fiber 3.3g Cholesterol 50mg Sodium 356mg
Exchanges: 1 Fruit, 1 Vegetable, 3 Lean Meat, 1 Fat

Cinnamon Ice Cream

2 cups vanilla fat-free ice cream, softened
1 teaspoon ground cinnamon

Combine ice cream and cinnamon in a medium bowl; stir until well-blended. Cover and freeze until ready to serve. Yield: 4 (½-cup) servings.

Per Serving: Calories 101 (0% from fat) Fat 0.0g (sat 0.0g) Protein 3.0g
Carbohydrate 23.5g Fiber 0.3g Cholesterol 0mg Sodium 45mg
Exchanges: 1½ Starch

Bring a touch of Indonesian flavor to your table with these sweet and spicy kebabs.

Chicken Satay
coconut-ginger rice
Grilled Pineapple Rings
serves 4

Look for a package of coconut-ginger rice in the grain section of the supermarket, and prepare it according to microwave directions.

menu plan

1. *Soak wooden skewers in water.*

2. *Cook rice in microwave.*

3. *Thread chicken on skewers.*

4. *Slice pineapple, and sprinkle with sugar.*

5. *Grill chicken and pineapple, adding pineapple when you turn the chicken.*

Chicken Satay

If you don't have time to thread chicken on skewers, brush ⅓ cup of the peanut sauce mixture over 4 (4-ounce) skinless, boneless chicken breast halves, and grill.

  3   tablespoons peanut sauce mix
         (such as A Taste of Thai)
  3   tablespoons low-sodium soy sauce
  2   tablespoons hoisin sauce
  2   tablespoons rice wine vinegar
  1   tablespoon pineapple juice
  1   tablespoon dark sesame oil
  1   pound chicken breast tenders
Cooking spray

Prepare grill.
Combine first 6 ingredients in a large bowl. Reserve ⅓ cup sauce mixture for dipping. Add chicken tenders to remaining sauce mixture, tossing to coat.

Thread chicken onto 10-inch wooden skewers.
Place chicken on grill rack coated with cooking spray; grill, covered, 3 to 5 minutes on each side or until done. Serve with reserved sauce mixture. Yield: 4 servings.

Per Serving: Calories 211 (30% from fat) Fat 7.0g (sat 1.5g) Protein 27.2g Carbohydrate 8.1g Fiber 0.8g Cholesterol 70mg Sodium 816mg
Exchanges: ½ Starch, 3 Lean Meat

Grilled Pineapple Rings

Buy a peeled and cored pineapple in the produce section of the grocery store.

  1   small peeled and cored pineapple
  2   tablespoons brown sugar

Prepare grill.
Cut pineapple into 8 (½-inch-thick) slices. Sprinkle slices with brown sugar.
Place pineapple slices on grill rack; grill, covered, 7 minutes or until tender. Yield: 4 servings.

Per Serving: Calories 80 (6% from fat) Fat 0.5g (sat 0.0g) Protein 0.5g Carbohydrate 20.2g Fiber 1.5g Cholesterol 0mg Sodium 3mg
Exchanges: ½ Starch, 1 Fruit

If you like a little fire in your dinner, here's your menu.

Cajun Fire Chicken
Creole Rice   Cucumber-Green Onion Salad
crusty French bread

serves 4

menu plan

1. *Prepare cucumber salad, and chill.*

2. *Cook rice.*

3. *Chop pepper, tomato, and cilantro for chicken dish.*

4. *Cook chicken dish.*

Cajun Fire Chicken

Cooking spray
- 4 (4-ounce) skinless, boneless chicken breast halves
- 1 green bell pepper, coarsely chopped
- 1 (14½-ounce) can stewed tomatoes, undrained and chopped
- 2 teaspoons hot sauce
- ⅓ cup chopped fresh cilantro, divided
- ½ teaspoon dried thyme
- 2 teaspoons olive oil

Additional hot sauce (optional)
Fresh thyme sprigs (optional)

Coat a large nonstick skillet with cooking spray; place over medium-high heat until hot. Add chicken, pepper, tomatoes, 2 teaspoons hot sauce, ¼ cup cilantro, and dried thyme. Bring to a boil; cover, reduce heat, and simmer 10 minutes. Uncover and simmer 10 minutes.

Stir remaining cilantro and olive oil into tomato mixture. Serve with additional hot sauce, and garnish with thyme sprigs, if desired. Yield: 4 servings.

Per Serving: Calories 192 (18% from fat) Fat 3.8g (sat 0.7g) Protein 27.6g Carbohydrate 11.8g Fiber 2.1g Cholesterol 66mg Sodium 323mg **Exchanges:** 2 Vegetable, 3 Very Lean Meat

Creole Rice

- 2¼ cups water
- 1 cup uncooked converted rice
- ½ teaspoon Creole seasoning

Bring water to a boil in a medium saucepan; stir in rice and Creole seasoning. Cover; reduce heat, and simmer 20 minutes.

Remove from heat; let stand, covered, 5 minutes or until water is absorbed. Fluff with a fork. Serve with pan juices from Cajun Fire Chicken.
Yield: 4 (¾-cup) servings.

Per Serving: Calories 185 (2% from fat) Fat 0.4g (sat 0.1g) Protein 3.8g Carbohydrate 40.1g Fiber 0.6g Cholesterol 0mg Sodium 80mg **Exchanges:** 2½ Starch

Cucumber-Green Onion Salad

- 2 large cucumbers, sliced
- 1 green onion, sliced
- ¼ cup light ranch dressing
- ¼ teaspoon cracked black pepper

Combine all ingredients in a medium bowl, tossing well. Cover and chill. Yield: 4 (1-cup) servings.

Per Serving: Calories 55 (58% from fat) Fat 3.6g (sat 0.3g) Protein 1.0g Carbohydrate 5.0g Fiber 1.1g Cholesterol 4mg Sodium 154mg **Exchanges:** 1 Vegetable, ½ Fat

A festive meal for holiday entertaining

Chicken with Gingered Cranberries
Nutty Brown Rice   Lemon Green Beans

whole-wheat rolls

serves 4

menu plan

1. *Make cranberry sauce, and let it simmer.*

2. *Chop and toast pecans.*

3. *While sauce simmers, cook rice in the microwave according to package directions.*

4. *Cook green beans in a saucepan.*

5. *Cook chicken while the green beans are cooking.*

Chicken with Gingered Cranberries

1½ cups fresh cranberries
½ cup fresh tangerine juice (about 2 tangerines)
⅓ cup honey
1 teaspoon grated peeled fresh ginger
4 (4-ounce) skinless, boneless chicken breast halves
¼ teaspoon salt
¼ teaspoon pepper
1 teaspoon olive oil

Combine first 4 ingredients in a small saucepan. Cover and bring to a boil; reduce heat to low and simmer 12 minutes or until cranberry skins pop and sauce thickens, stirring occasionally. Set aside, and keep warm.
Sprinkle chicken with salt and pepper. Heat oil in a large nonstick skillet over medium heat until hot. Add chicken, and cook 8 minutes on each side or until done. To serve, spoon warm sauce over chicken. Yield: 4 servings.

Per Serving: Calories 252 (10% from fat) Fat 2.7g (sat 0.5g) Protein 26.6g Carbohydrate 31.1g Fiber 1.7g Cholesterol 66mg Sodium 221mg Exchanges: 2 Fruit, 4 Very Lean Meat

Nutty Brown Rice

1 package boil-in-bag rice (such as Success Rice)
3 cups fat-free, less-sodium chicken broth
¼ teaspoon salt
⅛ teaspoon pepper
¼ cup chopped pecans, toasted

Prepare rice according to package directions for microwave, substituting chicken broth for water; drain well. Stir in salt, pepper, and pecans.
Yield: 4 (½-cup) servings.

Per Serving: Calories 138 (36% from fat) Fat 5.5g (sat 0.5g) Protein 3.5g Carbohydrate 19.0g Fiber 1.2g Cholesterol 0mg Sodium 382mg Exchanges: 1 Starch, 1 Fat

Lemon Green Beans

1 (16-ounce) package frozen green beans
Butter-flavored spray (such as I Can't Believe It's Not Butter)
2 teaspoons lemon pepper

Prepare beans according to package directions. Drain, and coat with butter-flavored spray. Sprinkle with lemon pepper. Yield: 4 (¾-cup) servings.

Per Serving: Calories 40 (9% from fat) Fat 0.4g (sat 0.1g) Protein 2.1g Carbohydrate 8.8g Fiber 3.2g Cholesterol 0mg Sodium 239mg Exchanges: 2 Vegetable

a dessert idea: *For an elegant dessert, make the Cherry Poached Pears with Dark Chocolate Sauce on page 193.*

A great alternative to Thai food takeout

Thai Chicken and Plums
Wilted Sesame Spinach rice vermicelli
gingersnaps
serves 4

You'll find rice vermicelli in the Asian section of the store or in an Asian market. Regular vermicelli will also be fine.

menu plan

1. *Boil water for vermicelli.*

2. *Prepare plums, and quarter chicken.*

3. *Prepare chicken.*

4. *While chicken cooks, cook vermicelli.*

5. *Cook spinach just before serving the meal.*

Thai Chicken and Plums

Ask your butcher to debone the chicken thighs.

1   tablespoon salt-free Thai seasoning (such as
      The Spice Hunter)
¼   teaspoon pepper
⅛   teaspoon salt
6   (3-ounce) skinless, boneless chicken thighs, quartered
1   teaspoon vegetable oil
4   plums, pitted and quartered
¼   cup fat-free, less-sodium chicken broth
¼   cup low-sugar apricot or peach preserves
1   tablespoon red wine vinegar

Combine first 3 ingredients in a heavy-duty, zip-top plastic bag, and add chicken. Seal bag; shake chicken to coat.
Heat oil in a large nonstick skillet over medium-high heat. Add chicken; cook 6 minutes, turning to brown all sides. Remove chicken from pan, and set aside.
Add plums to pan, scraping pan to loosen browned bits; cook 1 minute on each side, or until skins are browned. Add chicken broth to pan. Stir in apricot preserves and red wine vinegar; stir well. Return chicken to pan. Bring to a boil; cover, reduce heat, and simmer 5 minutes or until chicken is done.
Yield: 4 servings.

Per Serving: Calories 237 (25% from fat) Fat 6.6g (sat 1.5g) Protein 25.8g
Carbohydrate 18.2g Fiber 1.2g Cholesterol 106mg Sodium 232mg
Exchanges: 1 Fruit, 3 Lean Meat

Wilted Sesame Spinach

1   teaspoon dark sesame oil
2   teaspoons sesame seeds
½   teaspoon bottled minced garlic
1   (10-ounce) package spinach leaves
¼   cup fat-free, less-sodium chicken broth
½   teaspoon salt-free Thai seasoning (such as
      The Spice Hunter)
¼   teaspoon salt
⅛   teaspoon pepper

Heat oil in a large nonstick skillet over medium-high heat. Add sesame seeds and garlic; sauté 2 minutes or until browned. Add spinach and remaining 4 ingredients to pan; cover and steam 3 minutes or just until spinach wilts, stirring occasionally.
Yield: 4 (⅓-cup) servings.

Per Serving: Calories 37 (54% from fat) Fat 2.2g (sat 0.3g) Protein 2.4g
Carbohydrate 3.1g Fiber 2.9g Cholesterol 0mg Sodium 239mg
Exchanges: 1 Vegetable, ½ Fat

Add a touch of warmth to this sandwich and salad meal with a steaming bowl of tomato soup.

Zucchini-Turkey Melts

tomato soup

Cucumber-Carrot Salad

serves 4

We served the meal with a reduced-sodium canned tomato soup.

menu plan

1. *Slice cucumbers; prepare salad, and chill.*

2. *Dice zucchini, slice onions, and slice turkey for sandwich.*

3. *Prepare sandwiches.*

4. *While sandwiches cook, heat soup.*

Zucchini-Turkey Melts

Use a griddle to cook sandwiches all at one time.

1   (10-ounce) Italian cheese-flavored thin pizza crust (such as Boboli)
½   teaspoon olive oil
1   cup diced zucchini (about 2 small)
½   cup sliced green onions (about 4 onions)
¼   pound thinly sliced smoked turkey, cut into thin strips
⅓   cup freshly grated Asiago or Parmesan cheese
⅓   cup light mayonnaise
2   tablespoons sun-dried tomato sprinkles
¼   teaspoon pepper
Butter-flavored cooking spray

Cut pizza crust in half crosswise forming 2 half-moons; set aside.

Heat oil in a large nonstick skillet over medium heat. Add zucchini and onions; sauté 4 minutes or until tender. Add turkey, and sauté 1 minute. Set aside.

Combine cheese and next 3 ingredients; spread cheese mixture over one half of crust. Sprinkle turkey mixture over cheese mixture. Top with remaining half of crust, pressing gently. Cut sandwich in half.

Coat surface of sandwiches with cooking spray. Place skillet over medium-high heat until hot. Add one sandwich half; cook 2 to 3 minutes or until golden. Turn with a large spatula, and cook 2 to 3 minutes. Repeat procedure with other half of sandwich. Cut each half of sandwich in half to form 4 pie-shaped wedges. Yield: 4 servings.

Per Serving: Calories 346 (36% from fat) Fat 14.0g (sat 5.1g) Protein 18.7g Carbohydrate 35.6g Fiber 1.6g Cholesterol 29mg Sodium 927mg Exchanges: 2 Starch, 1 Vegetable, 2 Medium-Fat Meat, 1 Fat

Cucumber-Carrot Salad

2   small cucumbers, peeled, if desired, and sliced (about 3 cups)
20   small fresh mint leaves
½   cup shredded carrot
⅓   cup oil-free sweet-and-sour dressing (such as Old Dutch)
¼   teaspoon pepper

Combine cucumber and mint leaves; toss gently. Combine carrot, dressing, and pepper. Pour over cucumber mixture; toss gently. Cover and chill. Serve with a slotted spoon.

Yield: 4 servings (serving size: about ¾ cup).

Per Serving: Calories 51 (4% from fat) Fat 0.2g (sat 0.0g) Protein 0.7g Carbohydrate 12.4g Fiber 1.1g Cholesterol 0mg Sodium 325mg Exchange: 1 Starch

Creamy Wild Rice-Turkey Chowder
Grilled Three-Cheese Sandwiches
fresh pears

serves 4

menu plan

1. Dice turkey; chop onions and carrot for chowder.

2. Assemble sandwiches, and preheat griddle.

3. Cook sandwiches on griddle.

4. Cook soup.

5. Slice pears.

Creamy Wild Rice-Turkey Chowder

Smoked turkey adds a nice flavor to the chowder, but you can use any kind of cooked turkey.

Cooking spray
4 ounces smoked turkey, diced
1 cup chopped green onions (about 4 onions)
½ cup chopped carrot
1 (10¾-ounce) can condensed reduced-fat, reduced-sodium cream of mushroom soup (such as Healthy Request)
1½ cups 1% low-fat milk
⅓ cup quick-cooking wild rice
¼ teaspoon pepper

Coat a medium saucepan with cooking spray, and place over medium-high heat until hot. Add turkey, green onions, and carrot to pan; sauté 3 minutes or until carrot is tender.

a dessert idea: *If you've got the time, indulge in a Caramel-Chocolate Brownie (page 201).*

Add soup and milk, stirring well; bring mixture to a boil. Stir in rice; bring to a boil. Cover, reduce heat to medium-low, and simmer 5 minutes or until rice is tender. Stir in pepper. Yield: 4 (1-cup) servings.

Per Serving: Calories 167 (25% from fat) Fat 4.6g (sat 1.7g) Protein 12.7g
Carbohydrate 17.5g Fiber 2.0g Cholesterol 26mg Sodium 550mg
Exchanges: 1 Vegetable, 1 Starch, 1 Lean Meat

Grilled Three-Cheese Sandwiches

½ cup (2 ounces) shredded reduced-fat Swiss cheese
½ cup (2 ounces) shredded reduced-fat sharp Cheddar cheese
½ cup crumbled blue cheese
¼ cup fat-free mayonnaise
1 tablespoon finely chopped green onions
8 (1½-ounce) slices whole-grain bread
2 tablespoons yogurt-based spread (such as Brummel and Brown)

Preheat griddle.
Combine first 5 ingredients; stir well. Spread cheese mixture evenly over 4 slices of bread. Top with remaining 4 bread slices.
Spread tops of sandwiches with half of yogurt-based spread. Place sandwiches, spread side down, on a medium-hot griddle (325°). Cook 5 minutes or until bottom slices of bread are lightly browned. Spread remaining yogurt-based spread on tops of sandwiches; turn sandwiches. Cook 5 minutes or until bottom slices of bread are lightly browned and cheese melts. Yield: 4 sandwiches.

Per Serving: Calories 301 (41% from fat) Fat 13.8g (sat 6.6g) Protein 16.6g
Carbohydrate 27.9g Fiber 2.2g Cholesterol 29mg Sodium 823mg
Exchanges: 2 Starch, 2 Medium-Fat Meat

This thick and creamy chowder is a great way to use your leftover holiday turkey. It's also good with chicken instead of turkey.

Tacos with a turkey twist—plus sweet potato fries

Turkey Soft Tacos
Shoestring Sweet Potatoes   Amaretti Apples

serves 4

menu plan

1. *Slice sweet potatoes, and bake.*

2. *Brown turkey for tacos.*

3. *Slice onions, cilantro, and lettuce for tacos.*

4. *Warm tortillas, and assemble tacos.*

5. *Prepare apple dessert.*

Turkey Soft Tacos

1   pound ground turkey
1   (1.25-ounce) package 40%-less-salt taco
       seasoning mix
¾   cup water
¾   cup sliced green onions (about 3 onions)
½   cup sweetened dried cranberries
       (such as Craisins)
1   tablespoon sugar
1   tablespoon apple cider vinegar
4   (8-inch) fat-free flour tortillas, warmed
4   teaspoons chopped fresh cilantro
¼   cup fat-free sour cream
½   cup thinly sliced lettuce
Cilantro sprigs (optional)
Fat-free sour cream (optional)

Cook turkey in a nonstick skillet over medium-high heat 7 to 8 minutes or until browned, stirring until it crumbles. Stir in taco seasoning and next 5 ingredients; cover, reduce heat to medium, and simmer 2 minutes. Uncover and simmer 5 minutes or until mixture thickens, stirring occasionally.
Spoon turkey mixture evenly down centers of tortillas. Top each with 1 teaspoon chopped cilantro, 1 tablespoon sour cream, and 2 tablespoons lettuce. Roll up,

and serve immediately. Garnish with sour cream and cilantro sprigs, if desired. Yield: 4 servings.

Per Serving: Calories 340 (15% from fat) Fat 5.5g (sat 1.4g) Protein 28.9g Carbohydrate 42.0g Fiber 2.3g Cholesterol 74mg Sodium 741mg
Exchanges: 2 Starch, 1 Fruit, 3 Lean Meat

Shoestring Sweet Potatoes

2   large sweet potatoes, cut into very thin strips
Cooking spray
2   teaspoons olive oil
¼   teaspoon salt
¼   teaspoon pepper

Preheat oven to 450°.
Place potato strips on a baking sheet coated with cooking spray. Coat potatoes lightly with cooking spray. Drizzle with oil; sprinkle with salt and pepper. Bake at 450° for 20 to 25 minutes or until browned. Yield: 4 servings.

Per Serving: Calories 155 (16% from fat) Fat 2.7g (sat 0.4g) Protein 2.1g Carbohydrate 31.1g Fiber 3.9g Cholesterol 0mg Sodium 163mg
Exchanges: 2 Starch

Amaretti Apples

2   large Red Delicious apples, cored and thinly sliced
3   tablespoons amaretto (almond-flavored liqueur)
4   amaretti cookies, crumbled

Arrange apple evenly in 4 dessert dishes. Drizzle evenly with amaretto, and top with crumbled cookies. Yield: 4 servings.

Per Serving: Calories 123 (7% from fat) Fat 1.0g (sat 0.3g) Protein 0.6g Carbohydrate 23.9g Fiber 3.1g Cholesterol 0mg Sodium 0mg
Exchanges: ½ Starch, 1 Fruit

Celebrate the fall apple harvest by making a sweet apple topping to spoon over tender turkey.

Turkey Cutlets with Lady Apples
Garlic Mashed Potatoes
Lemon-Herb Broccoli

serves 4

menu plan

1. *Microwave potatoes.*

2. *Brown turkey cutlets.*

3. *Steam broccoli.*

4. *Slice apples, and combine with juice and cornstarch in skillet.*

5. *Mash potatoes, and steam broccoli while apple mixture simmers.*

sage

Sage is a strong-flavored herb that is most often used with poultry, lamb, and pork, and it's one of the prominent flavors in sausage.

You can identify sage by its oval, green-gray leaves which are slightly bitter and have a musty mint taste.

Sage's name comes from the Latin word *salvus*, which means safe, because the herb is believed to have healing powers.

Turkey Cutlets with Lady Apples

You can substitute two small Fuji or Gala apples for the lady apples.

1	teaspoon rubbed sage
½	teaspoon onion powder
½	teaspoon salt
¼	teaspoon pepper
1	pound turkey cutlets
1	teaspoon vegetable oil
1	cup apple juice
1	tablespoon cornstarch
4	lady apples, cut into wedges (about 1½ pounds)

Combine first 4 ingredients in a small bowl. Rub sage mixture on both sides of turkey cutlets. Heat oil in a large nonstick skillet over medium-high heat. Add turkey, and cook 3 minutes on each side or until browned. Remove turkey from skillet; set aside, and keep warm.

Combine apple juice and cornstarch, stirring until cornstarch dissolves. Add apple juice mixture and apple wedges to pan, scraping pan to loosen browned bits. Bring to a boil; reduce heat, and simmer, covered, 10 minutes or until apple is tender, stirring occasionally. To serve, spoon sauce over cutlets. Yield: 4 servings.

Per Serving: Calories 260 (12% from fat) Fat 3.5g (sat 0.9g) Protein 27.0g
Carbohydrate 30.5g Fiber 3.9g Cholesterol 68mg Sodium 367mg
Exchanges: 2 Fruit, 4 Very Lean Meat

Garlic Mashed Potatoes

Yukon Golds have a rich, buttery flavor and are great for mashing. If you don't have Yukon Golds, use baking potatoes.

- 1 pound Yukon Gold potatoes
- ¼ cup light cream cheese with garlic and spices
- ½ cup fat-free milk
- ⅛ teaspoon salt
- ¼ teaspoon pepper

Scrub potatoes; prick several times with a small knife. Place on a shallow microwave-safe platter. Cover loosely with wax paper. Microwave at HIGH 6 minutes, rotating dish a quarter turn after 3 minutes.
Mash potatoes slightly with a potato masher. Add cream cheese and remaining ingredients; mash to desired consistency.
Yield: 4 servings (serving size: about ½ cup).

Per Serving: Calories 125 (17% from fat) Fat 2.4g (sat 1.6g) Protein 4.6g
Carbohydrate 21.9g Fiber 2.1g Cholesterol 11mg Sodium174mg
Exchanges: 1½ Starch

Lemon-Herb Broccoli

You can also steam the broccoli in the microwave at HIGH for 7 to 8 minutes or until tender.

- 2 (16-ounce) packages frozen broccoli spears
- 1 teaspoon dried marjoram
- 1 tablespoon fresh lemon juice

Arrange broccoli in a steamer basket. Crumble marjoram over broccoli. Steam broccoli, covered, 5 minutes or until crisp-tender. Sprinkle broccoli with lemon juice. Yield: 4 servings.

Per Serving: Calories 43 (8% from fat) Fat 0.4g (sat 0.1g) Protein 4.4g
Carbohydrate 8.1g Fiber 3.0g Cholesterol 0mg Sodium 24mg
Exchanges: 2 Vegetable

fall apples

There are thousands of varieties of apples, ranging from tender to crisp and sweet to tart. Apples are available year-round, but they're at their best from September to November.

Lady Apples are small apples that range in color from yellow to brilliant red. They have a sweet, tart flesh and are great for cooking.

Fujis are harvested late in October. They are medium-sized apples with stripes and a light red blush over greenish-yellow skin. Fujis are sweet and have a dense flesh, so they may require additional cooking time.

Galas are originally from New Zealand and are usually available from August through April. Galas are golden yellow with red stripes and have a mild, sweet flavor and crisp texture.

Granny Smiths are green, crisp, and tart. They are great for baking because they hold their shape well.

Red Delicious are big, sweet, and juicy and have bright red skins. They are more suitable for eating raw than for cooking.

Rome Beauties are bright red apples that sometimes have yellow stripes. They are juicy, tart, and good for baking.

The sausage dish is really a meal in itself.

Turkey Sausage Couscous
Skillet Swiss Chard   Peppermint-Apple Cider
whole-grain rolls

serves 4

menu plan

1. Cook couscous.

2. Chop pepper for couscous, and chop chard.

3. While couscous stands, cook sausage mixture.

4. Combine couscous and sausage mixture, and let stand.

5. Prepare chard and cider while couscous mixture stands.

a few tips:
count on couscous

1 When you need an alternative to rice or pasta, keep couscous in mind. This staple of North African cuisine has found its way to the tables of Americans who like quick and easy cooking.

2 Couscous is granular semolina (coarsely ground durum wheat). Look for boxes of precooked couscous on the pasta and grain shelves of the supermarket.

3 You can have steaming couscous on the table in 10 minutes. Just add the dry grains to boiling water, remove the pan from the heat, cover, and let stand 5 minutes.

4 In addition to plain couscous, you can get flavored varieties such as roasted garlic and tomato-lentil.

Turkey Sausage Couscous

Look for turkey breakfast sausage either in the regular sausage section or in the frozen meats section of the supermarket.

1   cup water, divided
½   cup uncooked couscous
5   ounces reduced-fat turkey breakfast sausage
1   teaspoon fennel seeds
1   (8-ounce) package presliced mushrooms
1   red bell pepper, chopped
1   cup frozen green peas, thawed
¼   teaspoon salt
¼   teaspoon black pepper
¼   cup crumbled blue cheese

Bring ¾ cup water to a boil in a small saucepan; add couscous. Cover and remove from heat; let couscous stand 5 minutes.

Cook sausage and fennel seeds in a Dutch oven over medium-high heat 3 minutes, stirring until sausage crumbles. Stir in mushrooms, chopped bell pepper, and ¼ cup water; cover and simmer 6 minutes or until bell pepper is tender.

Fluff couscous with a fork. Add couscous, peas, salt, and black pepper to sausage mixture; stir well.

Remove from heat. Sprinkle with cheese; cover and let stand 5 minutes. Yield: 4 (1¼-cup) servings.

Per Serving: Calories 219 (31% from fat) Fat 7.5g (sat 2.7g) Protein 13.2g
Carbohydrate 26.1g Fiber 3.8g Cholesterol 32mg Sodium 504mg
Exchanges: 1 Starch, 2 Vegetable, 1 High-Fat Meat

Skillet Swiss Chard

2   teaspoons olive oil
1   bunch Swiss chard, chopped (about 8 cups)
¼   teaspoon salt

Heat oil in a large skillet over medium-high heat; add Swiss chard and salt. Sauté 2 to 3 minutes or until chard wilts. Yield: 4 (½-cup) servings.

Per Serving: Calories 34 (63% from fat) Fat 2.4g (sat 0.3g) Protein 1.3g
Carbohydrate 2.7g Fiber 1.2g Cholesterol 0mg Sodium 299mg
Exchange: 1 Vegetable

Peppermint-Apple Cider

You can use either apple cider or apple juice in this sweet and tangy beverage.

4   cups apple cider
4   peppermint sticks

Bring apple cider to a boil in a large saucepan over medium-high heat. Place peppermint sticks in individual cups. Pour hot cider over peppermint sticks. Yield: 4 (1-cup) servings.

Per Serving: Calories 157 (1% from fat) Fat 0.2g (sat 0.1g) Protein 0.1g
Carbohydrate 39.7g Fiber 0.5g Cholesterol 0mg Sodium 14mg
Exchanges: 1 Starch, 1 Fruit

Swiss chard

The use of chard has been traced back to the hanging gardens of ancient Babylonia, but the name "chard" is derived from the Latin and French word for "thistle." No one is really sure why the light green variety of chard is called Swiss chard.

varieties Although Swiss chard is a member of the beet family, this earthy-flavored leafy green is similar to spinach and can be used in most recipes calling for spinach. Swiss chard has crinkly green leaves and either silvery, celerylike stalks or bright scarlet stalks.

selection Chard is sold in bunches, with each bunch being about half stems and half leaves. If you buy a bunch with large leaves, it will be easier to clean. Look for crisp leaves with no dark or moist patches, and avoid bunches with cracked or dried stems. Most recipes just call for the leaves, but you can cook the stalks as you would cook asparagus.

win

Wintry winds howl, icicles glitter on the trees, and crackling logs beckon from the fireplace. Come sit for a while, and sustain yourself with robust flavors that offer comfort from the cold: spicy bean soup and chunky chili; roasted winter squash; sturdy winter greens; zesty citrus fruits; and warm, soothing chocolate.

ter

Treat yourself to a lazy Saturday special breakfast.

Bananas Foster French Toast

orange juice   southern pecan coffee

serves 2

Buy an unsliced loaf of French bread so you can cut the bread to
the right thickness—about ¾ inch for this recipe.

menu plan

1. *Slice and soak bread.*

2. *Peel and slice bananas.*

3. *Cook French toast.*

a few tips:
buying bananas

1 If you want ripe bananas, look for those that are plump, evenly colored yellow fruit with tiny brown specks. Avoid those with blemishes, which indicate bruising.

2 If you buy green bananas, you will need to ripen them further at home. (Bananas are one of the fruits that develop better flavor when ripened off the tree.) To ripen, keep the bananas uncovered at room temperature (about 70°F) until they are evenly yellow.

3 For quick ripening, put bananas in a brown paper bag, and store at room temperature.

Bananas Foster French Toast

Omit the rum for a kid-pleasing breakfast.

1   large egg, lightly beaten
⅓   cup 1% low-fat milk
2   tablespoons brown sugar
2   teaspoons light rum
2   (¾-inch-thick) slices French bread
1   small banana, diagonally sliced
2   tablespoons reduced-calorie syrup

Combine first 4 ingredients in a shallow dish, stirring well with a whisk.

Soak bread slices in milk mixture 1 minute; turn over, and let soak 1 minute or until all egg mixture is absorbed.

Heat a large nonstick skillet over medium heat until hot. Add bread, and cook 4 minutes on each side or just until lightly browned and center is set.

Place toast on serving plates; top with banana slices, and drizzle each serving with 1 tablespoon syrup. Yield: 2 servings.

Per Serving: Calories 261 (13% from fat) Fat 3.9g (sat 1.3g) Protein 7.1g
Carbohydrate 48.2g Fiber 2.1g Cholesterol 108mg Sodium 241mg
Exchanges: 2 Starch, 1 Fruit, 1 Fat

Warm up at lunchtime with a quick bean soup and some spicy cumin chips.

Spicy Two-Bean Soup
Cumin Chips   Orange-Onion Salad
serves 4

menu plan

1. *Peel and slice oranges; slice onion for salad; rinse and drain beans, and shred cheese for bean soup.*

2. *Prepare soup.*

3. *While soup simmers, prepare chips.*

4. *Toss salad.*

Spicy Two-Bean Soup

1   teaspoon olive oil
1   cup frozen chopped onion
½   teaspoon garlic powder
1   (19-ounce) can cannellini beans, rinsed and drained
1   (16-ounce) can kidney beans, rinsed and drained
1   (14½-ounce) can fat-free, less-sodium chicken broth
2   (4.5-ounce) cans chopped green chiles
1   tablespoon ground cumin
¼   teaspoon salt
½   cup (2 ounces) shredded Monterey Jack cheese with jalapeño peppers

Add oil to a large saucepan; place over medium-high heat until hot. Add onion and garlic powder; sauté until tender.
Mash half of cannellini beans; add to onion mixture. Add remaining cannellini beans and kidney beans. Stir in broth and next 3 ingredients. Bring to a boil; cover, reduce heat, and simmer 8 minutes. Sprinkle each serving with 2 tablespoons cheese. Yield: 4 (1½-cup) servings.

Per Serving: Calories 235 (25% from fat) Fat 6.6g (sat 3.2g) Protein 14.0g Carbohydrate 30.6g Fiber 6.5g Cholesterol 15mg Sodium 974mg
Exchanges: 2 Starch, 1 Medium-Fat Meat

Cumin Chips

4   (6-inch) corn tortillas
Garlic-flavored cooking spray
½   teaspoon ground cumin
¼   teaspoon salt

Preheat oven to 350°.
Cut each tortilla into 8 wedges using kitchen shears. Place tortilla wedges on a large baking sheet. Lightly coat wedges with cooking spray. Sprinkle evenly with cumin and salt. Bake at 350° for 6 minutes or until lightly browned and crisp.
Yield: 4 servings (serving size: 8 chips).

Per Serving: Calories 59 (11% from fat) Fat 0.7g (sat 0.1g) Protein 1.5g Carbohydrate 12.2g Fiber 1.4g Cholesterol 0mg Sodium 188mg
Exchange: 1 Starch

Orange-Onion Salad

6   cups torn romaine lettuce
2   oranges, peeled and sliced
½   cup sliced red onion
⅓   cup fat-free red wine vinaigrette

Combine first 3 ingredients; toss well. Add vinaigrette, and toss. Yield: 4 (1½-cup) servings.

Per Serving: Calories 72 (2% from fat) Fat 0.2g (sat 0.0g) Protein 1.8g Carbohydrate 17.4g Fiber 2.9g Cholesterol 0mg Sodium 205mg
Exchanges: 1 Vegetable, 1 Fruit

A simple steamed fish supper

Oriental Steamed Snapper
Broccoli Salad

serves 2

menu plan

1. Cook rice.

2. Mince ginger and garlic, and slice green onions for fish.

3. Section oranges, chop broccoli and red onion, and make dressing for salad.

4. Microwave broccoli for salad.

5. Place cooling rack in skillet, and make a foil tray.

6. Prepare fish.

7. Prepare salad while fish steams.

Oriental Steamed Snapper

You don't need a steamer to prepare this flavorful fish—you can make your own steamer with a cake cooling rack and aluminum foil.

2   (5-ounce) red snapper or grouper fillets
2   tablespoons rice wine vinegar
2   tablespoons reduced-sodium soy sauce
1   teaspoon minced peeled fresh ginger
1   large garlic clove, minced
½   teaspoon sesame oil
2   green onions, cut into 2-inch julienne strips
1   cup hot cooked instant brown rice (such as
      Success Rice)
¼   teaspoon pepper

Pour water into a large skillet to a depth of 1 inch. Place a small cake cooling rack in pan; roll edges of a large piece of aluminum foil to create a tray that fits on top of rack and within edges of pan. Place fish on foil tray.

Combine vinegar and next 4 ingredients in a small bowl; stir well with a whisk. Drizzle mixture evenly over fish. Sprinkle fish with green onions.

Bring water in pan to a boil over medium-high heat; cover, and steam fish 10 minutes or until fish flakes easily when tested with a fork.

Sprinkle rice with pepper; toss well. Place ½ cup rice on each serving plate. Place fish over rice; spoon juices from foil tray over fish. Yield: 2 servings.

Per Serving: Calories 285 (12% from fat) Fat 3.9g (sat 0.7g) Protein 32.0g Carbohydrate 26.8g Fiber 2.8g Cholesterol 52mg Sodium 703mg **Exchanges:** 2 Starch, 4 Very Lean Meat

Broccoli Salad

2   oranges
1   teaspoon vegetable oil
1   teaspoon prepared horseradish
1   teaspoon honey
⅛   teaspoon salt
Dash of pepper
2½ cups chopped broccoli florets
¼   cup finely chopped red onion

Peel and section oranges over a bowl to catch juice; set orange sections aside. Squeeze orange membranes over bowl to extract remaining juice; reserve 1 tablespoon juice. Combine oil, horseradish, honey, salt, pepper, and reserved juice. Set aside.

Place broccoli in a microwave-safe dish; cover and microwave at HIGH 2 to 3 minutes or until crisp-tender. Drain; rinse with cold water, and drain. Combine broccoli, onion, orange sections, and juice mixture; toss well. Yield: 2 (1-cup) servings.

Per Serving: Calories 129 (19% from fat) Fat 2.8g (sat 0.4g) Protein 4.4g Carbohydrate 25.9g Fiber 6.5g Cholesterol 0mg Sodium 179mg **Exchanges:** 2 Vegetable, 1 Fruit, ½ Fat

Simple elegance with an Asian flair

Mirin-Glazed Sea Bass with Noodles
Spinach-Mandarin Orange Salad
Fresh Pears with Ginger

serves 4

menu plan

1. *Prepare soy sauce mixture, reserving 2 tablespoons for salad dressing.*

2. *Brush soy sauce mixture on fish.*

3. *Slice onions and pears.*

4. *Combine pears with honey mixture.*

5. *Cook pasta.*

6. *Broil fish while pasta cooks.*

7. *Prepare salad.*

Mirin-Glazed Sea Bass with Noodles

- ¼ cup low-sodium soy sauce
- ¼ cup mirin (sweet rice wine)
- 2 teaspoons sesame oil
- 4 (6-ounce) sea bass fillets (about ¾ inch thick)
- Cooking spray
- 6 ounces uncooked vermicelli
- 1 (14½-ounce) can fat-free, less-sodium chicken broth
- ¼ cup sliced green onions

Preheat broiler.

Combine first 3 ingredients. Set aside 2 tablespoons for salad dressing. Brush both sides of each fillet with remaining soy sauce mixture. Arrange fish fillets on a 15 x 10-inch jelly-roll pan coated with cooking spray. Let stand 10 minutes.

Cook pasta according to package directions, omitting salt and fat. Place chicken broth in a small saucepan; bring to a boil. Cover, reduce heat, and simmer 5 minutes. Drain pasta, and add to broth.

Broil fish 11 minutes or until fish flakes easily when tested with a fork.

To serve, ladle broth and pasta evenly into 4 shallow bowls; place a fish fillet on pasta in each bowl. Sprinkle evenly with sliced onions. Yield: 4 servings.

Per Serving: Calories 378 (14% from fat) Fat 5.8g (sat 1.2g) Protein 38.8g Carbohydrate 37.0g Fiber 1.4g Cholesterol 70mg Sodium 796mg Exchanges: 2½ Starch, 4 Very Lean Meat

Spinach-Mandarin Orange Salad

- 2 tablespoons orange juice
- 2 tablespoons rice wine vinegar
- ½ (10-ounce) package fresh spinach
- 1 (11-ounce) can mandarin orange sections, drained

Stir orange juice and rice wine vinegar into reserved 2 tablespoons soy sauce mixture. Toss with spinach, and top with orange sections. Yield: 4 servings.

Per Serving: Calories 51 (14% from fat) Fat 0.8g (sat 0.1g) Protein 1.6g Carbohydrate 8.9g Fiber 2.1g Cholesterol 0mg Sodium 162mg Exchanges: ½ Fruit, ½ Vegetable

Fresh Pears with Ginger

- 2 tablespoons honey
- 2 tablespoons lemon juice
- 2 tablespoons minced crystallized ginger
- 3 ripe pears, sliced

Combine first 3 ingredients in a medium bowl. Add pears, and toss well. Yield: 4 servings.

Per Serving: Calories 121 (4% from fat) Fat 0.5g (sat 0.0g) Protein 0.5g Carbohydrate 31.7g Fiber 3.0g Cholesterol 0mg Sodium 2mg Exchanges: 1 Starch, 1 Fruit

Brighten your spirits in the middle of winter with this hearty seafood dinner.

Curried Sea Scallops
Microwave Risotto   Roasted Green Beans
serves 4

menu plan

1. *Melt butter, and sauté onions for risotto; start cooking risotto in the microwave.*

2. *Wash and trim beans; slice garlic; roast beans.*

3. *Prepare and cook scallops.*

4. *Finish cooking risotto.*

Curried Sea Scallops

1   pound sea scallops (about 1 inch thick)
2   teaspoons dark sesame oil
¼   cup orange juice
½   teaspoon curry powder
½   teaspoon freshly ground pepper
¼   teaspoon salt
Orange zest (optional)

Rinse scallops, and pat dry with paper towels. Combine scallops and oil, tossing to coat. Place a large nonstick skillet over high heat until hot. Add half of scallops; cook 2 minutes on each side or until browned. Remove scallops from pan; wipe pan clean with paper towels. Repeat procedure with remaining scallops.

Combine orange juice and next 3 ingredients. Add orange juice mixture to pan. Cook over medium-high heat 1 minute or until thoroughly heated, stirring often. Serve sauce with scallops. Garnish with orange zest, if desired. Yield: 4 servings (serving size: about 4 scallops and 2 tablespoons sauce).

Per Serving: Calories 129 (22% from fat)   Fat 3.2g (sat 0.4g)   Protein 19.2g
Carbohydrate 4.6g   Fiber 0.2g   Cholesterol 37mg   Sodium 328mg
Exchanges: ½ Fruit, 3 Very Lean Meat

Microwave Risotto

You may never make risotto the traditional way (with constant stirring) again when you see what creamy results you can get from the microwave.

2   tablespoons light butter
½   cup frozen chopped onion
1   cup uncooked Arborio rice
3   cups fat-free, less-sodium chicken broth
¼   teaspoon salt
¼   teaspoon freshly ground pepper
¼   cup preshredded fresh Parmesan cheese

Heat butter in a 1½-quart microwave-safe dish, uncovered, at HIGH 30 seconds or until melted. Add onion and rice, stirring to coat. Cook, uncovered, at HIGH 4 minutes.

Stir in chicken broth, and cook, uncovered, at HIGH 9 minutes. Stir well, and cook, uncovered, at HIGH 9 minutes. Remove from microwave, and let stand 5 minutes or until all liquid is absorbed. Stir in salt, pepper, and cheese. Yield: 4 (¾-cup) servings.

Per Serving: Calories 279 (16% from fat)   Fat 4.9g (sat 3.2g)   Protein 9.0g
Carbohydrate 47.0g   Fiber 1.3g   Cholesterol 15mg   Sodium 763mg
Exchanges: 3 Starch, 1 Fat

Roasted Green Beans

1   pound fresh green beans
2   garlic cloves, sliced
Olive oil-flavored cooking spray
2   teaspoons lemon juice
2   teaspoons olive oil
¼   teaspoon salt
¼   teaspoon pepper

Preheat oven to 450°.

Wash beans, and trim ends. Place beans in a 13 x 9-inch roasting pan; add garlic. Coat beans and garlic with cooking spray; toss well. Drizzle lemon juice and olive oil over beans. Sprinkle with salt and pepper.

Bake, uncovered, at 450° for 8 minutes or until beans are crisp-tender, stirring once. Yield: 4 servings.

Per Serving: Calories 58 (37% from fat)   Fat 2.4g (sat 0.3g)   Protein 2.1g
Carbohydrate 8.9g   Fiber 3.0g   Cholesterol 0mg   Sodium 152mg
Exchanges: 1 Vegetable, ½ Fat

Who doesn't crave a Reuben for lunch every now and then?

Fresh Slaw Reubens
low-fat potato chips   low-fat oatmeal cookies
sweet pickles

serves 2

If sodium is not a problem for you, enjoy a sweet crunchy
pickle with your sandwich and chips.

menu plan

1. *Make slaw for sandwiches.*

2. *Assemble sandwiches.*

3. *Grill sandwiches.*

Fresh Slaw Reubens

2   cups country-style shredded slaw mix
2   tablespoons white wine vinegar
3   tablespoons fat-free Thousand Island dressing
4   (1.1-ounce) slices rye bread
2   ounces thinly sliced low-fat deli corned beef (such as
      Healthy Choice)
2   (1-ounce) slices reduced-fat Swiss cheese
2   teaspoons yogurt-based spread (such as Brummel
      and Brown)

Combine slaw and vinegar in a medium bowl; toss well. (Discard slaw dressing envelope if there is one in the package.)

Spread dressing evenly on one side of bread slices. Top two slices evenly with corned beef and cheese slices. Spoon slaw evenly over cheese. Top with remaining bread slices, dressing side down. Spread both sides of sandwiches evenly with yogurt-based spread.

Place sandwiches in a large skillet over medium-high heat. Cook 1 to 2 minutes on each side or until golden. Yield: 2 servings.

Per Serving: Calories 349 (28% from fat) Fat 10.8g (sat 5.3g) Protein 19.5g Carbohydrate 43.2g Fiber 6.0g Cholesterol 35mg Sodium 919mg
Exchanges: 3 Starch, 2 Medium-Fat Meat

Get out your lap trays, and enjoy a bowl of beefy chili in front of a roaring fire.

Citrus-Jícama Salad
Butternut-Beef Chili   multigrain rolls
low-fat hot chocolate
serves 4

If you can't find the frozen vegetable blend, use 1 cup each of frozen chopped onion and frozen chopped green bell pepper.

menu plan

1. *Microwave squash; peel and cube squash for chili.*

2. *Brown meat for chili.*

3. *While chili is simmering, peel and cut oranges, jícama, and cilantro for salad; toss salad.*

4. *Prepare low-fat hot chocolate from mix.*

Citrus-Jícama Salad

3   large oranges, peeled and sliced crosswise
⅔   cup diced peeled jícama (about ½ small jícama)
⅓   cup orange juice
2   tablespoons chopped fresh cilantro
1   tablespoon lime juice
¼   teaspoon sugar

Cut orange slices in half; place oranges and jícama in a bowl. Combine orange juice and remaining 3 ingredients; pour over orange mixture, and toss.
Yield: 4 (¾-cup) servings.

Per Serving: Calories 74 (3% from fat) Fat 0.2g (sat 0.0g) Protein 1.4g
Carbohydrate 18.0g Fiber 4.0g Cholesterol 0mg Sodium 1.3mg
Exchanges: 1 Vegetable, 1 Fruit

Butternut-Beef Chili

1   small butternut squash (about ¾ pound)
¾   pound ground round
1   (10-ounce) package frozen chopped onion, celery, and pepper blend
2   (14.5-ounce) cans Mexican-style stewed tomatoes
¾   cup water
¾   teaspoon ground cumin
¾   teaspoon chili powder
1   (16-ounce) can kidney beans, drained
1   teaspoon bottled minced garlic

Pierce squash with a fork, and place on a paper towel in microwave oven. Microwave at HIGH 2 minutes. Peel and cube squash. Set aside 1½ cups cubed squash.
Cook beef and vegetable blend in a Dutch oven over medium-high heat until meat is browned, stirring to crumble. Add squash, tomatoes, and remaining 5 ingredients; bring to a boil. Cover, reduce heat, and simmer 17 minutes or until squash is tender, stirring occasionally. Yield: 4 (2-cup) servings.

Per Serving: Calories 310 (24% from fat) Fat 8.1g (sat 3.1g) Protein 23.0g
Carbohydrate 36.9g Fiber 7.9g Cholesterol 31mg Sodium 981mg
Exchanges: 2 Starch, 1 Vegetable, 2 Lean Meat

winter squash

Winter squash, unlike the squash of summer, have thick skins and large seeds. These squash are picked in the fall and stored until spring, so they are available in peak form throughout the winter.

varieties Each type of winter squash has its own distinct flavor, texture, and color. Some of the varieties are acorn, buttercup, butternut, hubbard, spaghetti, and turban. Pumpkins are also in the winter squash family.

Acorn is a ribbed squash shaped like a giant acorn and is usually green or orange, or a combination of both.

Buttercup is one of the sweeter varieties of winter squash. It looks like a dark green turban squash with pale stripes up and down the sides.

Butternut is one of the most available varieties in most parts of the country. It's a pale orange squash that looks like an elongated bell, usually about 12 inches in length.

Hubbard is a large, irregularly shaped squash that ranges from 8 to 25 pounds. This squash has a greenish-gray skin and a rich orange flesh.

Spaghetti is a yellow, elongated melon-shaped squash. After you cook it, you can separate the flesh into strands that resemble spaghetti noodles.

Turban is an orange squash with a flat, circular bumpy base topped with a smaller, turban-shaped section with blue-green stripes. The flesh is bright orange.

storage Because of its thick skin, winter squash can be stored longer than summer squash. You don't have to refrigerate winter squash; keep it in a paper bag in a cool, dark place (about 50°F) for about a month, or store it in the refrigerator. Don't store winter squash in plastic bags for more than 3 days because the plastic traps moisture and causes the squash to rot.

acorn (left) and butternut squash

acorn squash

clockwise from bottom left: acorn, spaghetti, and butternut squash

Savor a simple, down-to-earth meal.

Tenderloin Steaks with Garlic Sauce
Mashed Sweet Potatoes   Steamed Broccoli
raspberry sorbet
serves 2

Look for dried juniper berries in the spice section of the grocery store. Crush them before adding them to the recipe to release their pungent, ginlike flavor.

menu plan

1. *Peel and cube sweet potatoes; cook in boiling water.*
2. *Sear steaks.*
3. *Trim broccoli, and grate orange rind.*
4. *Steam broccoli.*
5. *Mash sweet potatoes.*
6. *Prepare garlic sauce.*

Tenderloin Steaks with Garlic Sauce

¼ cup fat-free beef broth
2 tablespoons dry red wine
1 tablespoon balsamic vinegar
⅛ teaspoon salt
1 large garlic clove, minced
1 teaspoon crushed juniper berries (optional)
¼ teaspoon salt
¼ teaspoon coarsely ground pepper
2 (4-ounce) beef tenderloin steaks (¾ to 1 inch thick)

Combine first 5 ingredients and juniper berries, if desired. Set aside.

Press ¼ teaspoon salt and pepper evenly onto steaks. Heat a heavy skillet over high heat until hot. Place steaks in pan; cook 3 minutes on each side or to desired degree of doneness. Transfer steaks to a plate; keep warm.

Reduce heat to medium; add broth mixture. Cook 2 minutes or until sauce is slightly reduced, scraping pan to loosen browned bits. Serve sauce over steaks. Yield: 2 servings.

Per Serving: Calories 190 (40% from fat) Fat 8.4g (sat 3.1g) Protein 24.5g Carbohydrate 2.3g Fiber 0.1g Cholesterol 70mg Sodium 512mg Exchanges: 4 Lean Meat

Mashed Sweet Potatoes

½ pound sweet potatoes, peeled and cubed
¼ cup (1 ounce) goat cheese
⅛ teaspoon salt
⅛ teaspoon pepper

Cook potato in a large saucepan in boiling water to cover 10 to 15 minutes or until tender. Drain; return to pan. Add cheese, salt, and pepper; mash well with a potato masher. Yield: 2 (½-cup) servings.

Per Serving: Calories 163 (25% from fat) Fat 4.6g (sat 3.0g) Protein 4.8g Carbohydrate 26.2g Fiber 1.9g Cholesterol 11mg Sodium 232mg Exchanges: 1½ Starch, 1 Fat

Steamed Broccoli

½ pound broccoli, trimmed
1 teaspoon grated orange rind

Steam broccoli, covered, 5 to 8 minutes or until crisp-tender. Drain well. Sprinkle with orange rind. Yield: 2 servings.

Per Serving: Calories 33 (11% from fat) Fat 0.4g (sat 0.1g) Protein 3.4g Carbohydrate 6.2g Fiber 3.5g Cholesterol 0mg Sodium 31mg Exchange: 1 Vegetable

A quick and easy beef stew brings you a taste of the tropics.

Island Beef Stew
mixed greens with fat-free vinaigrette   sourdough bread

serves 4

menu plan

1. *Chop garlic; slice peppers; and peel and cube sweet potato for stew.*

2. *Sauté vegetables for stew.*

3. *Cook stew.*

4. *Prepare salad while stew cooks.*

sweet potatoes

varieties The two most common varieties of sweet potatoes are a pale sweet potato and a darker skin variety which many people mistakenly call a "yam." (A true yam is not related to a sweet potato.) The pale sweet potato has a thin, light yellow skin and a pale yellow flesh. After it's cooked, it has a dry, crumbly texture, much like that of a white baked potato, and its flavor is not sweet. The darker variety has a thicker skin and a bright orange flesh that is very sweet and moist when cooked.

storage Store sweet potatoes in a cool, dry, dark place. If the temperature is just right (about 55°F) you can keep them for about 3 to 4 weeks. Otherwise, you need to use them within a week. Do not refrigerate sweet potatoes.

Island Beef Stew

> 3 garlic cloves, chopped
> 1 (8-ounce) package presliced mushrooms
> 2 red bell peppers, cut into 1-inch pieces
> Cooking spray
> 1 (1-pound) package refrigerated fully cooked pot roast (such as Jimmy Dean), cut into 1-inch cubes
> 1 large sweet potato, peeled and cut into 1-inch cubes (about ¾ pound)
> 1 (14.25-ounce) can no-salt-added beef broth (such as Health Valley)
> 1 tablespoon balsamic vinegar
> 1 teaspoon salt-free Jamaican jerk seasoning (such as The Spice Hunter)
> Fresh cilantro leaves (optional)
> Sliced green onions (optional)
> Salsa (optional)

Sauté garlic, mushrooms, and bell pepper in a large Dutch oven coated with cooking spray over medium-high heat 5 minutes or until vegetables are tender.

Add pot roast and next 4 ingredients; bring to a boil over high heat, stirring frequently. Cover, reduce heat, and simmer 15 minutes or until sweet potato is tender. Top with cilantro, green onions, and salsa, if desired. Yield: 4 (1½-cup) servings.

Per Serving: Calories 376 (23% from fat) Fat 9.4g (sat 3.3g) Protein 42.7g Carbohydrate 31.2g Fiber 3.5g Cholesterol 112mg Sodium 728mg
Exchanges: 2 Starch, 5 Very Lean Meat

a dessert idea: *For an island treat, try the Tropical Fruit Sundaes on page 194.*

When you're in the mood for Italian, this simple veal dish is always a good choice.

Italian-Style Veal
Spinach Salad with Citrus Vinaigrette
breadsticks   lemon sorbet

serves 4

menu plan

1. *Boil water for pasta.*

2. *Cook pasta.*

3. *Flatten, cut, and brown veal.*

4. *Prepare salad; slice peppers.*

5. *Cook veal mixture.*

Italian-Style Veal

4   ounces uncooked vermicelli
¾   pound veal cutlets
½   teaspoon black pepper, divided
2   teaspoons olive oil
2   large red or green bell peppers, cut into strips
¼   cup dry sherry
2   (14½-ounce) cans diced tomatoes with garlic and
       onion, undrained
1   teaspoon dried oregano

Cook pasta according to package directions, omitting salt and fat.
Place veal between 2 sheets of heavy-duty plastic wrap, and flatten to ¼-inch thickness using a meat mallet or rolling pin. Cut each cutlet into 2-inch-wide strips; sprinkle with ¼ teaspoon black pepper.
Heat oil in a large nonstick skillet over medium-high heat. Add veal; sauté 2 minutes or until done. Remove veal, using a slotted spoon; set aside.

Add bell pepper strips to pan; sauté 5 minutes or until lightly browned. Stir in sherry; cook 1 minute. Add tomato, oregano, and remaining ¼ teaspoon black pepper. Bring to a boil; reduce heat, and simmer, uncovered, 5 minutes. Return veal to pan; cook 1 minute or until thoroughly heated.
Drain pasta. To serve, spoon veal mixture over pasta. Yield: 4 servings (serving size: 1 cup veal mixture and ½ cup pasta).

Per Serving: Calories 414 (35% from fat) Fat 16.0g (sat 4.9g) Protein 28.0g Carbohydrate 41.6g Fiber 5.0g Cholesterol 78mg Sodium 1051mg
Exchanges: 2 Starch, 2 Vegetable, 3 Medium-Fat Meat

Spinach Salad with Citrus Vinaigrette

¼   cup orange juice
2   tablespoons balsamic or red wine vinegar
2   tablespoons minced green onions
1   tablespoon olive oil
¼   teaspoon salt
4   cups torn fresh spinach

Combine first 5 ingredients; stir well with a whisk. Pour over spinach; toss well. Yield: 4 (1-cup) servings.

Per Serving: Calories 50 (63% from fat) Fat 3.5g (sat 0.5g) Protein 1.0g Carbohydrate 4.1g Fiber 1.0g Cholesterol 0mg Sodium 172mg
Exchanges: 1 Vegetable, ½ Fat

A stick-to-your-ribs German-style supper for a blustery winter night

Beet Salad Potato and Sausage Skillet

pumpernickel bread   gingersnaps   warm apple cider or light beer

serves 4

menu plan

1. *Slice and cook sausage.*

2. *Cook sausage-potato mixture.*

3. *Prepare salad while sausage mixture cooks.*

Beet Salad

  1   cup canned sliced beets, drained
  6   cups mesclun salad greens
  ½   small red onion, chopped
  ¼   cup (1 ounce) crumbled blue cheese
  ¼   cup fat-free balsamic vinaigrette
Freshly ground pepper (optional)

Cut sliced beets into thin strips; set aside.
Combine salad greens and onion; toss.
Place 1½ cups greens mixture on each of 4 salad plates. Top evenly with beets and blue cheese. Drizzle each serving with 1 tablespoon vinaigrette. Sprinkle with freshly ground pepper, if desired.
Yield: 4 (1½-cup) servings.

Per Serving: Calories 74 (32% from fat) Fat 2.6g (sat 1.6g) Protein 3.0g
Carbohydrate 9.8g Fiber 2.7g Cholesterol 6mg Sodium 449mg
Exchanges: 2 Vegetable, ½ Fat

Potato and Sausage Skillet

Look for the refrigerated potato wedges on the shelves near the refrigerated biscuits and pizza crust.

Cooking spray
  1   (14-ounce) package light smoked sausage, sliced
  1   onion, cut in half and sliced
  1   (20-ounce) package refrigerated new potato wedges
       (such as Simply Potatoes)
  1   cup low-sodium chicken broth
  ½   cup light beer

Coat a large skillet with cooking spray; add sausage, and cook over medium-high heat 4 minutes or until sausage is browned, stirring frequently. Remove sausage, and set aside.
Add onion and potato to pan. Cook 10 minutes or until browned, stirring frequently. Return sausage to skillet. Add broth and beer. Increase heat to high, and cook 5 minutes or until liquid almost evaporates.
Yield: 4 (1¼-cup) servings.

Per Serving: Calories 236 (10% from fat) Fat 2.7g (sat 0.9g) Protein 17.1g
Carbohydrate 31.4g Fiber 3.8g Cholesterol 35mg Sodium 1028mg
Exchanges: 2 Starch, 2 Very Lean Meat

The savory pork rolls are similar to the ones featured at Chinese bistro chain restaurants.

Thai Pork Rolls   Chili Rice
fresh persimmons or oranges   lemon wafers
serves 6

menu plan

1. *Boil water for cabbage leaves.*

2. *Begin cooking pork mixture.*

3. *Cook rice in microwave.*

4. *Cook cabbage leaves.*

5. *Assemble pork rolls.*

persimmons

"If it be not ripe, it will draw a mans mouth awrie with much torment; but when it's ripe, it is a delicious as an Apricock." *Captain John Smith, 17th century*

Before you eat a persimmon, it must be ripened to the point of mushy softness, or the taste will be unpleasantly astringent.

Ripe American persimmons have yellowish-pink to orange-red smooth skins and are about the size of a large plum or a peach. The ripe flesh is jellylike and quite sweet.

You can ripen persimmons at room temperature, or store ripe fruit in the refrigerator for up to 3 days.

Thai Pork Rolls

You can use 12 smaller cabbage leaves instead of 6 large napa cabbage leaves. Place 2 leaves side by side, fill, and roll.

 8 cups water
 1 pound lean ground pork
 2 large garlic cloves, minced
 1 cup fresh bean sprouts
 ¼ cup chopped fresh cilantro
 3 tablespoons oyster sauce
 2 teaspoons salt-free Thai seasoning (such as The Spice Hunter)
 6 large napa (Chinese) cabbage leaves
Cilantro sprigs (optional)

Bring 8 cups water to a boil in a large Dutch oven.
Cook pork and garlic in a large nonstick skillet over medium heat until pork is browned, stirring to crumble. Drain and return pork to pan. Add bean sprouts and next 3 ingredients to pork mixture; cook until thoroughly heated.
Add cabbage leaves to boiling water, and cook 30 seconds. Drain.
Spoon about ½ cup pork mixture onto one end of each cabbage leaf; roll up, leaving ends open. Garnish with cilantro, if desired, and serve immediately. Yield: 6 servings.

Per Serving: Calories 163 (49% from fat) Fat 8.8g (sat 3.0g) Protein 17.0g
Carbohydrate 3.8g Fiber 0.7g Cholesterol 54mg Sodium 206mg
Exchanges: 1 Vegetable, 2 Medium-Fat Meat

Chili Rice

Look for hot chili oil in the Asian section of the grocery store or in an Asian market.

1 extra-large bag boil-in-bag instant rice (such as Success Rice)
2¼ teaspoons chili oil
¼ teaspoon salt

Cook rice according to microwave package directions.
Combine rice, chili oil, and salt.
Yield: 6 (½-cup) servings.

Per Serving: Calories 123 (13% from fat) Fat 1.8g (sat 0.3g) Protein 2.0g
Carbohydrate 24.0g Fiber 0.5g Cholesterol 0mg Sodium 98mg
Exchanges: 1½ Starch

Asian-style pork and sesame-flavored noodles pair perfectly for dinner.

Asian-Style Pork Medallions
Sesame Noodles with Vegetables
fresh orange wedges   fortune cookies

serves 4

menu plan

1. *Boil water for noodles.*

2. *Mince garlic, slice pepper, and rinse bean sprouts for noodle dish. Chop cilantro.*

3. *Prepare vinaigrette.*

4. *Cook pasta.*

5. *Cook pork while pasta is cooking.*

Asian-Style Pork Medallions

 2   teaspoons sesame oil
¼   teaspoon crushed red pepper
 1   large garlic clove, minced
 1   (1-pound) pork tenderloin, cut into ½-inch-thick slices
¼   cup dry sherry
 3   tablespoons low-sodium soy sauce
 1   tablespoon brown sugar

Heat oil in a nonstick skillet over medium-high heat. Add pepper and garlic; sauté 1 minute. Add pork, and cook 3 to 4 minutes on each side or until browned. **Remove** pork from pan, and keep warm.
Add sherry, soy sauce, and sugar to pan; cook over medium heat 2 to 3 minutes or until slightly thickened, stirring constantly. Add pork to pan, and cook 1 to 2 minutes or until thoroughly heated, stirring to coat pork with sauce. Yield: 4 servings.

Per Serving: Calories 165 (28% from fat) Fat 5.1g (sat 1.3g) Protein 23.9g Carbohydrate 3.2g Fiber 0.1g Cholesterol 74mg Sodium 351mg
Exchanges: 3 Lean Meat

Sesame Noodles with Vegetables

 2   tablespoons rice wine vinegar
 2   tablespoons low-sodium soy sauce
 1   teaspoon grated peeled fresh ginger
 2   teaspoons bottled minced garlic
½   teaspoon sesame oil
 4   ounces uncooked cappellini
 2   cups angel hair slaw
 1   red bell pepper, cut into julienne strips
½   cup fresh bean sprouts, rinsed and drained
 2   tablespoons chopped fresh cilantro

Combine first 5 ingredients in a small bowl; stir well with a whisk. Set aside.
Cook pasta in boiling water according to package directions, omitting salt and fat. Add slaw and pepper during last 30 seconds of cooking time. Place bean sprouts in a colander; pour pasta mixture over sprouts, and drain well. Transfer pasta mixture to a bowl, and toss with vinegar mixture. Sprinkle with cilantro. Yield: 4 (1-cup) servings.

Per Serving: Calories 131 (8% from fat) Fat 1.2g (sat 0.2g) Protein 4.4g Carbohydrate 24.9g Fiber 1.9g Cholesterol 0mg Sodium 205mg
Exchanges: 1 Starch, 2 Vegetable

A pork dinner with a perfect balance of savory and sweet

Pork Chops with Caramelized Onions
Couscous with Golden Raisins   Sparkling Ambrosia
serves 4

menu plan

1. *Prepare fruit mixture for ambrosia, and chill.*

2. *Boil water for couscous; toast almonds.*

3. *Brown pork chops.*

4. *Chop onion while chops are browning.*

5. *Prepare couscous.*

6. *Cook onion.*

7. *Pour gingerale over fruit just before serving.*

Pork Chops with Caramelized Onions

- 4 (4-ounce) lean boneless pork loin chops
- 3 tablespoons all-purpose flour
- 1 teaspoon olive oil
- 1 large onion, chopped
- ¼ cup balsamic vinegar
- 2 tablespoons brown sugar

Combine pork chops and flour in a heavy-duty, zip-top plastic bag. Seal bag, and shake to coat chops.
Place a large nonstick skillet over medium-high heat until hot; add oil. Add chops, and cook 6 minutes on each side or until done. Remove chops from pan, and keep warm.
Add onion to pan. Cook over medium-high heat 5 minutes or until tender. Add vinegar; cook 1 minute, stirring constantly. Sprinkle with brown sugar; cook 1 minute, stirring constantly. To serve, spoon onion mixture evenly over chops. Yield: 4 servings.

Per Serving: Calories 234 (27% from fat) Fat 7.1g (sat 2.3g) Protein 22.9g Carbohydrate 18.6g Fiber 1.2g Cholesterol 59mg Sodium 51mg **Exchanges:** 1 Starch, 3 Lean Meat

Couscous with Golden Raisins

Toast almonds in a nonstick skillet over medium-high heat for 1 minute.

- ¾ cup water
- ½ teaspoon instant chicken bouillon granules
- ½ cup uncooked couscous
- ½ cup golden raisins
- 2 tablespoons slivered almonds, toasted

Combine water and bouillon granules in a small saucepan. Bring to a boil. Add couscous; cover and remove from heat. Let stand 5 minutes. Fluff couscous with a fork. Stir in raisins and almonds.
Yield: 4 (½-cup) servings.

Per Serving: Calories 163 (13% from fat) Fat 2.4g (sat 0.2g) Protein 4.3g Carbohydrate 32.1g Fiber 2.2g Cholesterol 0mg Sodium 76mg **Exchanges:** 1 Starch, 1 Fruit, ½ Fat

Sparkling Ambrosia

Gingerale adds the bubbly to this ambrosia.

- 2 (11-ounce) cans mandarin oranges in light syrup, drained
- 1 (8-ounce) can crushed pineapple in juice, undrained
- 2 tablespoons honey
- 2 tablespoons coconut
- ½ cup gingerale

Combine first 4 ingredients in a small bowl, tossing well. Cover and chill. Add gingerale just before serving. Yield: 4 (½-cup) servings.

Per Serving: Calories 114 (6% from fat) Fat 0.8g (sat 0.7g) Protein 0.3g Carbohydrate 27.84g Fiber 0.9g Cholesterol 0mg Sodium 16mg **Exchanges:** 2 Fruit

If you're tired of the turkey hassle, this is a great menu for the holidays.

Coriander-Crusted Pork with Garlic Potatoes
Lemon Broccoli   whole-grain rolls

serves 4

menu plan

1. *Cut potatoes, and trim broccoli.*

2. *Prepare pork.*

3. *Steam broccoli while pork and potatoes are cooking.*

4. *Heat rolls in oven according to package directions.*

Coriander-Crusted Pork with Garlic Potatoes

   2   **tablespoons coriander seeds**
   2   **teaspoons freshly ground pepper**
   2   **tablespoons hot mustard**
   1   **(1-pound) pork tenderloin**
Cooking spray
   8   **small red potatoes**
   2   **teaspoons olive oil**
   2   **teaspoons bottled minced garlic**
   ¼   **teaspoon kosher salt**

Preheat oven to 475°.
Place coriander seeds in a spice or coffee grinder. Process until coarsely ground. Combine coriander and pepper.

Spread mustard on tenderloin; press coriander mixture into tenderloin. Place on a 15 x 10-inch jelly-roll pan coated with cooking spray. Bake at 475° for 5 minutes.
Cut potatoes into 1-inch pieces; toss with olive oil and garlic. Sprinkle evenly with salt. Add potato to pan; bake pork and potato at 475° for 18 additional minutes or until a meat thermometer inserted in thickest part of tenderloin registers 160°. Yield: 4 servings.

Per Serving: Calories 259 (22% from fat) Fat 6.2g (sat 1.4g) Protein 27.4g Carbohydrate 23.8g Fiber 3.4g Cholesterol 74mg Sodium 310mg **Exchanges:** 1½ Starch, 3 Lean Meat

Lemon Broccoli

   1   **pound fresh broccoli (15.3 ounces trimmed)**
   2   **teaspoons lemon juice**
   1   **teaspoon salt-free lemon-herb seasoning**
Lemon slices (optional)

Remove broccoli leaves, and cut off tough ends of stalks; discard. Arrange broccoli in a vegetable steamer over boiling water. Cover and steam 5 minutes or until crisp-tender. Sprinkle with lemon juice and seasoning. Garnish with lemon slices, if desired.
Yield: 4 servings.

Per Serving: Calories 33 (11% from fat) Fat 0.4g (sat 0.0g) Protein 3.3g Carbohydrate 6.3g Fiber 3.6g Cholesterol 0mg Sodium 29mg **Exchange:** 1 Vegetable

a dessert idea: *For a sweet holiday treat, prepare the Frozen Chocolate Mint Torte (page 202), and serve chocolate-flavored coffee.*

A hearty meal for two

Pork Medallions with Cherry Sauce
Sautéed Spinach   Herb-Roasted New Potatoes
serves 2

menu plan

1. *Cut potatoes, and place in oven to roast.*

2. *While potatoes cook, slice pork, and prepare cherry sauce.*

3. *Cook pork.*

4. *Sauté spinach.*

Pork Medallions with Cherry Sauce

    2   tablespoons all-purpose flour
    ¼   teaspoon salt
    ¼   teaspoon pepper
    8   ounces pork tenderloin, cut crosswise into
            ¼-inch-thick slices
    ¾   cup apple juice
    ½   cup fat-free, less-sodium chicken broth
    ½   cup dried cherries
    1   tablespoon Dijon mustard
    1   tablespoon apple jelly
Olive oil-flavored cooking spray
    2   tablespoons minced green onions

Combine first 3 ingredients in a heavy-duty, zip-top plastic bag. Add pork slices. Seal bag; shake well. Remove pork from bag; shake off excess flour.

Combine apple juice and next 4 ingredients in a 2-cup glass measure; set aside.

Coat a large nonstick skillet with cooking spray; place over medium-high heat until hot. Add pork; cook 1 minute on each side or until browned. Remove pork from pan.

Add apple juice mixture to pan; bring to a boil, scraping pan to loosen browned bits. Cook 5 minutes or until sauce is slightly thickened. Return pork to pan; reduce heat and cook 1 minute. Sprinkle with green onions. Yield: 2 servings.

Per Serving: Calories 374 (9% from fat) Fat 3.8g (sat 1.0g) Protein 25.9g Carbohydrate 55.9g Fiber 2.6g Cholesterol 74mg Sodium 731mg **Exchanges:** 2 Starch, 2 Fruit, 3 Very Lean Meat

Sautéed Spinach

    2   teaspoons olive oil, divided
    1   (10-ounce) package fresh spinach
    ¼   teaspoon salt
    ¼   teaspoon freshly ground pepper
    2   teaspoons fresh lemon juice

Heat 1 teaspoon olive oil in a large skillet over medium-high heat; add spinach. Sprinkle with salt and pepper. Cover and cook 3 to 4 minutes or until spinach is wilted, stirring once. Cook, uncovered, 1 minute or until liquid evaporates. Remove from heat; stir in lemon juice and remaining 1 teaspoon olive oil. Yield: 2 (¾-cup) servings.

Per Serving: Calories 73 (62% from fat) Fat 5.0g (sat 0.7g) Protein 4.1g Carbohydrate 5.6g Fiber 5.8g Cholesterol 0mg Sodium 405mg **Exchanges:** 1 Vegetable, 1 Fat

a dessert idea: *If you're entertaining, the Mocha Pudding (page 209) will be a hit with your guests.*

Herb-Roasted New Potatoes

1 **pound small red potatoes**
Olive oil-flavored cooking spray
1 **teaspoon dried thyme**
½ **teaspoon garlic salt**
¼ **teaspoon freshly ground pepper**

Preheat oven to 425°.

Cut potatoes into 1-inch pieces; spread on a 15 x 10-inch jelly-roll pan. Coat with cooking spray; sprinkle with thyme, garlic salt, and pepper. Toss well; spread in a single layer. Bake at 425° for 20 to 25 minutes or until golden. Yield: 2 (1-cup) servings.

Per Serving: Calories 174 (3% from fat) Fat 0.6g (sat 0.1g) Protein 5.1g Carbohydrate 38.3g Fiber 4.3g Cholesterol 0mg Sodium 539mg
Exchanges: 2 Starch

Start with a deli-roasted chicken for a simple supper.

Mustard-Roasted Chicken
Cheesy Garlic Mashed Potatoes
mixed greens with fat-free vinaigrette   crusty rolls

serves 4

menu plan

1. *Prepare chicken and vegetables; put in oven to bake.*

2. *Prepare potatoes in microwave.*

3. *Place rolls in oven during last 5 minutes of baking time for chicken.*

4. *Add remaining ingredients to potatoes, and let stand.*

5. *Toss greens with vinaigrette.*

Mustard-Roasted Chicken

¼ cup stone-ground mustard
1 tablespoon dried rosemary
2 teaspoons maple-flavored syrup
1 teaspoon cracked black pepper
1 (2½-pound) deli-roasted whole chicken, skinned
1 (8-ounce) package presliced mushrooms
1 onion, cut into 1-inch pieces
2 garlic cloves, quartered
Cooking spray

Preheat oven to 500°.
Combine first 4 ingredients. Spoon half of mustard mixture over chicken. Combine mushrooms, onion, and garlic in a bowl; add remaining half of mustard mixture, tossing well.

Place chicken in a 9-inch pan coated with cooking spray; place vegetables around chicken. Bake at 500° for 20 minutes or until thoroughly heated.
Yield: 4 servings.

Per Serving: Calories 274 (32% from fat) Fat 9.8g (sat 2.4g) Protein 35.6g Carbohydrate 10.3g Fiber 1.9g Cholesterol 101mg Sodium 830mg
Exchanges: ½ Starch, 4 Lean Meat

Cheesy Garlic Mashed Potatoes

½ (22-ounce) package frozen mashed potatoes
        (2⅔ cups frozen potatoes)
1¼ cups 1% low-fat milk
1 (2.3-ounce) package low-fat garlic and herb cheese
        spread (such as Fleur de Lis)
1 tablespoon chopped fresh or frozen chives
¼ teaspoon salt
¼ teaspoon pepper

Combine mashed potatoes and 1¼ cups milk in a large microwave-safe bowl. Microwave at HIGH 6 minutes, stirring after 3 minutes.
Stir in cheese spread and remaining ingredients; let stand 2 minutes. Stir well, and serve immediately.
Yield: 4 (½-cup) servings.

Per Serving: Calories 153 (33% from fat) Fat 5.6g (sat 3.0g) Protein 4.5g Carbohydrate 20.8g Fiber 1.1g Cholesterol 11mg Sodium 365mg
Exchanges: 1½ Starch, 1 Fat

A wonderful way to use sweet, tender winter pears

Chicken and Fruit Sauté with Couscous
Winter Green Salad

serves 4

menu plan

1. *Boil water for couscous.*

2. *Slice onion and pears; wash and tear greens.*

3. *Prepare couscous.*

4. *Sauté chicken and onion.*

5. *Cook chicken and fruit in cider mixture.*

6. *Prepare salad.*

Chicken and Fruit Sauté with Couscous

½ teaspoon salt
½ teaspoon dried thyme
⅛ teaspoon ground red pepper
1 pound chicken breast tenders
1 teaspoon vegetable oil
1 red onion, sliced
1 cup apple cider
1 teaspoon cornstarch
2 large ripe Bosc pears, thinly sliced
1 teaspoon cider vinegar
2 cups cooked whole-wheat couscous

Combine first 3 ingredients in a medium bowl; add chicken and toss to coat. Heat oil in a large nonstick skillet over medium-high heat. Add chicken and onion; sauté until chicken is golden.
Combine apple cider and cornstarch; stir until smooth.
Toss pear slices with vinegar.
Add cider mixture to pan; cook over medium heat 2 minutes or until thickened, stirring occasionally. Stir in pear; simmer 2 minutes, stirring occasionally. Serve over ½-cup portions couscous. Yield: 4 servings.

Per Serving: Calories 368 (9% from fat) Fat 3.5g (sat 0.7g) Protein 31.8g
Carbohydrate 53.5g Fiber 5.9g Cholesterol 66mg Sodium 376mg
Exchanges: 2 Starch, 1 Fruit, 4 Very Lean Meat

Winter Green Salad

Use fresh, refrigerated grapefruit sections from the jar, and buy a bag of prewashed torn romaine lettuce.

2 cups torn romaine lettuce
2 cups torn escarole
½ cup grapefruit sections
½ cup thinly sliced red onion
2 tablespoons coarsely chopped pecans or walnuts
¼ cup fat-free raspberry vinaigrette

Combine salad greens, grapefruit sections, onion, and nuts in a bowl; toss well. Drizzle with dressing, and toss. Yield: 4 (1¼-cup) servings.

Per Serving: Calories 65 (39% from fat) Fat 2.8g (sat 0.3g) Protein 1.4g
Carbohydrate 9.5g Fiber 2.3g Cholesterol 0mg Sodium 26mg
Exchanges: 2 Vegetable

escarole

Escarole, a variety of endive, is a wintertime green with broad, bright green leaves which grow in loose heads. Escarole is not as bitter as Belgian endive or chicory, other greens in the same family. Escarole is most often used in salads along with other types of greens.

A comfort menu with favorite familiar flavors

Sweet-and-Spicy Chicken and Vegetables
Blue Cheese-Pear Salad
Easy Fruited Rice Pudding

serves 4

menu plan

1. *Peel and slice pears, and prepare salad dressing.*

2. *Slice onion and celery for chicken dish.*

3. *Brown chicken.*

4. *Cook chicken and vegetable mixture.*

5. *Cook rice pudding mixture.**

6. *Assemble salads.*

*If you want to serve the rice pudding chilled, make it first, and let it chill while you prepare the rest of the meal.

Sweet-and-Spicy Chicken and Vegetables

   4   (4-ounce) skinless, boneless chicken breast halves
   ½   teaspoon pepper
   ¼   teaspoon salt
Cooking spray
   1   large onion, cut into thin vertical slices
   5   celery stalks, cut into 2-inch pieces
   ⅓   cup frozen Granny Smith apple juice concentrate, thawed
   3   tablespoons spicy brown mustard
   1   tablespoon balsamic vinegar

Place chicken between 2 sheets of heavy-duty plastic wrap, and flatten to ¼-inch thickness using a meat mallet or rolling pin. Sprinkle with pepper and salt.

Coat both sides of chicken with cooking spray. Place a nonstick skillet over medium heat until hot. Add chicken to pan, and sauté 1 to 2 minutes on each side or until lightly browned. Add onion and celery.

Combine apple juice concentrate, mustard, and balsamic vinegar. Add apple juice mixture to pan; bring to a boil. Cover, reduce heat, and simmer 8 minutes or until vegetables are tender. Yield: 4 servings.

Per Serving: Calories 271 (9% from fat) Fat 2.8g (sat 0.5g) Protein 29.3g Carbohydrate 31.3g Fiber 5.0g Cholesterol 66mg Sodium 616mg
Exchanges: 1 Starch, 1 Fruit, 3 Very Lean Meat

Blue Cheese-Pear Salad

   1   large pear, peeled, cored, and coarsely chopped
   2   tablespoons white wine vinegar
   1   tablespoon vegetable oil
   ½   teaspoon freshly ground pepper
   ¼   teaspoon salt
   8   cups gourmet salad greens
   1   red Bartlett pear, sliced
   ½   cup (2 ounces) crumbled blue cheese

Combine first 5 ingredients in a blender; process until smooth, stopping once to scrape down sides.
Place 2 cups salad greens on each of 4 plates. Arrange pear slices over greens, and top with cheese. Drizzle dressing evenly over salads. Yield: 4 servings.

Per Serving: Calories 141 (50% from fat) Fat 7.9g (sat 3.3g) Protein 4.4g Carbohydrate 14.4g Fiber 3.1g Cholesterol 11mg Sodium 350mg
Exchanges: 1 Vegetable, ½ Fruit, 1½ Fat

Blue Cheese-Pear Salad

Easy Fruited Rice Pudding

1   (5.5-ounce) package rice pudding mix with cinnamon
     and raisins (such as Uncle Ben's Rice Pudding Mix)
2   cups 1% low-fat milk
1   cup diced peeled apple

Prepare rice pudding according to package directions, using low-fat milk, omitting butter or margarine, and adding apple after 5 minutes. Serve warm or chilled. Yield: 4 (⅔-cup) servings.

Per Serving: Calories 216 (8% from fat)   Fat 1.9g (sat 0.8g)   Protein 5.9g
Carbohydrate 44.4g   Fiber 1.9g   Cholesterol 5mg   Sodium 192mg
Exchanges: 2 Starch, 1 Fruit

Get "simmering for hours" flavor in minutes with a pressure cooker.

Moroccan Chicken
garlic and olive oil couscous   frozen red grapes
serves 4

Check out the varieties of flavored couscous in the rice and grain section.

menu plan

1. *Place grapes in a single layer on a baking sheet, and freeze for at least 15 minutes.*
2. *Peel and cut onion, turnips, and potatoes.*
3. *Cook chicken in pressure cooker.*
4. *While chicken cooks, prepare couscous according to package directions.*

Moroccan Chicken

1	(14½-ounce) can diced tomatoes with jalapeño peppers, undrained
2	tablespoons currants
1½	teaspoons curry powder
¼	teaspoon salt
4	(4-ounce) skinless, boneless chicken breast halves
1	onion, cut into 1-inch pieces
2	turnips, peeled and cut into 1-inch pieces
2	sweet potatoes, peeled and cut into 1-inch pieces

Combine first 4 ingredients in a 4-quart pressure cooker; stir well. Add chicken, onion, turnip, and sweet potato, in order listed. Close lid securely; bring to high pressure over high heat (about 8 minutes). Adjust heat to medium or level needed to maintain high pressure, and cook 5 minutes. Remove from heat; place pressure cooker under cold running water. Remove lid. Spoon chicken mixture and juices evenly over ¾-cup portions of couscous. Yield: 4 servings.

Per Serving: Calories 335 (6% from fat) Fat 2.3g (sat 0.5g) Protein 30.9g Carbohydrate 47.9g Fiber 7.7g Cholesterol 66mg Sodium 603mg
Exchanges: 3 Starch, 3 Very Lean Meat

a few tips:
pressure cooking

If you've been reluctant to use a pressure cooker for fear it would explode—fear not. Today's new and improved models have safety devices that prevent the lid from blowing off, even if you make a mistake. Pressure cookers cut stovetop cooking time by about two-thirds, and give you a product that is unbelievably moist and tender.

1 Read the manufacturers' instructions before you start cooking so you'll understand the features of your brand. All of the new models have safety devices that allow the steam to escape, even if the lid is in place.

2 Follow the recipe for the required amount of liquid. You always have to have liquid in the cooker—either water, broth, or the juices from the food. The liquid boils and turns to steam, the cooker locks in the steam, and the pressure builds and allows the temperature inside to rise rapidly to cook the food quickly.

3 The foods that work best in a pressure cooker are meats, especially the tougher cuts, and long-cooking vegetables like potatoes. Don't use the pressure cooker for foods that cook quickly anyway because they'll get mushy.

No chopping required—this spicy soup is made from canned and frozen veggies.

Cajun Black-Eyed Soup
French bread
Apple-Granola Crisp

serves 4

menu plan

1. *Peel and slice apples for dessert.*

2. *Slice turkey sausage for soup.*

3. *Combine ingredients for soup and cook.*

4. *Combine ingredients for dessert.*

5. *Cook dessert in microwave.*

Cajun Black-Eyed Soup

1   teaspoon olive oil
1½ cups frozen chopped onion, pepper, and celery blend
       (such as McKenzie's)
¼   teaspoon garlic powder
¼   teaspoon ground red pepper
1¼ cups fat-free, less-sodium chicken broth
1¼ cups water
1   (14.5-ounce) can no-salt-added diced tomatoes,
       undrained
1   cup frozen cut okra
2   (16-ounce) cans black-eyed peas, rinsed and drained
2   ounces cooked smoked turkey sausage, halved
       lengthwise and sliced

Heat oil in a large saucepan over high heat. Add frozen vegetable blend, garlic powder, and red pepper; sauté until tender. Stir in broth and remaining ingredients. Bring to a boil; cover, reduce heat, and simmer 5 minutes or until okra is tender. Yield: 4 (2-cup) servings.

Per Serving: Calories 185 (12% from fat)   Fat 2.4g (sat 0.5g)   Protein 10.9g
Carbohydrate 30.9g   Fiber 7.4g   Cholesterol 5mg   Sodium 777mg
Exchanges: 2 Starch, 1 Vegetable

Apple-Granola Crisp

Apples that are good for cooking include Baldwin, Cortland, Granny Smith, Gravenstein, Jonagold, Rome Beauty, and York Imperial.

4   cups sliced peeled cooking apple
¼   cup golden raisins
1   tablespoon brown sugar
1   tablespoon cornstarch
1   tablespoon lemon juice
½   teaspoon vanilla extract
Butter-flavored cooking spray
1¼ cups low-fat granola without raisins (such as
       Healthy Choice)

Combine first 6 ingredients in a large bowl; toss well. Spoon mixture into an 11 x 7-inch baking dish coated with cooking spray. Cover with heavy-duty plastic wrap; microwave at HIGH 5 minutes or until apple is tender. Remove plastic wrap. Top apple mixture with granola; coat generously with cooking spray. Microwave, uncovered, at HIGH 2 minutes. Yield: 4 (1-cup) servings.

Per Serving: Calories 237 (10% from fat)   Fat 2.7g (sat 0.4g)   Protein 3.1g
Carbohydrate 53.8g   Fiber 4.3g   Cholesterol 0mg   Sodium 78mg
Exchanges: 2 Starch, 1½ Fruit

Prepare a holiday meal without spending hours in the kitchen.

Sage-Crusted Turkey Tenderloin
Savory Wild Rice   Marmalade Brussels Sprouts
whole-wheat rolls **Holiday Ambrosia (page 182)**
serves 4

menu plan

1. *Toast coconut for ambrosia in microwave at HIGH for 1 to 2 minutes.*

2. *Prepare ambrosia, and chill.*

3. *Dredge turkey, and bake.*

4. *Boil water for rice.*

5. *Prepare Brussels sprouts.*

6. *Cook rice.*

Sage-Crusted Turkey Tenderloin

    3   tablespoons finely chopped fresh sage
    3   tablespoons shredded three-cheese blend
          (such as Kraft)
    ¼   cup coarsely crushed cornflakes
    1   (1-pound) package turkey tenderloins
    1   tablespoon reduced-calorie margarine, melted
    ¼   teaspoon salt
Cooking spray
Sage sprigs (optional)

Preheat oven to 425°.
Combine first 3 ingredients in a shallow dish. Brush turkey with margarine; sprinkle with salt. Dredge turkey in sage mixture, coating well. Place on a baking sheet coated with cooking spray. Bake at 425° for 25 minutes or until meat thermometer registers 170°. Garnish with sage sprigs, if desired. Yield: 4 servings.

Per Serving: Calories 190 (24% from fat) Fat 5.0g (sat 1.6g) Protein 29.0g
Carbohydrate 6.0g Fiber 0.3g Cholesterol 71mg Sodium 371mg
Exchanges: ½ Starch, 4 Very Lean Meat

Savory Wild Rice

    1   (4-ounce) package long grain and wild rice mix
          (such as Success Rice)
    1   tablespoon yogurt-based spread (such as Brummel
          and Brown)

Prepare rice according to package directions, omitting butter and using only 1 tablespoon seasoning mix. Stir in yogurt-based spread. Yield: 4 (½-cup) servings.

Per Serving: Calories 106 (11% from fat) Fat 1.3g (sat 0.3g) Protein 2.5g
Carbohydrate 21.0g Fiber 0.5g Cholesterol 0mg Sodium 134mg
Exchanges: 1½ Starch

Marmalade Brussels Sprouts

    16 small Brussels sprouts
    ⅓ cup low-sugar orange marmalade

Trim ends of sprouts. Place in a 1½-quart microwave-safe dish; add water to cover. Microwave at HIGH 8 minutes or just until tender; drain. Add marmalade, and toss well to coat.
Yield: 4 (½-cup) servings.

Per Serving: Calories 36 (5% from fat) Fat 0.2g (sat 0.0g) Protein 2.6g
Carbohydrate 7.7g Fiber 3.1g Cholesterol 0mg Sodium 22mg
Exchange: 1 Vegetable

Holiday Ambrosia

Save time by purchasing grapefruit and orange sections in a fresh-pack jar (available at most supermarkets in the refrigerated section near the fresh produce or the dairy products).

1   (15¼-ounce) can chunk pineapple in juice, drained
1   cup pink grapefruit sections
1   cup orange sections
¼   cup coconut, toasted

Combine first 3 ingredients in a medium bowl; toss gently. Sprinkle with coconut. Cover and chill.
Yield: 4 (¾-cup) servings.

Per Serving: Calories 112 (18% from fat)   Fat 2.2g (sat 1.8g)   Protein 1.0g
Carbohydrate 23.5g   Fiber 2.9g   Cholesterol 0mg   Sodium 16mg
Exchanges: 1½ Fruit, ½ Fat

a dessert idea: *If you want to add another dessert for this holiday meal, serve the Cookies and Cream Pudding Pie (page 205) with your favorite flavored coffee.*

citrus fruit

Citrus fruit brings a bright splash of color and zesty flavor to dreary winter days. Since most citrus fruit is at its peak during the winter months, don't miss out on the variety of these great-tasting, great-for-you fruits with your meals.

grapefruit Yellow grapefruit has pale yellow skin and whitish yellow flesh; ruby red grapefruit is sweeter than yellow and has a reddish blush on its skin and red flesh.

navel oranges These winter oranges get their name from the indentation in the skin at the flower end. They have sweet, juicy flesh, few seeds, and are easy to peel.

blood oranges These small to medium-sized oranges have a reddish blush on their skin and deep red flesh and juice.

kumquats This fruit looks like an elongated miniature orange. It is usually eaten whole, and its skin is sweeter than the tart flesh.

pomelos Pomelos are the largest citrus fruit and have thick, bumpy yellow to pink skins. The flesh is seedless and slightly bittersweet.

tangerines Tangerines, clementines, and satsumas are varieties of the mandarin orange— all are small, loose-skinned oranges.

tangelos This sweet, tart fruit is a cross between a tangerine and a pomelo. The most common variety in the United States is the Minneola, distinguished by its nipple-shaped stem end.

winter produce

Vegetables	Fruits	Herbs
Baby Turnips	Apples	Bay Leaves
Beets	Blood Oranges	Chives
Belgian Endive	Bosc Pears	Parsley
Brussels Sprouts	Cranberries	Rosemary
Celery Root	Grapefruit	Sage
Chili Peppers	Kiwifruit	Thyme
Dried Beans	Kumquats	
Escarole	Lemons	
Fennel	Mandarin Oranges	
Frisée	Navel Oranges	
Kale	Persimmons	
Jerusalem Artichokes	Pomegranates	
Leeks	Pomelos	
Mushrooms	Tangelos	
Parsnips	Tangerines	
Potatoes	Quinces	
Rutabagas		
Sweet Potatoes		
Watercress		
Winter Squash		

Although many produce items are available year-round, this chart lists those that are at their peak during this season. Check with farmers' markets in your area for regional varieties.

des

serts

What says "dessert" to you? Chocolate anything? Silky, soothing pudding? Juicy, sweet fruit wrapped in a tender pastry, or melt-in-your-mouth cookies? You'll find it all here—a dessert for every season. They're all quick and easy, so you don't have to wait long to satisfy your sweet tooth. Pick your favorites for happy endings to your light and easy meals.

Fruit desserts

Some of the best desserts come from nature in the form of sweet, juicy fruit.

Use either Rome Beauty, Cortland, or Winesap apples
to get the best texture for your applesauce.

cooking apples

The best apples for cooking and baking are those that can maintain some texture and keep their flavor throughout the cooking process.

varieties A few of the more common cooking apples are Baldwin, Cortland, Northern Spy, Rome Beauty, Winesap, Granny Smith, and York Imperial.

If you have a farmers' market in your area, ask about the other varieties that are available in your part of the country.

Apples are available all year long, but most varieties are at their best from September through November when they are newly harvested.

storage Store apples in a cool, dark place or in a plastic bag in the refrigerator.

Apple Cider Applesauce

Use a potato masher to get the best chunky texture for the applesauce. If you don't have a potato masher, use a fork.

8 cups peeled, sliced cooking apple (about 2½ pounds)
½ cup apple cider or apple juice
¼ cup sugar
⅛ teaspoon ground nutmeg
¼ teaspoon ground cinnamon

Combine apple and apple cider in a large saucepan. Bring to a boil, stirring frequently; cover, reduce heat, and simmer 20 minutes or until apple is tender, stirring occasionally.

Add sugar and nutmeg to apple mixture; stir. Cook until sugar dissolves, stirring constantly. Mash apple mixture slightly with a potato masher until mixture is chunky. Cover and chill thoroughly. Sprinkle evenly with cinnamon before serving.

Yield: 6 (½-cup) servings.

Per Serving: Calories 117 (4% from fat) Fat 0.5g (sat 0.1g) Protein 0.3g
Carbohydrate 30.2g Fiber 3.5g Cholesterol 0mg Sodium 1mg
Exchanges: 2 Fruit

Apple Cider Applesauce

If you're buying berries packed in containers, check the bottom of the container for signs of fruit juice leakage. Visible juice indicates that there may be crushed or moldy berries in the container.

Fresh Strawberries with Orange Custard

Substitute your favorite berry in this superquick dessert. And for more variety, use either lemon or lime rind and juice instead of orange.

½ (8-ounce) carton fat-free sour cream
¼ cup fat-free sweetened condensed milk
½ teaspoon grated orange rind
1 tablespoon fresh orange juice
1½ cups sliced strawberries
Orange zest (optional)
Edible flowers (optional)
Mint sprigs (optional)

Combine first 4 ingredients in a small bowl.
Spoon ⅓ cup sour cream mixture into each of 2 (6-ounce) custard cups or dessert dishes.
Top each serving with ¾ cup strawberries and 2 tablespoons sour cream mixture. Garnish with orange zest, edible flowers, and mint, if desired. Yield: 2 servings.

Per Serving: Calories 185 (2% from fat) Fat 0.4g (sat 0.0g) Protein 7.7g
Carbohydrate 36.2g Fiber 2.4g Cholesterol 1mg Sodium 81mg
Exchanges: 1½ Starch, 1 Fruit

Fresh Berries with Ginger Cream

3 tablespoons sugar
4 teaspoons cornstarch
1 cup 1% low-fat milk
2 teaspoons minced crystallized ginger
1 large egg yolk, lightly beaten
¼ teaspoon vanilla extract
2 cups blackberries, raspberries, or blueberries

Combine sugar and cornstarch in a medium saucepan; gradually stir in milk. Add minced ginger. Bring to a boil over medium heat until mixture is thickened, stirring constantly.
Gradually stir one-fourth of hot mixture into beaten egg yolk; add to remaining hot mixture. Reduce heat to low, and cook 2 minutes, stirring constantly. Remove from heat; stir in vanilla. Cool slightly. Cover and chill.
To serve, spoon ¼ cup cream into each of 4 dessert dishes. Top each with ½ cup berries. Yield: 4 servings.

Per Serving: Calories 130 (15% from fat) Fat 2.2g (sat 0.8g) Protein 3.2g
Carbohydrate 25.2g Fiber 3.8g Cholesterol 57mg Sodium 34mg
Exchanges: 1 Starch, ½ Fruit, ½ Fat

Fresh Strawberries with Orange Custard

raspberries

Choose bright, plump raspberries without hulls. If the hulls are still attached, the berries were picked too early and will be tart.

Store raspberries in a single layer in a moisture-proof container in the refrigerator for 2 to 3 days. Rinse them lightly just before serving.

Melon-Raspberry Compote with Rum

Add the raspberries just before serving to prevent them from becoming soggy.

 ¼ cup sugar
 ½ cup water
 2 tablespoons white rum
 2 tablespoons fresh lime juice
 1½ cups cubed cantaloupe
 1½ cups cubed honeydew melon
 1½ cups raspberries
 Mint sprigs (optional)

Combine sugar and water in a small saucepan; bring to a boil over medium-high heat. Cook 1 minute or until sugar dissolves, stirring constantly. Remove from heat.

Stir in rum and lime juice. Cool 15 minutes or until mixture reaches room temperature.
Combine cantaloupe and honeydew melon in a medium bowl; add rum mixture. Cover and chill. Just before serving, add raspberries, and stir gently. Garnish with mint sprigs, if desired.
Yield: 4 (1-cup) servings.

Per Serving: Calories 138 (3% from fat) Fat 0.5g (sat 0.1g) Protein 1.3g
Carbohydrate 29.4g Fiber 4.0g Cholesterol 0mg Sodium 12mg
Exchanges: 1 Starch, 1 Fruit

Mixed Fruit with Vanilla-Apricot Syrup

Use any combination of fresh fruit you like to get a total of 5 cups fruit.

 ¼ cup sugar
 1 tablespoon vanilla extract
 1 cup apricot nectar
 1 cup blueberries
 1 cup blackberries
 1 cup strawberries, sliced
 ½ cup cubed pineapple
 ½ cup sliced peach (1 medium)
 ½ cup sliced plum (about 3 medium)
 ½ cup sliced apricot (about 2 medium)

Combine sugar, vanilla, and apricot nectar in a small saucepan; bring to a boil, stirring until sugar dissolves. Reduce heat, and simmer, uncovered, until mixture is reduced to ⅔ cup.
Pour syrup into a small bowl, and cool to room temperature. Layer fruit in serving bowls or stemmed glasses. Spoon syrup evenly over fruit.
Yield: 5 (1-cup) servings.

Per Serving: Calories 147 (4% from fat) Fat 0.6g (sat 0.0g) Protein 1.3g
Carbohydrate 35.5g Fiber 4.6g Cholesterol 0mg Sodium 4mg
Exchanges: ½ Starch, 2 Fruit

Mixed Fruit with Vanilla-Apricot Syrup

Cherry Poached Pears with Dark Chocolate Sauce

2 firm Bosc pears
1¼ cups cranberry-cherry juice
¾ cup white Zinfandel
⅓ cup sugar
1½ teaspoons cornstarch
2 tablespoons unsweetened cocoa
1 teaspoon light butter

Peel pears; remove core from bottom end, leaving stem intact. If needed, slice about ¼ inch from base of each pear so that it will sit flat.

Place pears, stem end up, in a deep saucepan. Combine juice and wine; pour over pears. Bring to a boil; cover, reduce heat, and simmer 15 to 20 minutes or just until pears are tender, basting occasionally.

Remove pears from liquid using a slotted spoon. Reserve 3 tablespoons poaching liquid; discard remaining liquid.

Combine sugar, cornstarch, and cocoa in a saucepan. Stir in reserved poaching liquid until smooth, using a whisk. Bring to a boil over medium heat until thickened, stirring constantly. Remove from heat; stir in butter until it melts.

To serve, spoon 1 tablespoon chocolate sauce onto each of 2 dessert plates. Place 1 pear over sauce on each plate. Drizzle remaining chocolate sauce evenly over pears. Serve immediately. Yield: 2 servings.

Per Serving: Calories 275 (8% from fat) Fat 2.4g (sat 1.1g) Protein 2.4g Carbohydrate 65.0g Fiber 4.0g Cholesterol 3mg Sodium 16mg
Exchanges: 2 Starch, 2 Fruit

Poached Pears with Marmalade

4 firm Bosc pears
1 cup water
⅓ cup sugar
1 teaspoon lemon juice
½ teaspoon vanilla extract
2 tablespoons low-sugar orange marmalade
4 teaspoons sliced almonds, lightly toasted

Peel pears; cut in half lengthwise, and remove cores. Set aside.

Combine water, sugar, and lemon juice in a large skillet, and bring to a boil. Reduce heat to medium-low; add pear halves. Cover and cook 10 minutes or until tender, turning once. Remove pears with a slotted spoon. Bring poaching liquid to a boil; cook 3 to 5 minutes or until reduced to about ½ cup. Remove from heat; stir in vanilla and marmalade.

Place 2 pears halves in each of 4 dessert dishes. Spoon sauce evenly over pears; sprinkle evenly with toasted almonds. Yield: 4 servings.

Per Serving: Calories 197 (11% from fat) Fat 2.5g (sat 0.2g) Protein 1.3g Carbohydrate 45.6g Fiber 4.4g Cholesterol 0mg Sodium 1mg
Exchanges: 2 Starch, 1 Fruit

Bosc pears

Bosc pears are winter pears and have long, tapering necks with slim stems. A ripe Bosc has golden brown to reddish brown skin and a tender, buttery-tasting flesh. This variety holds its shape well during baking and poaching.

Cherry Poached Pears with Dark Chocolate Sauce

Nectarine Melba Sundaes

These sundaes are also delicious with sliced peaches in place of the nectarines.

- ¼ cup all-fruit raspberry spread (such as Polaner's)
- 2 tablespoons water
- 1 cup raspberries
- 2 cups thinly sliced unpeeled nectarines
- 2 cups vanilla fat-free frozen yogurt

Combine raspberry spread and water in a small saucepan; bring to a boil over medium heat, stirring until smooth. Remove from heat; add raspberries, and stir gently.

Arrange nectarine slices evenly on 4 dessert plates; top each serving with ½ cup frozen yogurt. Spoon raspberry mixture evenly over yogurt.
Yield: 4 servings.

Per Serving: Calories 168 (3% from fat) Fat 0.6g (sat 0.1g) Protein 4.5g
Carbohydrate 39.2g Fiber 4.2g Cholesterol 0mg Sodium 76mg
Exchanges: ½ Starch, 2 Fruit

Tropical Fruit Sundaes

To toast the coconut, place it in a microwave-safe shallow dish and microwave at HIGH 1 to 2 minutes, stirring every 30 seconds.

- 1 cup chopped kiwifruit (about 2)
- 1 cup chopped mango (about 1 medium)
- 3 tablespoons orange juice
- 1 tablespoon lime juice
- 2 cups pineapple sherbet
- 4 teaspoons flaked sweetened coconut, toasted

Combine first 4 ingredients in a small bowl; cover and chill 30 minutes. Spoon ½ cup sherbet into each of 4 dessert dishes. Top sherbet evenly with fruit mixture, and sprinkle with coconut. Serve immediately.
Yield: 4 servings (serving size: ½ cup sherbet, ½ cup fruit, and 1 teaspoon coconut).

Per Serving: Calories 180 (10% from fat) Fat 1.9g (sat 1.1g) Protein 1.7g
Carbohydrate 41.7g Fiber 1.8g Cholesterol 0mg Sodium 38mg
Exchanges: 1 Starch, 1½ Fruit

a few tips:
chopping mangoes

It's a bit tricky to cut a mango because it has a large seed that grows horizontally inside the fruit. You have to cut around the seed on both sides.

1 To cut around the seed, hold the mango vertically on the cutting board. Use a sharp knife and slice the fruit lengthwise on either side of the flat pit (seed).

2 To chop or cube the mango, hold a mango half in the palm of your hand, and score the pulp in square cross-sections. Slice to the skin of the mango, but not through the skin.

3 Turn the mango half inside out, and cut the square chunks from the skin.

Tropical Fruit Sundaes

Frozen desserts

What better way to beat the heat than with a sweet frozen treat?

Refreshing Fruit Shake

Refreshing Fruit Shake

Freeze the strawberries and banana for 30 minutes; frozen fruit makes the shake thicker.

1½ cups halved strawberries
1 banana, sliced
1 (8-ounce) can crushed pineapple, undrained
2 tablespoons honey
3 cups vanilla fat-free ice cream

Combine all ingredients in a blender; process until smooth, stopping once to scrape down sides. Pour mixture into glasses. Yield: 5 (1-cup) servings.

Per Serving: Calories 198 (1% from fat) Fat 0.3g (sat 0.1g) Protein 3.2g Carbohydrate 46.4g Fiber 2.0g Cholesterol 0mg Sodium 50mg
Exchanges: 1 Starch, 2 Fruit

Café Mocha Granita

2 cups water
2 tablespoons sugar
2 tablespoons instant espresso granules
1 cup 1% low-fat milk
¼ cup chocolate syrup
¼ cup Kahlúa or other coffee-flavored liqueur

Combine water and sugar in a medium saucepan; bring to a boil. Cook, stirring until sugar dissolves. Remove from heat; stir in espresso granules. Stir in milk, chocolate syrup, and liqueur. Pour mixture into a 9-inch square pan. Cover and freeze 4 hours or until firm.
Remove mixture from freezer; let stand 10 minutes. Scrape mixture with a fork until fluffy. Spoon into goblets or dessert dishes. Yield: 4 (1-cup) servings.

Per Serving: Calories 153 (5% from fat) Fat 0.9g (sat 0.4g) Protein 2.9g Carbohydrate 25.6g Fiber 0.1g Cholesterol 2mg Sodium 44mg
Exchanges: 2 Starch

Café Mocha Granita

Cakes

For the occasions when you're pushed for time, but you must have cake.

Lemon Meringue Cakes

1 (5-ounce) package sponge cake or angel food cake shells
1½ cups lemon sorbet
6 tablespoons warm water
2 tablespoons egg white powder (such as Just Whites)
¼ teaspoon cream of tartar
3 tablespoons sugar
½ teaspoon vanilla extract
Lemon zest (optional)

Preheat oven to 500°.

Place cakes on an ungreased baking sheet. Spoon ¼ cup lemon sorbet into each cake. Place sorbet-filled cakes in freezer while preparing meringue.

Place warm water in a large bowl. Add egg white powder; beat at medium speed of a mixer until foamy. Add cream of tartar. Beat at high speed until soft peaks form. Gradually add sugar, 1 tablespoon at a time, beating 2 to 3 minutes or until stiff peaks form. Add vanilla, beating just until blended.

Spread egg white mixture over cakes, covering entire surface of sorbet and cakes. Bake at 500° for 2 minutes or until meringue is lightly browned. Garnish with lemon zest, if desired. Serve immediately.

Yield: 6 servings.

Per Serving: Calories 179 (4% from fat) Fat 0.8g (sat 0.3g) Protein 3.3g Carbohydrate 39.5g Fiber 0.0g Cholesterol 33mg Sodium 193mg **Exchanges:** 2½ Starch

Pumpkin Snack Cake

1 (18.25-ounce) reduced-fat yellow or white cake mix (such as Sweet Rewards)
2 teaspoons pumpkin-pie spice
1 cup canned pumpkin
1 cup water
2 tablespoons vegetable oil
2 large eggs, lightly beaten
1 cup raisins
Cooking spray
2 tablespoons powdered sugar

Preheat oven to 375°.

Combine cake mix and pumpkin-pie spice in a large bowl. Combine pumpkin and next 3 ingredients in a medium bowl; beat at medium speed of a mixer 2 minutes or until blended. Add pumpkin mixture to cake mix mixture; beat at low speed 1 minute or until combined. Stir in raisins.

Pour batter into a 15 x 10-inch jelly-roll pan coated with cooking spray. Bake at 375° for 15 to 17 minutes or until a wooden pick inserted in center comes out clean. Cool on a wire rack.

Sift powdered sugar over top of cake.

Yield: 24 servings.

Per Serving: Calories 121 (16% from fat) Fat 2.2g (sat 0.6g) Protein 1.9g Carbohydrate 24.8g Fiber 0.7g Cholesterol 18mg Sodium 147mg **Exchanges:** 1½ Starch

Coconut-Cranberry Cake

1   (16-ounce) carton vanilla low-fat yogurt
1   (10.5-ounce) loaf angel food cake
1   (16-ounce) can whole-berry cranberry sauce
½   teaspoon grated orange rind
¼   teaspoon ground nutmeg
1   (8-ounce) carton frozen reduced-calorie whipped
      topping, thawed
½   cup flaked sweetened coconut
Cranberries (optional)
Mint sprigs (optional)

Spoon yogurt onto several layers of heavy-duty paper towels. Spread to ½-inch thickness. Cover with additional paper towels; let stand 5 minutes. Scrape yogurt into a bowl, using a rubber spatula; set aside.

Slice cake horizontally into three equal layers, and set aside. Combine cranberry sauce, grated orange rind, and nutmeg.

Place bottom cake layer on a serving plate. Spread half of yogurt on bottom layer; top with one-third of cranberry mixture. Place middle cake layer over cranberry mixture. Spread remaining half of yogurt over layer; top with one-third of cranberry mixture. Top with remaining cake layer. Spread whipped topping evenly over top and sides of cake. Spoon remaining cranberry mixture on top of cake. Press coconut onto sides of cake. Cover and chill at least 2 hours. If desired, garnish with cranberries and mint. Yield: 10 servings.

Per Serving: Calories 257 (19% from fat) Fat 5.4g (sat 3.8g) Protein 5.0g
Carbohydrate 49.0g Fiber 0.4g Cholesterol 3mg Sodium 223mg
Exchanges: 2 Starch, 1 Fruit, 1 Fat

cranberries

Cranberries are also called *bounceberries* because the ripe berries bounce. These berries are grown on low vines in sandy bogs; they grow wild in northern Europe and in the northern parts of the United States. Most of the cultivated cranberries in this country come from Massachusetts, Maine, Wisconsin, Washington, and Oregon. The peak season for cranberries is October through December.

Look for fresh cranberries in 12-ounce plastic bags, and discard any that are discolored or shriveled. Refrigerate cranberries, tightly wrapped, for 2 months, or freeze them for up to a year.

Fresh cranberries are extremely tart, so they're usually combined with other fruits and/or some type of sweetener. In addition to fresh cranberries, you can buy canned cranberry sauce—either jellied or whole-berry—and dried, sweetened cranberries that can be used like raisins.

Cookies

Keep cookies on hand when you need "dessert-on-the-run."

Chocolate-Caramel Brownies

Applesauce replaces the fat in this recipe.

- ¾ cup unsweetened applesauce
- 1¾ cups sugar
- ½ cup egg substitute
- 1 teaspoon vanilla extract
- 1 cup all-purpose flour
- ⅔ cup unsweetened cocoa
- ½ teaspoon salt
- Butter-flavored cooking spray
- 3 tablespoons fat-free caramel apple dip (such as Marzetti's)

Preheat oven to 350°.

Pour applesauce into a wire-mesh strainer; drain 15 minutes. (There should be ½ cup applesauce after draining.)

Combine drained applesauce, sugar, egg substitute, and vanilla.

Lightly spoon flour into a dry measuring cup; level with a knife.

Combine flour, cocoa, and salt in a medium bowl. Add flour mixture to applesauce mixture, and stir just until moist. Pour batter into a 9-inch square pan coated with cooking spray.

Bake at 350° for 28 minutes. Remove from oven, and cool 10 minutes. Drizzle with caramel apple dip; cool. Cut into bars. Yield: 15 brownies.

Per Brownie: Calories 158 (4% from fat) Fat 0.7g (sat 0.3g) Protein 2.9g Carbohydrate 35.3g Fiber 0.3g Cholesterol 0mg Sodium 104mg
Exchanges: 2 Starch

Lemon Oatmeal Cookies

- ⅓ cup stick margarine, softened
- ½ cup sugar
- ⅓ cup packed brown sugar
- 2 large egg whites
- 1 tablespoon grated lemon rind
- ¾ cup all-purpose flour
- 1 cup regular oats
- Cooking spray

Preheat oven to 350°.

Beat margarine at medium speed of a mixer until creamy; gradually add sugars, beating well. Add egg whites and lemon rind; beat until smooth.

Lightly spoon flour into dry measuring cups; level with a knife. Add flour and oats to sugar mixture; beat until well-blended.

Drop dough by rounded teaspoonfuls, 1½ inches apart, onto cookie sheets coated with cooking spray. Bake at 350° for 11 minutes or until edges are golden. Remove from pans, and cool completely on wire racks. Yield: 44 cookies.

Per Cookie: Calories 43 (33% from fat) Fat 1.6g (sat 0.3g) Protein 0.7g Carbohydrate 6.8g Fiber 0.2g Cholesterol 0mg Sodium 19mg
Exchange: ½ Starch

Chocolate-Caramel Brownies

Pies

Use packaged crusts, ice creams, and puddings to make some mighty pleasing pies.

Turtle Pie

4   cups chocolate low-fat ice cream
¾   cup fat-free caramel topping, divided
1   (6-ounce) package reduced-fat graham cracker crust
⅔   cup frozen reduced-calorie whipped topping, thawed
2   tablespoons chopped pecans, toasted

Place an extra-large bowl in freezer. Remove ice cream from freezer; let stand at room temperature 15 minutes.
Spoon ice cream into chilled bowl; stir in ¼ cup caramel topping. Spoon ice cream mixture into pie crust; cover and freeze at least 2½ hours.
Before serving, place pie in refrigerator 10 minutes to soften slightly. Heat ½ cup caramel topping according to package directions. Top each serving with 1 tablespoon whipped topping. Sprinkle evenly with pecans, and drizzle with caramel topping.
Yield: 10 servings.

Per Serving: Calories 234 (2% from fat) Fat 5.2g (sat 2.1g) Protein 3.0g
Carbohydrate 43.1g Fiber 0.9g Cholesterol 4mg Sodium 205mg
Exchanges: 3 Starch, 1 Fat

Frozen Chocolate Mint Torte

½   (20.5-ounce) package fudge low-fat brownie mix
       (about 2½ cups mix)
⅓   cup water
Cooking spray
6   (1.5-ounce) chocolate-covered peppermint patties
       (such as York), chopped
6   cups chocolate low-fat ice cream, softened
½   cup crushed hard peppermint candies (about 18)
⅓   cup fat-free hot fudge topping
Additional crushed hard peppermint candies (optional)

Preheat oven to 350°.
Combine brownie mix and water, stirring just until moist. Pour batter into a 9-inch springform pan coated with cooking spray. Bake at 350° for 15 to 20 minutes or until edges begin to pull away from pan.
Sprinkle chopped mint patties over warm brownie; let stand 5 minutes. Spread melted mint patties over surface of brownie using a small spatula or the back of a spoon; cool in pan on a wire rack.
Combine ice cream and peppermint candies in a large bowl. Spread ice cream mixture over brownie. Freeze at least 2 hours or until firm.
Remove sides of pan. Place fudge topping in a small heavy-duty, zip-top plastic bag; snip a tiny hole in 1 corner of bag. Drizzle fudge sauce over torte. Serve immediately. Garnish with additional crushed candies, if desired. Yield: 12 servings.

Per Serving: Calories 267 (13% from fat) Fat 3.9g (sat 2.1g) Protein 3.8g
Carbohydrate 54.8g Fiber 1.5g Cholesterol 5mg Sodium 173mg
Exchanges: 3½ Starch, ½ Fat

Frozen Chocolate Mint Torte

Cookies and Cream Pudding Pie

Vary this recipe by using chocolate pudding mix and a graham cracker crust, or vanilla pudding and cream-filled vanilla sandwich cookies.

1¾ cups 1% low-fat milk
2 (3.3-ounce) packages white chocolate instant
    pudding mix
1 cup frozen fat-free whipped topping, thawed
8 reduced-fat cream-filled chocolate sandwich cookies
    (such as reduced-fat Oreos), crushed
1 (6-ounce) package chocolate crumb crust
Additional crushed reduced-fat cream-filled chocolate
    sandwich cookies (optional)

Place milk in a medium bowl; add pudding mix. Beat at medium speed of a mixer until smooth.

Fold in whipped topping and crushed cookies. Spoon pudding mixture into chocolate crust. Cover and chill at least 4 hours. Garnish with additional crushed cookies, if desired. Yield: 10 servings.

Per Serving: Calories 218 (21% from fat) Fat 5.0g (sat 1.1g) Protein 2.9g Carbohydrate 40.9g Fiber 0.3g Cholesterol 2mg Sodium 453mg
Exchanges: 2½ Starch, 1 Fat

Blueberry Cream Cheese Pie

½ cup graham cracker crumbs (4 crackers)
2 tablespoons margarine, melted
2 tablespoons cornstarch
½ cup water, divided
2 cups fresh or frozen blueberries, thawed
⅔ cup sugar, divided
1 teaspoon lemon juice
1 (8-ounce) block ⅓-less-fat cream cheese, softened
4 ounces frozen fat-free whipped topping, thawed

Combine graham cracker crumbs and margarine in a small bowl. Press mixture into bottom of a 9-inch shallow pie plate. Bake at 350° for 7 minutes or until lightly browned. Let cool.

Combine cornstarch and ¼ cup water; stir well and set aside. Combine blueberries, remaining ¼ cup water, ⅓ cup sugar, and lemon juice in a saucepan. Cook over medium-high heat 7 to 8 minutes or until blueberries are soft. Reduce heat to low, and add cornstarch mixture. Bring to a boil; cook 1 minute or until thickened. Remove from heat and cool slightly.

Combine cream cheese and remaining ⅓ cup sugar; beat at medium speed of a mixer until smooth. Fold in whipped topping. Spoon cream cheese mixture over graham cracker crust. Spread blueberry mixture over cream cheese mixture. Cover and chill at least 2 hours or until set. Yield: 8 servings.

Per Serving: Calories 247 (38% from fat) Fat 10.4g (sat 4.8g) Protein 3.6g Carbohydrate 35.0g Fiber 1.2g Cholesterol 22mg Sodium 202mg
Exchanges: 1 Starch, 1 Fruit, 2 Fat

Pastry

Layers of phyllo give you a crisp, flaky crust.

You can buy fresh phyllo pastry in Greek markets; it's also available frozen in most supermarkets. Once you open the package, use the phyllo within 2 to 3 days. You can keep frozen phyllo for up to a year, but don't refreeze it or the dough will be brittle.

Apple Turnovers

We like the tartness a Granny Smith apple adds to these turnovers, but a Rome or a Winesap apple will give you more sweetness.

1   large cooking apple, peeled, cored, and quartered
¼   cup chopped dates
2   tablespoons brown sugar
¼   teaspoon salt
4   sheets frozen phyllo dough, thawed
Butter-flavored cooking spray
¼   cup sifted powdered sugar
½   teaspoon water
⅛   teaspoon vanilla extract

Preheat oven to 400°.
Place apple in food processor; pulse 4 times or until apple is finely chopped. Spoon apple into a bowl. Stir in dates, brown sugar, and salt.
Place 1 sheet of phyllo on a damp towel (cover remaining dough to keep from drying). Lightly coat with cooking spray. Place second sheet of phyllo over first sheet; coat with cooking spray. Cut stacked sheets lengthwise into 3 equal strips (each about 4½ inches wide).
Working with 1 strip at a time, place 2 tablespoons apple mixture at base of strip (cover remaining strips). Fold the right bottom corner over apple mixture to form a triangle. Continue folding triangle back and forth to end of strip. Place triangles, seam sides down, on a baking sheet coated with cooking spray. Repeat procedure with remaining phyllo sheets and apple mixture. Coat triangles with cooking spray.
Bake at 400° for 12 minutes or until golden. Remove from pan, and cool 5 minutes on a wire rack.
Combine powdered sugar, water, and vanilla, stirring until smooth. Drizzle sugar mixture evenly over turnovers. Serve warm. Yield: 6 turnovers.

Per Turnover: Calories 107 (10% from fat) Fat 1.2g (sat 0.1g) Protein 1.1g Carbohydrate 23.8g Fiber 1.2g Cholesterol 0mg Sodium 160mg
Exchanges: ½ Starch, 1 Fruit

Apple Turnovers

Mocha Pudding

Puddings

Nothing says "comfort" like a cup of creamy pudding.

Mocha Pudding

- ⅓ cup sugar
- 2 tablespoons cornstarch
- 1 tablespoon instant coffee granules
- ⅛ teaspoon salt
- 2 cups 1% low-fat milk
- ¼ cup semisweet chocolate minichips
- 1 large egg yolk, beaten
- 1 teaspoon vanilla extract

Combine first 4 ingredients in a medium saucepan. Gradually add milk, stirring with a whisk until blended.

Stir in chocolate. Cook over medium heat 7 minutes or until mixture comes to a boil, stirring constantly. Reduce heat and simmer 1 minute, stirring constantly.

Gradually stir about one-fourth of hot mixture into egg yolk; add to remaining hot mixture. Cook 2 minutes, stirring constantly. Remove from heat, and stir in vanilla. Pour into a bowl; cover with plastic wrap, gently pressing plastic directly on pudding. Chill until set. Yield: 4 (½-cup) servings.

Per Serving: Calories 219 (29% from fat) Fat 7.1g (sat 4.0g) Protein 5.7g Carbohydrate 35.3g Fiber 0.2g Cholesterol 59mg Sodium 135mg
Exchanges: 2 Starch, 1½ Fat

Rice Pudding with Honey

- 2 tablespoons sugar
- 2 tablespoons cornstarch
- ⅛ teaspoon salt
- 1¾ cups 2% reduced-fat milk
- 1 cup cooked medium-grain rice
- 1 teaspoon vanilla extract
- 2 tablespoons raisins
- 4 teaspoons honey
- ¼ teaspoon ground cinnamon

Combine first 3 ingredients in a medium saucepan. Stir in milk and rice. Bring to a boil over medium-high heat, stirring constantly. Reduce heat, and simmer 10 minutes or until thickened.

Remove pudding from heat, and stir in vanilla and raisins. Pour into a bowl; cover and chill.

To serve, spoon pudding evenly into 4 dishes. Drizzle each serving with 1 teaspoon honey, and sprinkle with cinnamon. Yield: 4 (½-cup) servings.

Per Serving: Calories 185 (10% from fat) Fat 2.1g (sat 1.3g) Protein 4.7g Carbohydrate 36.7g Fiber 0.5g Cholesterol 9mg Sodium 125mg
Exchanges: 2½ Starch

Gingered Banana Pudding Parfaits

Crystallized, or candied ginger, is fresh ginger that has been cooked in a sugar syrup and then coated with coarse sugar. Look for it in the spice section of the supermarket.

- 1 (3.4-ounce) package vanilla instant pudding mix
- 2 cups fat-free milk
- 2 tablespoons chopped crystallized ginger
- 1 cup gingersnap crumbs (about 16 cookies, finely crushed)
- 2 small bananas, sliced

Prepare pudding mix according to package directions using fat-free milk. Stir in chopped ginger. Cover and chill 10 minutes.

Layer pudding, gingersnap crumbs, and banana evenly into four parfait or stemmed glasses.
Yield: 4 servings.

Per Serving: Calories 292 (13% from fat) Fat 4.3g (sat 1.2g) Protein 6.1g Carbohydrate 59.0g Fiber 1.1g Cholesterol 11mg Sodium 448mg
Exchanges: 3 Starch, 1 Fruit, 1 Fat

Summer Pudding with Vanilla Custard Sauce

6   thin slices firm white bread
2   cups blueberries
2   cups raspberries
⅓   cup sugar
⅓   cup water
Vanilla Custard Sauce

Trim crusts from bread; reserve crusts for another use. Cut 2 bread slices in half diagonally; cut 2 bread slices each into 4 triangles.

Line a 4-cup, steep-sided bowl with plastic wrap, leaving a 3-inch overhang around the edges. Place 1 bread slice in bottom of bowl. Line sides of bowl with bread halves and triangles, arranging to completely cover sides of bowl. Set aside.

Combine berries, sugar, and water in a medium saucepan. Bring to a boil; reduce heat, and simmer, uncovered, 10 minutes. Pour berry mixture over bread slices in prepared bowl. Top with bread slice. Fold plastic wrap over bread slice, and place a small plate on top of pudding. Set an unopened 19-ounce can on plate to weight. Chill, weighted, 24 hours.

To serve, unmold pudding onto a serving plate, removing bowl and plastic. Cut pudding into wedges; serve with Vanilla Custard Sauce.

Yield: 6 servings (serving size: 1 wedge pudding and about 3 tablespoons custard sauce).

vanilla custard sauce

3   tablespoons sugar
2   teaspoons cornstarch
1¼   cups 1% low-fat milk
1   large egg, lightly beaten
2   teaspoons margarine
1½   teaspoons vanilla extract

Combine sugar and cornstarch in a medium saucepan; gradually add milk, stirring with a whisk. Bring to a boil over medium heat, stirring constantly with a wooden spoon. Cook 1 to 2 minutes or until thickened, stirring constantly.

Gradually stir about one-fourth of hot milk mixture into egg; add to remaining hot mixture, stirring constantly. Cook 3 minutes, stirring constantly; remove from heat, and stir in margarine and vanilla. Transfer to a small pitcher or dish; cover and chill. Yield: 1 cup plus 3 tablespoons.

Per Serving: Calories 193 (15% from fat) Fat 3.3g (sat 0.9g) Protein 4.8g Carbohydrate 36.5g Fiber 3.2g Cholesterol 29mg Sodium 193mg
Exchanges: 1½ Starch, 1 Fruit, ½ Fat

Banana Cream Trifle

1   (5.1-ounce) package vanilla instant pudding mix
3   cups fat-free milk
1   (13.6-ounce) fat-free golden loaf (such as Entenmann's)
⅓   cup packed brown sugar
1   tablespoon water
5   bananas, sliced
1   (8-ounce) container frozen reduced-calorie whipped topping, thawed
2   (1.4-ounce) chocolate-covered, toffee-flavored candy bars, chopped (such as Skor bars)

Prepare pudding mix according to package directions using 3 cups milk. Cover and chill.

Cut cake into 1-inch cubes; set aside.

Combine brown sugar and water in a large nonstick skillet; place over medium heat. Cook 2 minutes or until sugar dissolves. Add bananas; cook until bananas are glazed, stirring frequently. Remove from heat.

Arrange half of cake cubes in a 3-quart trifle bowl or straight-sided glass bowl. Spoon half of banana mixture over cake. Top with half of pudding mixture. Repeat layers with remaining cake, banana mixture, and pudding. Spread whipped topping over final layer of pudding, and sprinkle with candy pieces. Cover and chill.

Yield: 15 servings (serving size: about ¾ cup).

Per Serving: Calories 230 (15% from fat) Fat 3.8g (sat 2.4g) Protein 3.8g Carbohydrate 45.0g Fiber 1.0g Cholesterol 3mg Sodium 300mg
Exchanges: 2 Starch, 1 Fruit, ½ Fat

Banana Cream Trifle

vegetable purchasing guide

How much do I need to buy? What do I do with it? Here's what you
need to know about buying and preparing fresh vegetables.

Vegetable	Approximate Servings	Preparation*
Artichoke, globe	2 servings per pound (2 artichokes)	Wash; cut off stem and ½ inch off top. Remove loose bottom leaves. Cut off thorny tips with scissors. Rub cut surfaces with lemon.
Artichoke, Jerusalem	3 servings per pound	Wash; peel. Leave whole or slice.
Asparagus	3 to 4 servings per pound	Snap off tough ends. Remove scales, if desired.
Beans, dried	6 to 8 servings per pound	Sort and wash. Cover with water 2 inches above beans; soak overnight. Drain. Or, cover with water, bring to a boil, and cook 2 minutes. Remove from heat, and let stand 1 hour. Drain.
Beans, green	4 servings per pound	Wash; trim ends, and remove strings.
Beans, lima	2 servings per pound unshelled 4 servings per pound shelled	Shell and wash.
Beets	3 to 4 servings per pound	Leave root and 1 inch of stem; scrub with vegetable brush.
Broccoli	3 to 4 servings per pound	Remove outer leaves and tough ends of lower stalks. Wash. Cut into spears or chop.
Brussels sprouts	4 servings per pound	Wash; remove discolored leaves. Cut off stem ends.

*The preparation instructions are general; refer to your recipe for more detailed directions.

vegetable purchasing guide (continued)

Vegetable	Approximate Servings	Preparation*
Cabbage	4 servings per pound	Remove outer leaves; wash. Shred, chop, or cut into wedges.
Carrots	4 servings per pound	Scrape; remove ends, and rinse. Leave tiny carrots whole; large: slice, chop, or cut into strips.
Cauliflower	4 servings per head	Remove outer leaves and stalk; wash. Leave whole, or break into florets.
Celery	4 servings per bunch	Separate stalks; trim off leaves and base. Rinse. Slice diagonally, or chop.
Corn	4 servings per 4 large ears	Remove husks and silks. Leave corn on cob, or cut off tips of kernels, and scrape cob with dull edge of knife.
Cucumbers	2 servings per cucumber	Peel, if desired; slice, or chop.
Eggplant	2 to 3 servings per pound	Wash and peel, if desired. Cut into cubes, or cut crosswise into slices.
Greens	3 to 4 servings per pound	Remove stems; wash thoroughly. Tear into bite-size pieces.
Kohlrabi	3 to 4 servings per pound	Remove leaves; wash. Peel; dice, slice, or cut into strips
Leeks	3 servings per pound	Remove root, tough outer leaves, and tops, leaving 2 inches of dark leaves. Wash thoroughly. Slice, if desired.
Mushrooms	4 servings per pound	Wipe with damp paper towels, or wash gently and pat dry. Cut off tips of stems. Slice, if desired.

Vegetable	Approximate Servings	Preparation*
Okra	4 servings per pound	Wash and pat dry. Trim ends.
Onions	4 servings per pound	Peel; cut large onions into quarters or slices, or leave small onions whole.
Parsnips	4 servings per pound	Scrape; cut off ends. Slice or chop.
Peas, black-eyed, fresh	2 servings per pound unshelled 4 servings per pound shelled	Shell and wash.
Peas, dried	6 to 8 servings per pound	Sort and wash. Cover with water 2 inches above peas; soak overnight. Drain. Or, cover with water, bring to a boil, and cook 2 minutes. Remove from heat; cover and let stand 1 hour. Drain.
Peas, green	2 servings per pound unshelled 4 servings per pound shelled	Shell and wash.
Peas, snow	4 servings per pound	Wash; trim ends, and remove tough strings.
Peppers, bell	1 serving per pepper	Cut off top, and remove seeds and membranes. Leave whole to stuff, slice into thin strips, or chop.
Potatoes, baking	2 to 3 servings per pound	Scrub potatoes; peel, if desired.
Potatoes, new, red	3 to 4 servings per pound	Scrub potatoes; peel, if desired. Leave whole, or slice or cut into chunks.
Potatoes, sweet	2 to 3 servings per pound	Scrub potatoes. Leave whole to bake, or peel, if desired, and slice or cut into chunks.

*The preparation instructions are general; refer to your recipe for more detailed directions.

vegetable purchasing guide (continued)

Vegetable	Approximate Servings	Preparation*
Pumpkin	4½ to 5 cups cooked, mashed per 5-pound pumpkin	Slice in half crosswise. Remove seeds.
Rutabagas	2 to 3 servings per pound	Wash; peel, and slice or cube.
Squash, spaghetti	2 servings per pound	Rinse; cut in half lengthwise, and discard seeds.
Squash, summer	3 to 4 servings per pound	Wash; trim ends. Slice or chop.
Squash, winter (acorn, butternut, hubbard)	2 servings per pound	Rinse; cut in half, and remove seeds.
Tomatoes	4 servings per pound	Wash; peel, if desired. Slice or chop.
Turnips	3 servings per pound	Wash; peel, and slice or cube.

*The preparation instructions are general; refer to your recipe for more detailed directions.

fruit purchasing guide

How much do I need to buy? What do I do with it? Here's what you need to know about buying and preparing fresh fruits.

Fruit	Approximate Servings	Preparation*
Apples	3 to 4 servings per pound	Wash. Peel and core as required, and cut as desired.
Apricots	3 to 4 servings per pound	Wash. Cut in half, remove pit, and slice as desired.
Bananas	3 to 4 servings per pound	Peel, and cut as desired.
Blackberries	4 servings per pound	Rinse lightly just before serving.
Blueberries	4 servings per pound	Wash and drain; sort and remove stems.
Cherries	4 servings per pound	Wash; sort and remove stems and pits.
Cranberries	8 servings per pound	Sort, wash and drain.
Figs	6 servings per pound	Rinse gently just before serving. Peel, if desired.
Grapefruit	2 servings per pound	Cut into halves, or peel and cut into sections.
Grapes	4 servings per pound	Wash thoroughly. Remove stems; leave whole or halve.
Kiwifruit	3 to 4 servings per pound	Peel and slice. Or, cut off top and use a spoon to scoop out flesh.
Lemons	4 lemons per pound	Wash. Slice or cut into wedges. Grate rind, if desired.

Fruit	Approximate Servings	Preparation*
Oranges	2 servings per pound	Wash. Cut into halves, peel and cut into sections, or slice.
Peaches	4 servings per pound	Blanch to remove skin. Cut to remove seed. Chop or slice.
Pears	4 servings per pound	Wash. Peel and core as required, and cut as desired.
Pineapple	3 servings per pound	Cut off top, bottom, and skin. Chop or slice as desired.
Plums	4 to 5 servings per pound	Wash. Keep whole, or cut in half and remove pit.
Raspberries	4 servings per pound	Rinse lightly just before serving.
Rhubarb	4 to 8 pieces per pound	Remove leaf and hard area at base of stem. Wash and cut across stem into desired width.
Strawberries	2 to 3 servings per pound	Rinse and remove stems. Leave whole, slice, or chop.

*The preparation instructions are general; refer to your recipe for more detailed directions.

basic ingredients: weights & yields

ingredient	weight or count	yield
Apples	1 pound (about 3)	3 cups sliced
Bananas	1 pound (about 3)	2½ cups sliced or about 2 cups mashed
Bread	1 pound 1½ slices	12 to 16 slices 1 cup soft crumbs
Butter or margarine	¼-pound stick 1 pound	½ cup (1 stick) 2 cups (4 sticks)
Cabbage	1-pound head	4½ cups shredded
Carrots	1 pound	3 cups shredded
Cheese American or Cheddar low-fat cottage cheese reduced-fat cream cheese	 1 ounce 16-ounce carton 8 ounces	 about ¼ cup shredded 2 cups about 1 cup
Cocoa	16-ounce can	5 cups
Coconut, flaked or shredded	1 pound package	5 cups
Coffee, ground	1 pound	80 tablespoons (40 cups brewed)
Corn	2 ears	1 cup kernels
Cornmeal	1 pound	3 cups
Crab, in shell	1 pound	¾ to 1 cup flaked

basic ingredients: weights & yields (continued)

ingredient	weight or count	yield
Crackers and Wafers		
chocolate wafers	19 wafers	1 cup crumbs
graham crackers	14 squares	1 cup fine crumbs
saltine crackers	28 crackers	1 cup finely crushed
vanilla wafers	22 wafers	1 cup finely crushed
Dates, pitted	8-ounce package	1½ cups chopped
	1 pound	3 cups chopped
Eggs	5 large	1 cup
whites	8 to 11	1 cup
yolks	12 to 14	1 cup
Flour, all-purpose	1 pound	3½ cups unsifted
cake	1 pound	4¾ to 5 cups sifted
whole-wheat	1 pound	3½ cups unsifted
Bell peppers	1 large	1 cup diced
Lemons	1 medium	2 to 3 tablespoons juice; 2 teaspoons grated rind
Lettuce	1-pound head	6¼ cups torn
Limes	1 medium	1½ to 2 tablespoons juice; 1½ teaspoons grated rind
Macaroni	4 ounces dry (1 cup)	2 cups cooked
Milk		
fat-free evaporated	12-ounce can	1½ cups
fat-free sweetened condensed	14-ounce can	1¼ cups
Mushrooms	3 cups raw (8 ounces)	1 cup sliced, cooked

ingredient	weight or count	yield
Nuts		
almonds	1 pound unshelled	1¾ cups nutmeats
	1 pound shelled	3½ cups
peanuts	1 pound unshelled	2¼ cups nutmeats
	1 pound shelled	3 cups
pecans	1 pound unshelled	2¼ cups nutmeats
	1 pound shelled	4 cups
walnuts	1 pound unshelled	1⅔ cups nutmeats
	1 pound shelled	4 cups
Oats, quick-cooking	1 cup uncooked	1¾ cups cooked
Onions	1 medium	½ cup chopped
Oranges	1 medium	½ cup juice; 2 tablespoons grated rind
Peaches	2 medium	1 cup sliced
Pears	2 medium	1 cup sliced
Potatoes		
white	3 medium	2 cups cubed cooked or 1¾ cups mashed
sweet	3 medium	3 cups sliced
Raisins, seedless	1 pound	3 cups
Rice, long grain	1 cup uncooked	3 to 4 cups cooked
Shrimp, raw, unpeeled	1 pound	8 to 9 ounces cooked, peeled, deveined
Spaghetti	8 ounces uncooked	about 3½ cups cooked
Strawberries	1 quart	4 cups sliced
Sugar		
brown	1 pound	2⅓ cups firmly packed
powdered	1 pound	3½ cups unsifted
granulated white	1 pound	2 cups

the well-stocked pantry

Use this handy list to keep your kitchen stocked with the basic ingredients you need for quick and healthy cooking.

in the pantry

baking supplies
- baking powder
- baking soda
- cocoa, unsweetened
- cornstarch
- flour: all-purpose and whole-wheat
- honey
- milk: nonfat dry milk powder, fat-free evaporated
- oats: quick-cooking
- oils: olive, sesame, and vegetable
- sugar: brown, granulated, powdered

fruits and vegetables
- canned beans
- canned tomato products: paste, sauce, whole, diced, and seasoned tomatoes
- canned vegetables
- dried fruits

grains and pastas
- bulgur
- couscous
- dry pastas
- rice and rice blends

condiments and seasonings
- dried herbs and spices
- mayonnaise: low-fat or reduced-fat
- mustards
- salad dressings and vinaigrettes: fat-free and reduced-fat
- seasoning sauces: hot sauce, ketchup, low-sodium soy sauce, low-sodium Worcestershire sauce, vinegars

miscellaneous
- bouillon granules: chicken, beef, and vegetable
- broth, canned: reduced-sodium chicken and beef, vegetable
- minced bottled garlic
- minced bottled ginger
- unflavored gelatin

in the refrigerator
- cheeses, reduced-fat
- eggs and egg substitute
- milk: fat-free, 1% low-fat, and low-fat buttermilk
- margarine or light butter
- sour cream, low-fat
- yogurt, low-fat and fat-free

in the freezer
- cooked chicken: diced or strips
- egg substitute
- frozen fruits
- frozen vegetables
- juice concentrates
- phyllo pastry

metric equivalents

The recipes that appear in this cookbook use the standard United States method for measuring liquid and dry or solid ingredients (teaspoons, tablespoons, and cups). The information in the following charts is provided to help cooks outside the U.S. successfully use these recipes. All equivalents are approximate.

Equivalents for Different Types of Ingredients

A standard cup measure of a dry or solid ingredient will vary in weight depending on the type of ingredient.

A standard cup of liquid is the same volume for any type of liquid. Use the following chart when converting standard cup measures to grams (weight) or milliliters (volume).

Standard Cup	Fine Powder (ex. flour)	Grain (ex. rice)	Granular (ex. sugar)	Liquid Solids (ex. butter)	Liquid (ex. milk)
1	140 g	150 g	190 g	200 g	240 ml
¾	105 g	113 g	143 g	150 g	180 ml
⅔	93 g	100 g	125 g	133 g	160 ml
½	70 g	75 g	95 g	100 g	120 ml
⅓	47 g	50 g	63 g	67 g	80 ml
¼	35 g	38 g	48 g	50 g	60 ml
⅛	18 g	19 g	24 g	25 g	30 ml

Liquid Ingredients by Volume

¼ tsp					=	1 ml
½ tsp					=	2 ml
1 tsp					=	5 ml
3 tsp	=	1 tbls		=	½ fl oz	=	15 ml
		2 tbls	= ⅛ cup	=	1 fl oz	=	30 ml
		4 tbls	= ¼ cup	=	2 fl oz	=	60 ml
		5⅓ tbls	= ⅓ cup	=	3 fl oz	=	80 ml
		8 tbls	= ½ cup	=	4 fl oz	=	120 ml
		10⅔ tbls	= ⅔ cup	=	5 fl oz	=	160 ml
		12 tbls	= ¾ cup	=	6 fl oz	=	180 ml
		16 tbls	= 1 cup	=	8 fl oz	=	240 ml
		1 pt	= 2 cups	=	16 fl oz	=	480 ml
		1 qt	= 4 cups	=	32 fl oz	=	960 ml
					33 fl oz	=	1000 ml = 1 liter

Dry Ingredients by Weight

(To convert ounces to grams, multiply the number of ounces by 30.)

1 oz	=	¹⁄₁₆ lb	=	30 g
4 oz	=	¼ lb	=	120 g
8 oz	=	½ lb	=	240 g
12 oz	=	¾ lb	=	360 g
16 oz	=	1 lb	=	480 g

Length

(To convert inches to centimeters, multiply the number of inches by 2.5.)

1 in				=	2.5 cm	
6 in	= ½ ft			=	15 cm	
12 in	= 1 ft			=	30 cm	
36 in	= 3 ft	= 1 yd		=	90 cm	
40 in				=	100 cm	= 1 meter

Cooking/Oven Temperatures

	Fahrenheit	Celsius	Gas Mark
Freeze Water	32° F	0° C	
Room Temperature	68° F	20° C	
Boil Water	212° F	100° C	
Bake	325° F	160° C	3
	350° F	180° C	4
	375° F	190° C	5
	400° F	200° C	6
	425° F	220° C	7
	450° F	230° C	8
Broil			Grill

guide to healthy meals

Light and Easy Menus helps you meet the healthy eating recommendations of the U.S. Dietary Guidelines. All of the menus are reduced in calories, cholesterol, and sodium; have no more than 30 percent calories from fat; and are high in fiber. Use the nutrient analysis following each recipe to see specifically what nutrients the recipe contributes to the menu.

Total calories for each serving

Percentage of calories from fat

Grams are abbreviated "g"

Values for one serving of the recipe →

Per Serving: Calories 368 (9% from fat)   Fat 3.5g (sat 0.7g)   Protein 31.8g
Carbohydrate 53.5g   Fiber 5.9g   Cholesterol 66mg   Sodium 376mg ← Milligrams are abbreviated "mg"
Exchanges: 2 Starch, 1 Fruit, 4 Very Lean Meat

Fruits and Vegetables

The meals in *Light and Easy Menus* feature a variety of seasonal fruits and vegetables that not only taste great, but also help fight diseases such as heart disease, diabetes, obesity, hypertension, and certain types of cancer.

The National 5-A-Day Program advises all Americans to eat at least five servings of fruits and/or vegetables every day. Other health programs advocate a minimum of 10 servings a day for optimal health. So, as you plan your meals, don't skip the suggestions for salads, steamed vegetables, and fresh fruits listed in the menus.

Sodium

The current dietary recommendations advise us to limit sodium to 2,400 milligrams a day. As you enjoy the ease of using convenience products, be aware that many of them are high in sodium, even when they're low in fat and calories.

If you're watching your sodium intake carefully, read food labels and note the sodium value in the nutrient analysis following each recipe. We use reduced-sodium products when possible to help you keep your daily intake of sodium close to the recommended level. And remember that fresh fruits and vegetables are very low in sodium.

Diabetic Exchanges

Exchange values are provided for people who use them in meal planning for diabetes or weight control. The values are based on the *Exchange Lists for Meal Planning* developed by the American Diabetes Association and The American Dietetic Association.

Fat

Your daily fat intake should be 30 percent or less of your total calories for the day. This doesn't mean that every single food you eat has to be under 30 percent.

Recipes with over 30 percent calories from fat can still be healthy. For example, salmon is higher in fat than other fish, but it is omega-3 fat, a healthier kind of fat. And for recipes with very low-calorie foods like vegetables, the total amount of fat can be low but still make up a large percentage of the calories.

Here's how the 30 percent recommendation translates to actual fat grams per day:

If you should eat 2,000 calories per day, you can have up to 67 grams of fat:

2,000 calories x 30% = 600 calories

600 calories ÷ 9 calories per gram = 67 grams fat

Calories

Calorie requirements vary according to your size, weight, and level of physical activity. The calorie levels in the chart below are general guides; you may need more calories if you are pregnant, breast-feeding, or trying to gain weight, or less if you are trying to lose or maintain weight. Talk to your physician if you plan to start a reduced-calorie weight loss plan.

Nutrient Analysis

The nutrient values used in our calculations come from three sources: (1) a computer program by Computrition, Inc., (2) Food Processor®, a computer program by ESHA Research, and (3) manufacturers' information.

Our calculations are based on the following three assumptions: (1) when we give a range for an ingredient, the lesser amount is calculated; (2) only the amount of marinade absorbed by the food is calculated; (3) if alcohol is used, some of the calories evaporate during cooking, and the analysis reflects this reduction.

daily nutrition guide

Use the values from the U.S. Dietary Guidelines in the chart below to determine your daily nutrient needs.

	women ages 25 to 50	women over 50	men over 24
Calories	2,000	2,000 or less	2,700
Protein	50g	50g or less	63g
Fat	67g or less	67g or less	90g or less
Saturated Fat	22g or less	22g or less	30g or less
Carbohydrate	299g	299g	405g
Fiber	25g to 35g	25g to 35g	25g to 35g
Cholesterol	300mg or less	300mg or less	300mg or less
Sodium	2,400mg or less	2,400mg or less	2,400mg or less

index

D

P

acknowledgments & credits

Oxmoor House wishes to thank the following merchants and individuals:

Cyclamen Studio, Inc., Berkeley, CA

Horchow Collection, Dallas, TX

Mariposa, Manchester, MA

Smyer Glass, Benicia, CA

Union Glass, San Francisco, CA

Additional photography:

Beth Maynor: page 145

Randy Mayor: page 10

Howard L. Puckett: pages 6, 115, 236

Becky Luigart-Stayner: pages 6, 12, 34, 53, 54, 61, 65, 102,

111, 115, 146, 183, 212, 217, 220, 228, 232

Additional photo styling:

Cindy Manning Barr: pages 6, 18, 115

Cathy Muir: page 6

Fonda Shaia: pages 6, 18, 115